On Call

Val Inchley OBE

Onwards and Upwards Publishers
3 Radfords Turf, Cranbrook, Exeter,
EX5 7DX, United Kingdom.
www.onwardsandupwards.org

This first edition published in the United Kingdom by Onwards and Upwards Publishers (2018).

Printed in the United Kingdom.

ISBN:	978-1-911086-94-9
Typeface:	Sabon LT
Graphic design:	LM Graphic Design

Colour photograph attributions from the insert pages:

SPECIAL OCCASIONS	
Top left	Simpsons of Liverpool
Top right	Ede & Ravenscroft
Middle left	Rowan Butler
Middle right	Charles Green
DIASPORA	
Left side, 2nd photograph up	Usha
TRANSPORT	
Right side, 1st and 2nd photographs up	INF
Left side, 4th photograph down	Chris Dixon
Bottom left	Morna Lincoln
INF CENTRES	
Left side, 2nd photograph up	Chris Dixon
NEPALI CHURCHES	
Left, side 2nd photograph down	INF

Acknowledgements for other photographs and logos.

p6.	Ruth Watson photograph	INF
p155.	Centre photograph	R Dhewajoo
p266.	NeMUN logo	NeMUN
p29.	INF logo	INF
p250.	BaYaN logo	BYN
p280.	Prayer Group photograph	Lennox Smith

The author and publisher gratefully acknowledge the permission granted to reproduce the copyright material in this book.

Endorsements

Val's gentle, gracious humility – so true to her as a person if you ever get to meet – shines through the pages of her fascinating autobiography, the story of her call to, work in, and return from Nepal.

Val writes with a delightful light touch, weaves in her fabulous humour, and cuts to the core of what it means to love and serve Jesus, no matter the circumstances. Proselytism, as she explains early on, is very different from "living a life that attracts people to Jesus, telling them about him, and offering to pray for them when they are in need". Val has certainly led that life.

Enjoy her rich descriptions of living in Nepal and laugh-out-loud anecdotes; feel exhausted but enthused by her relentless schedule and responsibilities; learn from her depth of wisdom and spiritual insight; be challenged by her honesty, vulnerability and integrity; and be inspired, to press on to pursue all that God has called you to be and do.

Anne Le Tissier
Author, writer, speaker, with a passion and call to disciple others in their ongoing walk with God

Val Inchley captures perfectly the feel of life and pace of change in Nepal over her 43 years of ministry there. And she captures the reality of being a medical missionary, with all of life's ups and downs honestly and graphically described. This is an inspiring story of a life of Christian service and sacrifice, but also of the joy and wonder of living in such a fabulous land serving such a marvellous people. This is a personal story that is also the story of how God has been at work in Nepal over many years. Reading Val's account just makes me want to go back to Nepal again!

Venerable Bob Jackson
Author of *Higher than the Hills* and many other books

My first memories of Val were at the Himalayan Helper youth camps. Little did I know then that one day we would share a room at missionary training college (Mount Hermon that was) and be on the same team for local evangelism/church purposes.

During those days I was often asked the question, "Do you think that in 20 years' time she will still be running?" I can assure you that in more ways than one Val was still running then, and I am sure you will be convinced as you read this book that nearly 50 years later she still is. (Perhaps not at the same rate!)

Val has faithfully "run with perseverance the race marked out for [her]."[1] Where others might have given up she stuck at it during difficult days.

Val was able to be faithful because the word of God says, "The one who calls you is faithful and he will do it."[2]

Dorothy Evans
Former colleague

Dr Val has written an honest account of her adventure in faith. It is light and yet profound, humorous yet moving. The astonishing development of the Nepali church from mustard seed beginnings to global burgeoning is observed from within. Above all, this is an account of God's faithfulness and transforming power – in the midst of the Nepali people and in the lived experience of someone who was willing to be *On Call.*

Steve Aisthorpe
Former INF Director;
now Mission Development Worker with the Church of Scotland

---

1 Heb. 12:1.
2 2 Thess. 5:24.

In *On Call* Val describes with honesty and humour her experiences doing medical, administrative and teaching work for 43 years in the beautiful country of Nepal. Her book is a fund of information and should be required reading for anyone going to work in Nepal or indeed in any developing country. It is also a challenging read to any committed Christian for two reasons: one is Val's example of obedience, unflagging energy and long-term commitment; the other is the example and vitality of the Nepali church which, in spite of persecution, has multiplied a thousand-fold in the last 50 years.

Joan Kearney MA BD
Former colleague

A unique missionary autobiography.

For 43 years *On Call* letters brought news of Val and Nepal, and I was happy to distribute these for 25 years. I am so glad that 'Inch' has completed this comprehensive story of her life and work herself. Written in her own inimitable style, she weaves a wonderful picture of the beautiful land of Nepal – its geography, history, language – and of its resilient and hospitable people whom she was called to serve.

Judy (Judith M) Crook
Friend

Dedicated to

my parents,
Brenda Swann,
and Ruth Watson,
who were all key players in my life;

Left to right: Brenda Swann; Frank and Margaret Inchley; Ruth Watson

and with heartfelt thanks to all who supported me over the years with gifts and especially with prayer.

Contents

Preface

Don't you just love the story of Elijah! Backed up into a corner with an important task to complete, the Bible says: "Elijah, ... *human just like us,* prayed hard that it wouldn't rain, and it didn't – not a drop for three and a half years. Then he prayed that it would rain, and it did."[3] He was just an ordinary guy, like us, but he had an extraordinary God. That is my story too, though not quite so dramatic. So, anything good that has come out of my somewhat out-of-the-ordinary life is not because I am extraordinary but because I have been trying to follow and serve the same extraordinary God that Elijah knew.

Dr Valerie M. Inchley OBE

[3] Jas. 5:18 (MSG).

An approximate map of Nepal (2014)

1

Air Raids, Abersoch and Art

How it all began

(1944-1962)

Valerie with parents, Frank and Margaret, shortly after birth in 1944.

"IT'S ALRIGHT SO LONG AS YOU'RE not a missionary!" was the considered (or perhaps unconsidered) opinion of Carina, my best friend from Guides and Bible Class, somewhere back in the late 1950s. This was slightly disturbing as that was exactly what I was beginning to think of as a career, although I'm not sure that either of us really knew enough to pontificate about whether such an option would be alright or all wrong. I did know a bit, for in Bible Class and at Camp I had met many missionaries and heard their stories. My favourite books were *By Searching* and others by Isobel Kuhn of Lisuland, and those about the mid-century martyrs in Ecuador. However, I suspect the romance of darkest Africa and the mysterious Orient had more than a little to do with my ambitions at that time.

Born in central London in the middle of an air-raid, my life began with a bang. This fact, according to some of my 'friends', explains a lot. Maybe it does. Maybe it doesn't. It certainly gives away my age.

As soon as my father was demobbed from the Royal Air Force, we moved back to the Midlands, and so I spent all my childhood in Sutton Coldfield – and I'm proud to be a Suttonian: proud to have lived in the Royal Town; proud to have climbed trees in the largest natural park in the British Isles; proud to have gone to school just round the corner from where the first bit of white central road marking was tried out.

I was an only child with no older siblings to keep me out of (or perhaps lead me into) mischief. My earliest memory – or was it something I was later told? – concerns a jar of face cream. That day my mother must have been wholly distracted by one of the many household tasks mothers still had to do in the mid-1940s. She must have been or I'm sure she would never have let her precious infant roam the house alone and especially not climb the stairs when each step was bigger than one of my eighteen-month-old legs. The adventure led me into my parents' bedroom where I lurched towards the solid mahogany dressing table and grabbed at it to steady myself. From behind all the bottles and brushes a pair of hazel eyes in a round, ruddy face stared at me. Putting out my hand to touch this face, my small fingers closed instead around a jar of face cream. Too big to fit into my tiny fist, it fell onto the floor and rolled away into the corner. An inquisitive child, I dropped onto my well-upholstered bottom and crawled after the jar into the corner behind the dressing table. With two hands I tried to seize it and then the impossible happened: the jar came unscrewed. Wedging one thumb inside, at last I was able to get it near my nose for inspection. Nice smell! I promptly pulled out my thumb and put it into my mouth. Nice taste too! In case you're wondering, I ate the whole of it, but it made no significant difference to my complexion – or my digestion!

When I was small my mother used to tell me tales about David, my teddy bear, while my father invented an imaginary family with three children – Stanley, Valerie and Noreen – whose adventures always bore remarkable resemblance to my own exploits. Once I was old enough to read for myself, I began to devour books, usually by torchlight under the bedclothes when I was supposed to be going to sleep. Ever since then, stories have played a big part in my life, but nowadays I write them as well as read them.

My first school was Central High School (aka Keyes) which was run by the then minister of Sutton Coldfield Baptist Church. The girls' section was sited in the family home, Brook House, in Manor Road – so called because the Ebrook flowed through the garden. Not surprisingly, the stream and beyond was "out-of-bounds". The boys' section was at the back of the church on Sutton Parade. The only times I visited that were for dancing class (!) and 11-plus coaching.

I had scarcely started school when family problems interrupted my education. My mother somehow contracted double pneumonia followed by a DVT[4], both serious conditions in those days. After some months, and with the help of an early antibiotic, M & B 693, she pulled through, but while she was still recovering I was sent to a small boarding school. Although my favourite aunt, Aunty Eva, was a teacher there, I hated every minute of it, so wisely my father took me away and sent me to stay with an uncle on my mother's side in Stratford-upon-Avon. I assume I coped better with that as I was there for the rest of the term.

I have four distinct memories of that time – two good, two not so good. Like my dad, I hated milk and had vomited my first precious bottle of post-war nutritious milk all over the steps of Brook House. Here I was offered the alternative of a bottle of orange juice – bliss. Not so happy were arithmetic lessons. I was good at maths and invariably managed to complete a whole page before I remembered that the rule was to get each sum checked before going on to the next. I was always in trouble, but the school walks, past a fascinating hollow oak tree, partly made up for my misery. Anne (my cousin) was six years older than me but I loved doing everything she did. One day, while my uncle was building a garage extension, Anne wandered out there barefoot. I started to follow but my aunt told me to put my shoes on. Disobedience predictably led to a cut foot and an important lesson learnt (at least for a short while) the hard way.

While my mother was convalescing, I learnt to ride a bicycle – round and round and round on the lawn. By the time school reconvened I was no longer falling off and, to my delight, I was allowed to ride it to school

4 DVT – deep venous thrombosis.

– so long as I was with some older people and rode only on the pavement. This was almost certainly why I had my one and only accident – a somewhat painful encounter with a bumpy bit of footpath. After that I always rode a bicycle to school; in fact, I rode everywhere, even to the pillar box fifty yards down the road. By the time I was at secondary school, I considered myself an expert, so when, for some inexplicable reason, I failed the Cycling Proficiency Test first time round, it was particularly humiliating. Happily, I passed it the second time without any obvious change to my style and was again allowed to take the bike to school. Ever since then I have continued to enjoy life on two wheels – with pedal power or something stronger.

The rest of my early schooldays were happy and unremarkable except that my teachers described me as talkative (many times), very good at art (only ever one time!) and knowledgeable about Scripture (almost all the time).

Holidays spent only a minute from the beach at a caravan camp in Abersoch in North Wales were cool (literally and in modern idiom) and fun, but 1954 was especially important for me. With no siblings I would have been lonely without the activities of the CSSM[5] beach mission: sand modelling, games, sausage sizzles and even daily Bible talks. One day the leader of the team of Cambridge students conducting the mission stood on the sand pulpit and held up a picture of two roads. One was wide and heavily populated, the other narrow and traversed only by a few people. It was the road to heaven. Mike explained that we had to choose which road to travel in our lives. Of course, I already knew about God and Jesus and the Bible. My parents had taken me to church and sent me to Sunday school (as did almost all parents of their generation) but this idea of making a definite choice to follow Jesus, rather than just doing what was expected of me, was new and challenging. That day I asked Jesus to come into my heart and life. And he did. It was the best thing I ever did.

I learnt something else very important at the beach mission. Every day we had what was called 'Secret Service' in the sand dunes before breakfast. It was when the leaders helped us to form a habit of reading a bit from the Bible each day, and I've been doing it ever since. I guess I must have read the whole Bible well over a dozen times, and parts of it

---

[5] CSSM – Children's Special Service Mission.

many more times by now, but still God surprises me with new truths and new lessons – and sometimes old ones I need to relearn.

In the 1950s the Warren caravan site, at the tip of the Llyn Peninsula in North Wales, was an idyllic spot set in the sand dunes and favoured by families like mine who just wanted a simple holiday by the seaside. The highlights were walking over the headland to Llanbedrog, eating special homemade '99' ice creams in Abersoch, and one day falling off the rocks there. I still have the scar on my thumb. At other times we visited the Whistling Sands, Port Ceiriad or Aberdaron and Hell's Mouth Bay where all sorts of things got washed up by the tide. To my great delight my father drove the car on the beach at Black Rock Sands and at other times took us over the causeway to Mocras or Shell Island, although I was a bit disappointed he never let us get marooned there. We explored the exotic Italian village at Portmerion and rode on the little Festiniog Railway with my cousins, and when I was ten I climbed Snowdon with the CSSM. Some evenings we chased the chip van around the winding Welsh lanes to purchase a dinner my mother didn't have to cook, but once something went wrong with the car and my father had to drive it backwards all along the little narrow lane to a garage. One year my father offered Carina and me half a crown if we could get from the sea, over the dunes and back to the caravan without getting any sand on our feet. Over an hour later, and with very sore knees, we were both two and sixpence better off.

Many other happy memories flood back from those early years. Wearing a smart uniform and winning badges in the Brownies, where (don't laugh) I was a Sixer in the Fairies and later 'flew up' to the Guides; there I became leader of the Chaffinch Patrol, though obviously not because of my singing skills. Attending Health and Beauty classes, though I'm not sure they had much effect on me as I was healthy before I started and never likely to be beautiful. Getting a commendation from the Natural History Society for my seashell collection. Winning a hairbrush in a Mason's fizzy drinks decoding competition, even though I usually drank Corona dandelion and burdock. Working my way through all the News Chronicle *I-Spy* books. Cycling all around Sutton in the halcyon days before the roads became clogged with vehicles; that was when there were no shopping precincts, no one-way systems, no Sutton bypass and definitely no spaghetti junction. Having a budgie called Billy – and a goldfish, until it committed suicide by jumping out onto my bedroom floor. Buying my first aniseed balls after sweets came off ration. Eating my first bit of white chocolate, bought in a tiny Welsh shop in the middle of nowhere. Reading the Children's Newspaper and brazenly entering their annual handwriting competition; I guess they never awarded booby prizes or I would have won one. (Years later, after I had left home, my father ungraciously told me he took all my letters to the chemist to be made up – as if they were prescriptions!)

Every year I had several highlights to look forward to. Around February we always drove to Shropshire to the villages of West Hope and Ticklerton, where, beside the little stream, we picked snowdrops – it was quite legal in those days – and picnicked in the cold. March brought my birthday, when my mother excelled herself in arranging fantastic parties; one year she even made little wool doll badges for us all. Usually the festivities took place in a local church hall and the traditional party fare in the 50s was jelly and blancmange, fish paste sandwiches and birthday cake. We thought we were eating like kings. Easter, usually sometime in April, was when we paid our first visit of the year to the caravan. Sometime each year we drove out to the little village of Barnwell, where my father had been billeted for part of the war. We visited his old landlady who kept the village shop. Mrs Pask was a welcoming rotund lady who always had a black velvet choker around her neck; I never discovered why. Come November, and before all the plots in our road were built on, the families joined together to build a huge bonfire. The fathers lit the pooled fireworks, we children were allowed to hold the sparklers and Bengal matches, and our mothers produced mugs of hot cocoa and sooty baked potatoes from the bonfire ashes. In those days Christmas didn't begin until late December, but as soon as school finished I remember going with my father to buy a tree and collect our allocation of holly from Sutton Park – and then decorating the house. On Christmas Day I accompanied him to collect our big turkey which had been roasted in the local baker's oven. The year finished with a posh 'do' in town. My father, an electrical engineer and radio ham, was a member of the Birmingham and Midland Institute, and so every year he would exhibit some electrical 'mystery' at the Conversazione. I loved wandering around all the fascinating scientific exhibits, and then the evening – and thus the year – concluded with Auld Lang Syne.

On 7th September 1958, at the age of fourteen, I was baptized at Six Ways Baptist Church, Erdington, Birmingham and became a church member the following week. I knew I was a Christian but looking back, I feel sad that the church did not insist on us speaking out our testimony before baptism. Had I been required to do that, I think it would have helped me put my faith into words, not just on that special day but on many other subsequent occasions. Several Bible verses were given me at that time: "...because I know whom I have believed, and am convinced that he is able to guard what I have entrusted to him until that day." (2 Tim. 1:12); "What shall I return to the LORD for all his goodness to me? ... I will fulfil my vows to the LORD in the presence of all his people." (Psa. 116:12-14); and "...he who began a good work in you will carry it on to completion until the day of Christ Jesus." (Phil. 1:6). I have never forgotten them for they sum up God's faithfulness, something that has never failed even when I have made mistakes.

For a few years prior to that I had attended GCU[6] summer house parties and met various missionaries. My interest changed with each one I met – China, Africa, India... Then, the following year, I went with a group of church youth to a BMS[7] Summer School where I met Stanley Thomas, a missionary doctor from India. Perhaps some of what I felt was hero-worship, but I believe it was also the beginning of God telling me what he wanted for my life.

In 1955 I had passed the 11-plus, and the comment in my final primary school report was, "...very promising for the future," but *what future?* At 'Sutton High'[8] I don't think I really excelled at anything in particular until my final year, when I achieved 90% for Scholarship Biology, much to the amazement and initial disbelief of my headmistress. My memories don't seem to include much about our lessons – more about the pranks or games we played. We had phases of playing jacks or, later, chess before each teacher arrived for her respective class – except for Maths when we were expected to do mental arithmetic while waiting. I remember 'shooting' the inside of a biro at the Physics master, a small Welshman who was a particularly uninspiring teacher. I regularly learnt

6 GCU – Girl Crusaders Union.

7 BMS – Baptist Missionary Society.

8 Sutton Coldfield High/Grammar School for Girls.

my Latin vocabulary while riding my bike down Jockey Road on the way home from school – a harbinger of things to come with Nepali and Greek. Almost every week, the Latin master reminded us that "books are living things". I didn't learn much Latin but I did gain a love for books. In Geography one year, we all cheated; we used our textbooks to write our notes when we had been told to do it from memory. Well, what on earth would have been the use of poor notes (from faulty memories) when it came to exam revision? Usually I managed to stay out of trouble, but one Scripture lesson was an exception. When I politely tried to point out to the teacher that she had taught us the same lesson the previous week, she fixed me with an imperious stare and said, "I am not in my dotage yet." In fact, if she wasn't, she was pretty near it. We always had to sit in alphabetical order, presumably because our teachers found it easier to remember our names that way. Thus, Christine H., who sat immediately behind me, became a friend; but, perhaps surprisingly, Judy, who sat on the extreme right and Ruth, who sat way across the room on the extreme left, also became friends.

Most of the time I came no higher than seventh in the class; not bad but not spectacular, and particularly unspectacular in art and languages. This did not bode well for life as a missionary. What if the new language I had to tackle was even harder than French? What if it was tonal? One teacher had already noted that I had "no ear for music" – and that was putting it politely. At primary school I had been told repeatedly to stop singing as it put the pianist off; at secondary school the French Mistress tried to teach me to sing, the result being that I lost my voice. Since then I have only met one person who sings more out of tune than I do: Di cannot even clap in time. Inevitably, we became friends, but that was much later.

I also had no eye for art.

"Have you ever seen trees like that?"

As I looked again at my drawing, I was forced to admit that the Art mistress had a point: I had never seen such limbless specimens of giant flora, and I suddenly felt as sorry for them as for myself. They were as unlikely to produce leaves and fruit as I was to produce a Picasso! But, I wondered, what if such absurd arboreal amputees did exist somewhere? That inkling turned out to be correct. Within fifteen years my derided artwork became a prophetic picture fulfilled; in the 1970s all over rural

Nepal there were trees like that, sacrificing their lives to give humans firewood and animals fodder.

I was a member of the school Christian Union and there is one important thing I remember about that. It was where I learnt to pray out loud. As almost everyone else was initially as shy as I was, we had a method by which we would go around the group and pray in turn. We could have missed our turn but that would have been 'chicken'.

My fascination with the Himalayas had begun in Coronation year, when for a while I nurtured a childhood dream of being the first person to conquer Everest. With that vision vanquished by Tenzing and Hillary, I thought perhaps I might become the first woman on the summit, but before I was even old enough to don a pair of mountaineering boots, that fantasy too was shattered and I was left with the much easier (and safer) alternative of trekking in the foothills and enjoying the snows from afar.

The Shining Hospital, the pioneer medical project of the mission I later joined, had opened in that same year, 1953. Amazingly, but no doubt engineered by God, a further link with Nepal and the Himalayas was nurtured by Brenda Swann, my Bible Class leader. She got us all knitting blankets for the hospital as she had friends who were supporting this new mission. My knitting skills were akin to my artistic talent and singing ability but I could just about manage a nine-inch square without dropping a stitch. Doubtless, the early patients in Pokhara were appreciative, but I myself gained more through Brenda's Bible teaching. Even now, although I can't tell you the exact lessons, I vividly remember a series about life on three planes: ordinary life, life that anyone can live and most people do live; a sort of minimalistic religious life, where one is a Christian in name only; and a passionate Christian life, seeking to live like Jesus and for him. That became my aim.

Despite a total lack of any linguistic ability or musical talents, I was well-equipped for Nepal in some small ways. My head, I discovered, was half a size smaller than they block hats, though I have no recollection at all of why I needed to buy a hat. My legs were also smaller than average. I had been almost the shortest in my class at school and borne my inevitable nickname of "Inch" with a remarkable degree of fortitude and good humour. This diminutive stature was to come in useful in the future; being only slightly taller than most of my generation of Nepali ladies, I didn't stick out head and shoulders above them. And, unlike most of my expatriate friends, I found that I easily fitted into Nepali bus seats, although not having my knees tightly wedged against the seat in front meant I had a tendency to fall into the aisle every time the bus spun around one of the innumerable bends. But I also had some small hang-ups when it came to considering life in the subtropics. I suffered (and still do to a certain extent) from arachnophobia – fear of spiders, to you and me. On childhood holidays at the caravan, every night I would insist that my father swept around the windows to make sure none of these eight-legged beasties came into my boudoir.

Several years in the Guides should perhaps have prepared me for roughing it in a Nepali village. Sadly, I never mastered the art of rubbing two Boy Scouts together to start a fire; and the first time I attempted my Cook's badge, I dropped the cake while putting it into the oven. But I did win my Cyclist's badge honestly and fairly.

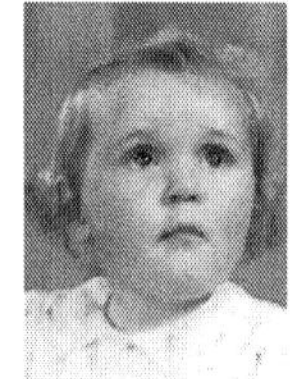

Left to right: 1946 (2 yr.); 1949 (5 yr.); 1952 (8 yr.); 1955 (11 yr.); 1962 (18 yr.).

In my penultimate year at Grammar School, we suffered under a series of Biology teachers and for one term were even taught by the headmistress. It was not a good experience. I liked Biology and was good at it and eagerly noted down all the gems she was passing on until she noticed...

"What are you writing?"

"Some biology notes."

"You are not meant to be writing notes. Go and stand outside in the corridor."

To this day I remain puzzled as to why I was not supposed to be writing notes in class, but I guess there are some mysteries in life that never do get solved.

I do have one rather strange regret about my later school days. At the end of my lower sixth year, it was time for another school photo – that fascinating old-fashioned kind where the camera revolves in the arc of a circle but, amazingly, still produces a rectangular picture. Fate decreed that I was seated at the very beginning of the row from where the camera was due to begin its operation. Having studied halfway to 'A' level Physics, I was at least half aware that after the black box had passed me I could disappear around the back and emerge to be re-snapped as the camera reached the end of its arc. Almost certainly I could have achieved this at the time without discovery, but once the photograph was developed there would be no escaping recognition. But (and it's a very big 'but'), my headmistress was not known for her tolerant sense of humour and so a prank like that would doubtless have jeopardised my becoming a prefect the following term. I flunked it and became a cowardly prefect. Or was it perhaps an act of supreme self-sacrifice that helped towards my university entrance and medical career?

2

Where Grandma Comes Into It

My call to mission in Nepal

(1962-1970)

Grandma Vince.

TO THIS DAY I CANNOT RECOLLECT why I chose medicine as a career. It was certainly not a carefully researched and prayed-through decision, but I do believe God had his hand in it. I have a feeling that it was the most illustrious choice I could come up with to silence my mother, who was worried that I was slow in defining my ambitions. In retrospect, I can understand her concern; she herself had been denied even a full school education although she was undoubtedly very bright and worthy of it, and so she did not want me to lose the amazing opportunity I had in my generation. It was far from easy for a girl from a non-medical family to gain entrance to medical school in the 1960s, but the State Scholarship – courtesy, I think, of my Biology marks – did the trick, and I was offered a place in Liverpool, the city of my father's birth.

Those five-plus years in Scouseland have left me with many happy memories and generated a number of good friends, most of whom also continued to pray faithfully for me all the time I was in Nepal.

I was such a conscientious student that I had hardly any social life at university; instead I ended up wearing glasses, possibly from eyestrain. I think I had been brainwashed into feeling I was not up to scratch and so was far too scared of failing my exams to do anything other than study. Even though I passed well in my first year, studying had become a habit; and looking back now, I regret I did not 'live it up' a bit more. I was also such a thrifty student that I rode my bicycle instead of forking out for bus fares; and instead of purchasing innumerable notebooks, I used to write my revision notes in pencil on the Formica table in my room in the hall of residence. The highlights of my first two years are equally weird: being introduced to peanut butter sandwiches (which I loved); and Chinese food (which I hated at first). But I did become active in the Christian Union and later was asked to join the leadership committee. One year I was missionary secretary (which was fine); the next year, in my absence, I was elected as treasurer (which was not quite so fine). At the end of the year, the auditor declared that had I entered the figures in the correct columns, his task would have been considerably easier.

After some time in Liverpool, I found a church that provided me with a vibrant fellowship where I was able to grow as a Christian while immersed in my medical studies. As they did with many other students, the pastor and his wife (Robert and Ruth Rowland) took me under their wing and fed me with Sunday lunches after interesting sermons. Even today I continue to visit the 'Tab' (Toxteth Tabernacle Baptist Church) where a diminishing number of members still remember me as a student.

During my one and only 'long vac' from university (Medical Students have to work so much harder than all others), I went to the Keswick Convention. It was neither the rain nor the deeply theological or spiritually inspiring messages that I remember, nor even the challenging missionary meeting, but rather a personal meeting with Dr Ruth Watson, one of the NEB (Nepal Evangelistic Band) pioneers. She became my heroine and from then on, my sights were increasingly set on Nepal. Along with friends in the university Christian Union, I began to pray regularly for the work of the NEB.

In my second year, I took driving lessons and passed the test first time, so I could have left bicycles behind for ever. It didn't quite work out like that. Without the necessary funds to purchase a car, I bought a little blue Honda 50, which I learnt to ride in a one-way street in the centre of Liverpool. It made travelling all over the city to complete my various medical assignments so much easier and quicker. But then, one dark and stormy night, I was riding it across town to visit friends in the north of the city when somewhere along the Scottie Road a dog dashed out in front of me. I braked, skidded and ended up in the gutter with bruised knees and ragged nylons, but luckily there was no car on my tail. A kindly local couple rushed out to pick me up, took me into their flat, gave me some new stockings and sent me happily on my journey. The following week I ventured that way again to take them some chocolates as a 'thank you'. As for the dog, I assume it came off better than I did.

In Third Year, in 1964, I was called for a distinction *viva voce* in Biochemistry. They asked me about the danger of microbial contamination from another planet, and I said I thought it was quite a possibility. My examiner countered that surely any micro-organisms carried on the outside of the spacecraft would be destroyed by heat on re-entering the earth's atmosphere. Undeterred, I argued that they could instead be carried on the inside, after man's walk on the moon. The interview ended and I was ushered out, suffering a sinking feeling of naïve stupidity. A few weeks later the worst was revealed: they had given me not only a distinction, but the prize as well. A few years later, the facts themselves were also revealed: I was all set for a career at NASA[9], but the fresh air and slightly less ambitious heights of the Himalayas were already beckoning.

The following year, while on an exchange scholarship in India, I had a particularly vivid dream in which the central and only memorable feature was that my name was not on the pass list for Pathology. This so terrified me that I spent the remaining two and a half months of the student elective with my nose in a textbook and missed some of the otherwise exciting smells of the east. Does God speak through dreams? I believe he did on this occasion – so that I would study and pass my exam. Later, in Nepal, I discovered that he does this far more often than I had

[9] NASA – National Aeronautics and Space Administration.

ever imagined. How else can he communicate with people who cannot read or have never heard of him?

My time in India taught me several other important lessons. Little green bits in Asian omelettes are not beans – but chillies. Ants (like me) are fond of Golden Syrup and so make the most of it when some visiting idiot (again, like me) leaves the top off the jar. Mosquito and flea bites can be survived... just. Putting on a sari is not an impossible task and the result can even be quite pleasing. Above all, I discovered that I could live in Asia – for three months, at least.

That year was also my 21st birthday, the big landmark in those far-off days. My parents had arranged a car treasure hunt but I remember little of that – only the argument I had with my mother about what I should wear for the great occasion. It was one of many we had had regularly over the previous few years, but I felt that having at last 'come of age' I should be allowed to choose my own wardrobe – but it was 1965, after all. A month later, I committed the "unforgivable sin", whatever that might be. I had never been a rebellious teenager, apart from where clothes were concerned, but what I did then apparently more than made up for it. All I did, in fact, was to borrow my mother's car and drive it to Liverpool and back at Easter. She'd given me permission to drive it while she and my father were away over the weekend, but had not specified that that only meant local trips – and of course I never asked. Strictly speaking, therefore, I had not done anything wrong. In fact, had my parents not phoned up on the Sunday to see how I was, I would have been home before them and they would have been none the wiser. My exploit would have remained undiscovered and yet another important lesson (though I'm still not quite sure what that was) left unlearnt.

In due course I graduated with honours and a warning from my father to be very careful as it is well known that doctors bury all their mistakes. I started to practise my new skills on the unsuspecting sick population of the north of England, for which I was paid the princely sum of around £90 a month. If on call time is included, this works out at less than five shillings old money (or around 25p new money) an hour. To be fair, in 1969, after half an hour's work, i.e. with two and sixpence in my pocket, I could buy a gallon of petrol to feed my little green Triumph Herald. At last I had four-wheels, a fantastic graduating present from my generous father. I didn't make a fortune but I really enjoyed my two years in the NHS and believe that some (at least) of my patients appreciated me. The mother of my first Caesarean section baby has remained in touch and prayed for me for over forty years. I was no medical genius but I do remember impressing my consultant by tentatively diagnosing a cancer of the neck of the womb. That lady was pathetically grateful that it was found early but, sadly, I have no idea what happened to her. Sometimes the long hours got to me – as they did (and still do) to all junior doctors. With a due degree of shame, I remember shouting at the night nurse down the phone when she woke me at around 2am, wanting me to come and look at a patient. What I said was absolutely correct – there was nothing more I could do medically – but it was the way I said it and my careless attitude towards a dying patient that led her to rebuke me. Happily, she was a lot older and wiser than me and bold enough to tell me off; and I managed to find sufficient humility to apologise, get out of bed and go to the ward. It was a hard lesson but, perhaps surprisingly, it also led to a good friendship with that nurse.

In 1967, the summer that I graduated, I had volunteered to be chief bottle-washer and assistant to head cook Joyce at a Himalayan Helper house party. This was a summer camp for youngsters interested in Nepal and the NEB, and there I met more missionaries from Nepal and other people like Joyce and myself who were wondering if God wanted us to go and work in that country. From then on I was even more keen to go to Nepal, but I knew that this was not enough. If I was to overcome the hurdle of learning a new language, cope with a lot of strange pathology, and survive in a land of large spiders, and all with no guaranteed salary, I needed a clear direction from God. He gave it on the weekend of my grandmother's 90th birthday.

By then I was working as a surgical houseman and, happily, that was my weekend off, although as Monday was our theatre day, all new patients had to be checked on the Sunday, regardless of which weekend it was. That meant I returned to Liverpool after the party and was up early on Sunday to do all the pre-ops before going (I hoped) to church. As I knelt by my bed and committed the day to God, I confess to getting a bit impatient with him. I told God that the time was well overdue for him to inform me whether he wanted me in Nepal or not. Then I went down to the ward, where, to my amazement, I discovered that every single new admission had already been clerked in. This had never happened before, and never happened again, but just on that very day my opposite number had kindly seen all my patients for me. Very happy, I dashed off to church in time to attend the pre-service prayer time. I had completely forgotten my earlier prayer until one of the church leaders read Psalm 138 verse 3. It says, in the Authorized Version, which we were still using in those days, "In the day when I cried thou answeredst me..." and it felt like a kick in the spiritual solar plexus. I just knew that by the end of that day, I would have my answer about Nepal, and suddenly, I wasn't so sure that I wanted it. It came anyway – at the very end of the service as we sang a hymn that symbolised Nepal for me in the words, "Green pastures are before me, which yet I have not seen," Green Pastures being the name of the leprosy hospital run by the mission I was hoping to join.

After gaining my full registration as a doctor, I spent six months on an Obstetric Unit, delivering babies and eventually acquiring a diploma to prove I could do this safely and satisfactorily. In general, I had been taught that as a Christian I should pray about every step of my career, but this was one I decided could be exempted. Wherever God wanted me to work there would always be babies; in fact, in Nepal in those days there was a superabundance of them, partly due to the lack of any serious family planning programmes. I have since learnt that this is not a good way to make decisions. However, all through my working life I think the job I enjoyed the most was delivering babies.

Sometime later, as preparation for returning to Asia, I spent a year at Bible College where, amongst many other worthier pursuits, I learnt how to *leepnu*[10] a floor. In fact, they almost succeeded in also teaching me how to shampoo a carpet, but this has not been of nearly as much subsequent use to me as the former, and at the time it was a near disaster for the whole college. My enthusiasm for the task meant that I soon ran out of the pressurised foam cleaner. To get more I descended to the basement, the floor of which I had recently *leepnu*-ed. The first container refused to function; the second I knocked over, and it rolled under the cupboard and immediately began to exude bubbly foam everywhere, including over me and my beautifully *leepnu*-ed floor. But then my

---

[10] Leepnu – besmear with mud. (In England, I did it with polish.)

emergency mode kicked in; I grasped the can and rushed upstairs so that what remained of the foam could get to work on my dirty bit of carpet. After that I had to mop up the *Yeti*-tracks[11] I had made in the basement and re-*leepnu* the floor. It was a miracle that I got a reasonable reference from the college, but then, I wasn't likely to be using an aerosol carpet cleaner in rural Nepal.

Among the more valuable skills I picked up at Bible College was a deeper knowledge of the Bible, although this could not be passed on in Nepal for several decades, there being in force until the 1990s a strict law against proselytism. But, you may ask, "How can you be a missionary if you can't proselytise?" The answer is simple: "Real missionaries don't proselytise." What I mean is, we don't force anyone to believe, or allure converts by paying them to join up – that's proselytism, and it's very different from living a life that attracts people to Jesus, telling them about him, and offering to pray for them when they are in need.

When I had enrolled in Bible College, I was a confident (and, I suspect, proud) young professional, so when someone shared 2 Cor. 12:9 with me I appropriated the first half of the verse – "'My grace is sufficient for you...'" – and essentially ignored the second half – "'...for my power is made perfect in weakness.' Therefore, I will boast all the more gladly of my weaknesses, so that Christ's power may rest on me." It has taken me all the years since then to accept that if I want Christ to work in me and through me, the whole of the verse is important – and I'm still learning it.

After Bible College I spent the summer learning how to learn a foreign language. Phonetics reinforced what everyone already knew – that I was tone-dumb as well as tone-deaf – but Phonemics was fun, like solving a code. My previous experience of English had shown me how irregularly irregular grammar could be, yet obviously God knew which country had a language that was phonetic and its grammar regular. But more of linguistics later...

---

[11] Yeti – abominable snowman.

3

Boats, Bombay and the Nepal Border

En route to Nepal

(Late 1970)

Left: Val in 1970. Right: Fishtail mountain with the International Nepal Fellowship compound in the foreground.

BY 1970 I HAD BEEN ACCEPTED to work with the NEB and began saying my farewells and enrolling friends, family and churches to pray and give towards my financial support. There were many things to buy and to pack because little was available in Nepal in the early 70s. There was a rule in the mission that all those going to Nepal for the first time had to pay for their own fare and provide all their own kit – the idea being that it would increase our trust in God to provide the necessary funds and also confirm that we were really doing what God had directed, not just following our own romantic ideas. This was a valuable experience as in the future there was no guaranteed salary attached to the post I was going to. Because I was no longer working in the NHS, this was a challenge, to put it mildly, but I discovered a strange fact: it seemed that whenever I purchased one lot of things 'in faith', funds started to come in for the next lot, and so on. I collected drums, trunks and boxes and began to fill them – with books and a bookcase, a table and chair, curtain material, underwear, marmite, camera films; almost everything except the kitchen sink. I particularly remember stocking up with 'feminine care' essentials for the next five years. Dot, a friend from Bible College, who also had her sights fixed on Nepal, came with me and nipped into Boots to pick up two giant boxes of Tampax while I drove the car around the block. The alternative (which, understandably, I rejected) was to buy yards of muslin for a do-it-yourself kit. Various churches arranged farewells for me but the occasion I remember best is the day I said goodbye to Grandma. She was now over ninety and my last words to her were, "I'll see you in heaven, if not before." Now I'm looking forward to that.

At last in November I was again heading east, this time by ship, but as Britain was no longer an empire, and P & O[12] no longer operated liners from Southampton, Peppy and I had first to travel overland to Venice. I have never suffered from home sickness so with characteristic lack of emotion I bade my parents farewell at Victoria Station. Little did I know that that would be the last time I would ever see my father – on earth. I was far too excited to remember much of the journey, except for boarding the ship. The MV Victoria was anchored out in deep water and to reach her we were taken from the canal in a small boat together with our cabin luggage. It was simple enough for me to climb the ladder from boat to ship but a far more faith-challenging, prayer-stimulating exercise to watch my case being carried up that same wobbly ladder.

Lloyd-Triestino was an Italian line, but judging by the length of its spaghetti, the quality of its pizza, and the flavour of its coffee, no one would have guessed. Nearing the equator, I suddenly produced a crop of itchy spots, thought originally to be bites sustained during our last port of call and a foretaste of life to come in tropics. But then, Peppy, studying my back in detail one day, diagnosed chickenpox and so I was automatically and humiliatingly debarred from the aquatic festivities of crossing the line. Nevertheless, it was a good time to relax (I would have said 'chill out', but one didn't do that in 1970, especially on the equator) and get into gear for the next phase of my life. Shipboard life was mostly fun, except for the time when I must have upset Doreen, a young

[12] P & O – originally Peninsular & Oriental Steam Navigation Co.

Salvation Army missionary travelling out to India. I have no recollection of what I had done or said; all I remember is that when it came to the church service on the boat, I had a really bad feeling and realised I could not take communion before I had apologised to her. Clearly, I did not learn this lesson properly at the time; at least two more times in the future I had to eat humble pie and say sorry to colleagues under similar circumstances.

Two other quite different incidents have also stuck in my memory. The first was in Cape Town. I still find it hard to describe the horror I felt when I saw apartheid in action – "Whites Only" labels on taxis... The second was in Karachi. Peppy and I had befriended an elderly gentleman and so accompanied him on a shore visit. As it turned out, the fact that he had a doctor and a nurse with him was providential. While we were all sitting in a not very salubrious restaurant having a snack, he suffered what was probably a TIA[13] (i.e. a transient mini-stroke), but happily, we were able to get him safely back to the boat – all very nerve-racking for us, but by the next day he seemed none the worse for his experience.

My memories of Bombay (now Mumbai) docks have largely been washed away in gallons of sweat, but the one impressive thing that has stayed with me is our tour of the city by night with our shipping agent. With due ethnic pride he showed us the Parsee cemetery, a tower in which the bodies are hung as food for the vultures; and, more pleasant, he drove us around the harbour where the lights shining around the semicircular bay were like an expensive crystal necklace against the silky black evening gown of the Indian Ocean. Then, after three days of sticky confusion, we left the city behind and headed north, enjoying the smuts and idiosyncrasies of Indian Rail. One main recollection is that both the flavour of Indian Railways' coffee and the length of its stations are far in excess of anything British Rail can offer, despite both having a common progenitor back in the days of the British Raj.

I was no stranger to the wiles of Indian trains. In South India, when I was a student, my friend and I had been advised to find a 'ladies only' compartment, which we dutifully did and spent a very pleasant journey sharing an almost empty compartment with an elderly Indian matron,

---

[13] TIA – transient ischaemic attack.

whose only demand was that we read the Bible to her. Naïvely expecting to be able to repeat this same good fortune at will, I suggested we try the same tactic again. But this second time there were 18 female adults and 8 children plus 1 extra person lying full-length on the luggage rack. When morning came and he rolled away his blanket, his beard showed that he had no right to be in that carriage at all, let alone occupying the luggage rack.

One of the many good things about Indian Rail is the vast quantity of *chha*[14] that continually runs up and down the corridors, although actually, it's the *peon*[15] with the big teapot and little clay cups that does the running – unless the train stops with a sudden lurch. The bad thing about our journey was that we had to make two changes, and this was when the fun began. We were travelling on a smaller, loop-line mail train with no corridor, and were approaching our second change, by way of several small stations that we knew we would have to retrace eventually on the third, north-bound narrow-gauge track.

Suddenly, at one stop, the guard popped his head into our compartment and conversationally, and quite logically, enquired, "Why didn't you get off at the previous station with your luggage?"

We replied with equal logic, "No one told us our luggage had disembarked."

In fact, we had been specifically directed to continue to the bigger station where there would be sufficient porters and time to deal with our 29 boxes, barrels and cases. As station succeeded station the conversation continued while the guard ran up and down the platform to communicate with us every time the train stopped. Our luggage got left farther and farther behind.

"Yes, your luggage did get off earlier."

"Oh dear, what happens now?"

"You'll have to pay a surplus charge as you are travelling beyond your luggage."

"But that's hardly fair."

"It's the rule."

---

[14] Chha – Hindi for tea (Nepali: Chiya) [chha also means 'is' in Nepali].

[15] Peon – general factotum, odd-job man etc.

"OK, but can't you make an exception – a reduction – as we were not told this had happened?"

"I'll have to check..."

We alighted at the main station and duly caught the narrow-gauge train back towards the north. As it drew into the little halt for a brief stop, we saw all our luggage piled up on the platform. That was both reassuring and challenging. How were we to get all 29 pieces onto the train in 5 minutes? The station authorities protested that they were not set up to handle that amount of luggage, which made us wonder who had earlier manhandled it off the other train in such a remarkably short time and without us noticing. They further stated categorically that they could do absolutely nothing to help us. But in the East there is always a way around a problem, if only you can find it, and the solution here, unfair though it seemed, proved to be that we hire private porters. Had we only had to haggle over the cost, it might have been relatively simple, but the scheduled stop proved just too short for the porters to finish their task. This was largely because most of the time was taken up, not with loading, but with an argument about where to put the boxes, and then, when that had apparently been settled and when almost all were aboard, another official appeared and reversed the decision. The inevitable happened. The guard blew his whistle and the train started to draw out of the platform with half our porters on and half our luggage off, until one of the private porters proved he was worth what we were paying him by pulling the communication cord. While that was being investigated, the loading was completed, the porters paid, and we breathed a huge sigh of relief.

Eventually, we arrived at the end of the line, long after all the officials had retired, and we had to spend the night in the station with an extended family of over-welcoming mosquitoes.

The next morning we anticipated problems crossing the border, but in the event, entering Nepal was ridiculously easy. As we were very obviously not loaded with umpteen cameras, various tape-recorders and a miscellany of firearms, our rickshaws were allowed to trundle across with a minimum of fuss and we were even in time for a late breakfast at our colleague's home.

We were fortunate; not everyone used to get across so easily. In the pioneer era, when faced with a large white box, one customs man asked, "What is it?"

"It's a refrigerator."

"What's a refrigerator?"

"Um... It's a sort of box."

"What's it made of?"

"Metal."

"And what's it used for?"

"Storing food."

"So, it's a metal box for storing food."

"Yes, I suppose you could describe it like that."

And so our first mission refrigerator had entered Nepal as a metal box for storing food – and at an accordingly low rate of duty. This was no deliberate deception; how else could one categorise a refrigerator for someone who had never seen one before?

It was Christmas Day 1970. I had reached Nepal but we still had to get to Pokhara, up in the hills. When the first mission team had arrived in 1952, they had walked in, but twenty years on there was a new road from the border. However, I discovered it would still take us all day to get to our destination, partly because of one big obstacle: a vital bridge had not yet been completed. Leaving behind 27 of our 29 boxes, and being assured they would follow in a few days, we caught a bus from Bhairawa. All very civilised – apart from the goats and chickens who shared our journey. At Butwal, the end of the road for the bus, we decamped into a small jeep, together with more passengers than seats, and set off again. At the river at Ramdi Ghat, we crossed by means of a hand-pulled ferry and then, after zooming around more than 1,200 Z-bends, we reached Pokhara just as our colleagues were about to sit down to their Christmas meal.

And so I arrived in Nepal – a land where the men wore the hats, where examinations and their results affected only a privileged few, where a journey over the next hill was for some a more major achievement than a walk on the moon, where there were no carpets to shampoo but thousands of mud floors to *leepnu,* where there was only one railway line, where they store most of their ice above the snow line rather than in refrigerators, but knowing that I was in the place where God wanted me to be. That was really important, especially as my first house in Nepal was a tiny mud and thatched hut which I just knew was infested with spiders. Apart from God, I would probably have turned tail and run home immediately. In fact, several times I seriously considered doing just that, always when confronted with an eight-legged challenge. One time, in desperation, I woke up a friend and, presuming on her courage and Christian character, succeeded in getting her out of her sickbed to come and kill the creature for me. Another time I remember standing in my mud hut shaking uncontrollably, watching the progress of a large arachnid all too near my bed. I clutched my big black bible in both hands (to stop them trembling) and prayed as never before.

4

Jai Nepal

The history and development of Nepal

Left: Hindu temple. Middle: Everest. Right: Buddha.

NEPAL MAY BE PICTURED AS a slightly lop-sided rectangle, tilted down at the eastern end. Quite simply, it may be divided east to west into four sections by means of its five main river systems, all draining south into the sacred and rather murky Ganges, and north to south into three divisions: the high Himalayas, a natural barrier to the Chinese; the hills and valleys, where all sensible people live; and the southern plains (the *Terai*), continuous with the mosquitoes of India. King Prithvi Narayan Shah, the founder of modern Nepal, spoke of it as a garden in which there are four castes and twenty-four sub-castes – a picturesque but still problematic description. Nepal, with its 50,000 or so square miles, is not a big country; though if all the hills and valleys were ironed out flat it would be considerably larger – and a lot less interesting.

There are some things that (almost) everyone knows about Nepal, even if they know nothing else. It is the land of Everest, the world's highest mountain. It is the home of the famous Gurkha soldiers. And it is the birthplace of Siddhārtha Gautama Shakyamuni – better known as the Buddha. It was also (at the time I arrived) the only Hindu kingdom in the world and very proud of being so.

Until the middle of the 18th century, Nepal was not even one kingdom. It was a conglomeration of around 53 tiny feudal hill states, whose borders were habitually changing. 'Nepal' meant not the nation but the Kathmandu Valley, a small area bounded on the east by the Sunkosi River and on the west by the Trisuli. It had been ruled by a succession of dynasties over possibly the last two thousand years. Little is known about the very early history of Nepal, and of the Gopal and Mahispal dynasties; it is lost in the mists of time and the myths of religion. The Hindu and Buddhist legends are fascinating – and unbelievable, probably because they are just that. A bit more is known of the eastern Kirants, who seem to have migrated to Nepal from Mongolia around the time Moses was migrating from Egypt to Israel; and of the Lichavis, who came from India at the time the Roman Empire was celebrating its millennial birthday. They ruled for almost as long but over a vastly smaller territory, and were followed by the Mallas (Newars) who were civilising Nepal during the centuries that Europe was mired in the Middle (or Dark) Ages. They were still going strong when Columbus sailed the ocean blue and Luther nailed up his *95 Theses*. They continued until almost the time that William Carey arrived in India and began, among many other things, to translate the Bible into Nepali.

The latter days of the Mallas saw the establishment of the very first (Roman Catholic) church in Nepal. This period was an amazing example of modern religious tolerance, such that a small number of Capuchin monks had been allowed to live in each of the three major kingdoms of the Kathmandu Valley. Perhaps because of their medical and other skills, they were respected and even permitted to preach. Sadly, however, once the Shahs came to power they not only ousted the Mallas but also all the Christians. For the next two hundred years, it looked as though God had forgotten Nepal. He hadn't.

1768/9 was a crucial period in Nepali history. King Prithvi Narayan Shah from Gorkha invaded and conquered the three main and other smaller kingdoms of the Kathmandu Valley and made plans to unify the whole country. Unfortunately, he died before completing this scheme, although he did establish the Shah dynasty, which lasted until 2008. These two initial years were also globally significant. Captain Cook set out on his first voyage of discovery, but westerners were no longer allowed to enter Nepal. The first edition of the Encyclopaedia Britannica was published in weekly instalments in Scotland, but there were no schools in Nepal. James Watt patented improvements for his steam engine and Richard Arkwright his spinning frame, so ushering in the Industrial Revolution, but Nepali villagers still lived in an Iron-Age-style agricultural society. Napoleon was born, but European politics only began to impact Nepal during the 1814-16 Anglo-Nepali War. By 1806, King Prithvi Narayan's successors had extended his territory to the borders of Sikkim and Bhutan in the east, to that of Kashmir in the west, and southwards to around Gorakhpur. This was the period of Great Nepal, but it was doomed to last less than a decade.

The Nepalis had expanded their borders too rapidly and, despite heroic skirmishes, were pushed back by the troops of the British Raj. The war ended in a semi-stalemate but with the Brits in a superior position. According to the Treaty of Sugauli, Nepal lost a third of its land mass, but as a consequence of their battle bravery, the 'Gurkhas' began to be enlisted in the British army. 'If you can't beat 'em, then get 'em to join you' seems to have been the motto! It paid off magnificently for both sides. The Gurkhas helped the British during the 1857 'Indian Mutiny' and were rewarded with getting back the south-west corner of their country, so giving Nepal its present-day boundaries.

Only four kings into the Shah dynasty, 'prime minister' Jung Bahadur violently seized power from them in the infamous Kot massacre, a foretaste and pattern perhaps for the equally scandalous palace massacre – the assassination of the royal family – in 2001. Following the original massacre, the nepotic Rana regime of hereditary prime ministers held sway for 104 years until the Revolution of 1950/1, when King Tribhuvan of the Shah dynasty was restored to power. The restoration of the monarchy meant that Nepal began to open up to the outside world, which in turn led to two very important events. The first was of global significance: it became possible to climb Everest from the south (Nepali) side and this in turn led to its conquest in 1953. The second was of eternal significance: two Christian missions were allowed to begin work predominantly in the health sector – the INF (International Nepal Fellowship) in 1952 and the UMN (United Mission to Nepal) in 1954. This in turn meant that Nepali Christians were also allowed to enter the country and work with these organisations. Ramghat, the first protestant church in Nepal, was established in Pokhara in 1952, and before long other churches sprang up in Kathmandu and Tansen. Bizarrely, and presumably for tortuous political reasons, while Tribhuvan had been away in India, his little four-year-old grandson, Gyanendra, had been crowned in Nepal. When Tribhuvan returned to Kathmandu and to sovereignty, he came hand-in-glove with the Nepali Congress Party, but failed to hold a general election and establish true democracy. Like his ancestor, Tribhuvan died early (but under mysterious circumstances) in Switzerland.

His son, Mahendra, almost immediately asserted himself; he sacked the Nepali Congress, imprisoned its leaders and instituted the one-party Panchayat[16] system, a sort of 'guided democracy' with himself as absolute monarch. In 1960 this may have been excusable as hardly anyone outside Kathmandu had been to school; the country was clearly not ready for universal suffrage. Even in local elections, the only way many villagers could identify their candidates was through the use of little symbols on the voting slips – all very sensible to choose between the sun, a tree, a sickle, a drum or an umbrella, although surely including the sacred cow was allowing bias into the ballot. Over the next thirty years, while this regime became progressively more repressive, the church became increasingly numerous. Sadly, the regime specialised, amongst other injustices, in locking up growing numbers of Christians. More positively, this king is remembered for the construction of the Mahendra (or East-West) Highway. Once again the King died prematurely, but this time from a very modern myocardial infarction. Power passed to his son, Birendra.

This Eton and Harvard educated king looked as though he might succeed in dragging Nepal into the 21st century, although his queen remained a very conservative Hindu. One of the very first things he did was to introduce the idea of Nepal as a Zone of Peace, but sadly this was not wholly consistent with the flagging political stability in his own country. By 1980 Nepal had changed beyond all recognition and the new educated middle class demanded a Referendum. It was pretty peaceful

[16] Panchayat – unit of local government from 1960 to 1990, after which they were renamed Village Development Committees (VDCs) until 2017.

(compared with similar upheavals in other countries) and rigged (or so they say); the Panchas continued for a further decade.

However, as the 80s progressed, the mood in the country subtly changed – until in 1990 the people erupted and the second Revolution (far more violent than the first in 1950-51 or the Referendum in 1980) ushered in a new era of freedom. King Birendra strategically changed tactics at just the right moment; he announced a constitutional monarchy and there was a second chance at multiparty democracy. From almost fifty potential parties, Nepal ended up with Congress (moderately right wing, and pro-India) in power and the Communists (who varied from red to very red, and generally pro-China) as opposition, plus a variety of other little parties. It was also a wonderful opportunity for the church. The Christians in prison were released, leaders and members became even bolder, the church started to grow exponentially, and many Bible training centres and parachurch organisations developed – or came out of the woodwork. Once again, however, the political leaders made a complete hash of things, and for many years there was a new government approximately every six months. As democracy was interpreted as freedom for everyone to do their own thing, including protest, one of my Nepali friends renamed it 'demo-crazy'. The resulting lack of progress, especially in the rural areas, triggered the Maoist People's War, and then the events of 1st June 2001 (the assassination of the royal family) marked the beginning of the end of the Nepalese monarchy. Maintaining the family tradition, Birendra died in his fifties – assassinated, it is claimed, by his son Deependra, who was also mortally wounded in the debacle.

Gyanendra (hugely unpopular from the word go) succeeded his unfortunate brother to the throne and was crowned for the second time! In 2005 he tried to do the impossible and turn back the clock, while, at the same time, turning off everyone's mobile phones for a while. He seized all the governing power into his own hands but a year later was forced to backtrack himself. In 2008 he had to abdicate; the monarchy was abolished, and Nepal became a democratic federal republic. All this explains why nowadays Nepal celebrates two separate Democracy Days: Republic Day and Martyrs' Day. But why not – the King's and Queen's birthdays are no longer holiday options!

For the next seven to eight years, the politicians tried, unsuccessfully, to write a new Constitution. Should the country be divided geographically or along ethnic lines? In fact, the political divisions made this an almost unresolvable issue. Should Nepal opt for secular status or return to being a Hindu nation? And, if so, would that mean a return to restrictions on the practice of the Christian faith? Although many Christians imprisoned for their faith were released in 1990, ever since then some opposition – even persecution – has continued within families and in subtler ways from officialdom.

According to the 2011 census, Nepal is more than 80% Hindu, but I prefer to describe the dominant religion as Animistic Buddho-Hinduism, with today an increasing amount of secular materialistic atheism thrown in for good measure. There is an old saying that in Nepal (Kathmandu) there are more temples than houses and more gods (or idols) than people. In the past it was literally true; today I'm not so sure. The human population has rocketed from just over 10 million when I arrived in 1970 to almost 29 million now, and many ancient temples were reduced to rubble during the 2015 earthquake.

Over the years I have tried hard to learn about Hinduism and understand Hindu beliefs, and consequently, I probably now know as much, if not more, than the average Nepali villager – very little! In comparison with Christianity, there is no universally accepted creed summarising the theology, no weekly congregational meetings to explain the faith. Hinduism is mostly a syncretistic conglomeration of rituals and rites passed down from father to son, mother to daughter. It's more about what you do – when you feast and when you fast and which festivals you celebrate – than in which deity you trust. In fact, you can believe in many gods, one god or even no god at all, and still be a devout Hindu – which perhaps explains why the Maoists continue to celebrate the annual *Desai* festival.

In his letter to the Romans, St Paul expressed his distress that so many of his Jewish compatriots were rejecting Christ although they were deeply and sincerely religious. While I have nowhere near his level of empathy, this describes in a manner how I feel about my Hindu friends, who, unlike so many people in the UK, have a genuinely spiritual outlook on life. It's quite natural to talk of the supernatural, and you can mention God without bringing the conversation to a complete standstill, although you can never be quite sure you are both talking about the same god.

Everyone from my generation onwards in the West has summer holidays. Not so in Nepal, but not because the summer is too hot and the monsoon too wet; with 33 *crode*[17] gods to keep on the right side of, there's some kind of religious festival or public holiday to celebrate at least every week. Rice has to be planted and harvested around these so there's hardly any time left for the luxury of an annual holiday.

However, the country comes to a standstill for ten days at *Desai.* No, that's not true. It used to be, but now it comes to a gridlock as everyone is trying to travel to and from their scattered families for the celebration. *Desai* is the time for flying kites and playing on *pings*[18]. In the old days, flying off the *ping,* over the cliff and straight to heaven was a bizarre tradition which thankfully is no more. Rather, *Desai* is a happy time for millions of Hindu Nepalis but not quite so happy for the millions of goats they sacrifice to the goddess Durga/Kali. One weird custom is that they go around with a sprig of etiolated seedlings stuck behind their ears (the Nepalis, I mean, not the goats) and then give each other massive *tikas*[19], made of red powder and rice grains, on the forehead. In contrast, the Christians have no *tikas* because they do no *pujas*[20], and this marks them out as different. Hardly surprising then that in the 1970s most of them tried to avoid a family gathering where they would be pressurised into eating the goat meat offered to the idols and receiving a *tika.* So, there was always a big Christian conference at *Desai* time. Nowadays, with a much larger Christian community, many Christians are brave enough to try to join their families but still steer clear of any of the Hindu rituals. That's easier said than done! It's easier than it was, but still not easy. Since then I have wondered about this; Nepali Christians stand out from Nepali Hindus because they don't have *tikas,* but in the West, where we don't have *tikas,* is it as obvious from my life that I have spent time with the Lord Jesus?

The second most important festival is *Tihar* (or *Deepawali/Diwali*) – also known as the festival of lights. Over the first three days, they worship crows, dogs and cows, no matter that for the rest of the year they can

---

17 1 Crode – 10 million.
18 Ping – swing.
19 Tika – religious mark on the forehead denoting Hindu worship.
20 Puja – Hindu worship.

throw stones at the crows, kick the dogs and underfeed the cows. During the final two days, they worship the goddess Laxmi and their brothers, and decorate their houses with little lamps. Traditionally these were small butter lamps in clay pots but now in the towns they are more likely to be strings of fairy lights. This is the one time in the year when you can be absolutely sure there will be no load shedding[21].

Hindus describe Christmas as the Christian *Desai,* but that's because they don't understand. The festivals have only two things in common – a family gathering and a big feast. The difference is that Christmas is about a loving God sending his son into this world while *Desai* is about war between the gods and the demons, and about appeasing an angry goddess Kali. Christmas is all about love, *Desai* all about fear. A Nepali (Hindu) proverb apparently says, "Without fear there is no love," but the Bible (1 John 4:18) says, "There is no fear in love; but perfect love drives out fear..."

Holi is the festival of colour, a day when no one wears their best clothes. For one or perhaps two days, grown men (and it *is* usually men rather than women) become little boys again, buy fancy water pistols, fill them with coloured water and spend the time shooting everyone in sight as well as throwing coloured powders at each other. It sounds like great fun but it's better not to enquire into the origin. One legend equates the red powder with the blood of a demon; another is a sort of pied piper tale in which the female devil abducting the children is herself destroyed by children's games. This explains why children from Christian families don't join in these festivities, but still it's often so difficult to know what is innocent merriment and what is Hindu *puja* by another name.

One other important festival, for the women, is *Teej.* Superficially it is all about beautiful women in gorgeous red saris fasting for the good of their menfolk and then rejoicing with feasting and dancing. A more perceptive look shows that it is really about the inferior status and oppression of women and how they are expected to smear themselves with red mud and then bathe 360 times in the river to cleanse themselves from the possible 'sin' of having touched a man during their 'unclean' period times of the last year. It's perhaps significant that in Hinduism there is no equivalent festival for ridding the men of their misdeeds! I'm

---

[21] Power cuts.

glad that Christianity is different; Jesus came and took on himself the punishment for both men and women so all of us can get back into a right relationship with God.

You've probably heard the opening lines of J. Milton Hayes' 1911 poem *The Green Eye of the Little Yellow God:*

> *There's a one-eyed yellow idol to the north of Khatmandu,*
> *There's a little marble cross below the town...*

But if you stop and read it all[22] you may be surprised to see what insight it gives into the tension between East and West, Hinduism and Christianity.

Living and working in a Hindu environment, I found to be at the same time both depressing and stimulating. Depressing, because of the almost universal fatalism and resignation to what was but could have been made so much better; stimulating, because of the comprehensive spirituality. It was thrilling to speak to people for the very first time about the Lord Jesus – not that I was very good at doing this.

The cataclysmic earthquake of 25th April 2015, with its hundreds of aftershocks, landslides and avalanches, will be remembered by the surviving victims and their families probably for even longer than their forebears talked of the 1934 quake. The shattering effects of this recent disaster are well known, less so the devastation that did *not* occur. It happened on a Saturday when children were at home, not in school; when families were together and Christians mostly worshipping in small, single-storey church buildings. The good news was that because of the scientific characteristics of the quake, it was not nearly as widespread nor as destructive as had been forecast. It killed a total of nearly 9,000 but the predicted figure for Kathmandu alone had been 40,000. The bad news is that because the tectonic forces that produce quakes have not been sufficiently dissipated, Nepal can anticipate further tragedies like this in the unknown future.

In the aftermath of this disaster, the Government of Nepal (GON) promised compensation to 2 million families who had lost their homes – but more than six months later nothing had been received. Over 4 billion dollars had been pledged by the international community, but I

---

[22] The full lyrics can be found in the Appendix.

understand much less had been received by GON, who had problems deciding how the funds should be disbursed. I have also been told that if individuals started to rebuild their own homes independently, they would automatically forfeit the compensation and so not be able to build stronger (earthquake-proof) structures that would last. One year on and thousands were still without permanent new homes.

Also, following the earthquake, the four main political parties at last got together and began to get their act together to complete the Constitution and reconstruct their country – with what will hopefully be better building standards and improved preparedness for future calamities. After innumerable delays and discussions, the new Constitution was eventually promulgated on 20th September 2015. Nepal was formally declared a secular republic, but at the last minute an extra clause was inserted, once again stating that conversion was illegal and punishable. The way the country was divided into seven new regions infuriated the *Terai* peoples and soured relationships with India. This led to revolts and strikes, and many months of border closure, which added an extra unnecessary burden onto people still struggling to recover from the earthquake.

In 2014 Nepal was ranked 145 on the global Human Development Index (HDI), compared with the UK at 14. However, a joint UN and Nepal National Planning Commission report in 2010 had optimistically predicted that Nepal would reach most of its Millennium Development Goals by 2015. It looked as though the country was at last climbing the ladders of progress, but then no one had reckoned with the bite of the big slippery snake that in April 2015 took many villages effectively back to square one.

Statistics (which we all know can lie) showed that Nepal was on target to eradicate extreme poverty and hunger. What we also know now is that 20% of this decline of poverty has been due to the remittances (25% of the GDP[23]) sent home by labour migrants. Economic poverty is thus being held at bay at the expense of rich family relationships – husbands and wives, parents and children separated for years on end.

Net enrolment in primary education was nearing 100% when 90% of schools in the three worst-hit districts in the earthquake were

[23] GDP – gross domestic product.

destroyed, leaving almost a million children with no schools in which to enrol.

Women are s-l-o-w-l-y getting a better deal, although more than a third are still illiterate. Maternal mortality has dropped from around 1,500/100,000 live births in 1970 to maybe 190 in the best-served areas of the country, but still, low-caste or Muslim women living in a village in the high hills or *Terai* plains are three times as likely to die as a result of pregnancy than their luckier 'sisters' in urban Kathmandu – and up to 24 times as likely as a mother in the UK. If I'd been born in Nepal, even though I never married and had children, I would still mostly likely have expired by now. Life expectancy is up from 42 to 68 but still lags 15 years behind that of the UK.

All child mortality rates have improved so much (down from around 300 in the 1970s to about 40) that it's tempting to wonder if they are too good to be true. To be fair, the average figures (which are the ones most widely circulated) are probably approximately accurate, but sadly, the indices for children from poor, low-caste remote villages are lagging far behind; and all small Nepali children are still far more likely to succumb to a host of infectious nasties than their 'cousins' in the UK.

Malaria is declining although I'm not sure the mosquitos know that yet. So too is TB[24], but that might be partly because some people have not received treatment! It's actually better *not* to treat TB than to treat it badly. This is because if you don't discover and diagnose at least 70% of the infectious cases and then ensure that 85% of these patients are cured by taking their medicines regularly, you are actually helping the resistance forces of the mycobacteria. The result is that the disease spreads in an antibiotic-resistant form, which is just as infectious but a lot harder to treat. On the other hand, if you don't treat them, they will die sooner, before spreading it quite so much, and the disease they spread is invariably the original, non-resistant, somewhat-easier-to-treat variety. Leprosy has been eliminated but not eradicated. Confused? Linguistically they are synonyms but not in Public Health terminology. There is now less than 1 case per 10,000 of the population, which means it has been eliminated as a public health problem, but thousands of people are still

[24] TB – tuberculosis.

living with the aftermath of the disease, and complete eradication, they say, may take as long as another twenty years.

The INF (formerly the NEB) has now operated as an international non-government organisation alongside the Government of Nepal in the health and development sector for more than sixty years. I worked as a doctor with INF for twenty-six of those. Perhaps we can take a little bit of the credit for these extraordinary improvements, especially in TB and leprosy, but undoubtedly God should take most of the glory for sending us all there in the first place.

5

The Hospital that Shines

The Shining Hospital, Pokhara

(Early 1970s)

The Shining Hospital (1970s).

AFTER ONLY ONE WEEK IN THE COUNTRY, I was set to work part-time in the Shining Hospital female outpatient clinic. Three of us shared one small consulting room: my senior colleague, another new doctor and me. Beryl was linguistically gifted and she was soon responding fluently to her patients, though I have a suspicion that for a while, at least, she had no idea what she was saying; it just sounded right and, what's more, it *was* right. I, on the other hand, was linguistically challenged and had to work exceptionally hard to communicate with my patients. Unless I understood what I heard and said, there was no way I could remember it. But once I had grasped the grammar, I knew exactly what I was saying even if it didn't sound very eloquent. Dr Ruth Watson, our senior doctor, role model and mentor, in addition to dealing with her own patients, took it on herself to correct both our Nepali and our medical practice, the latter being rather different from what we had been used to in the UK. Before long, I had an extensive vocabulary which included being able to describe D & V[25] in at least ten different ways, such as 'the ups and downs' which was pretty self-explanatory and 'outside-outside' which could also be fairly easily understood in the context of a developing country with few indoor privies.

I was working in the Shining Hospital – so named, not by its founders, but by former patients who had noticed the huts shining in the sun as they set out from their hill villages. It was a group of aluminium Nissan huts on the *Tundikhel* (the old parade ground) at the northern extent of Pokhara bazaar and conveniently next to one of the funeral *ghats*[26] on the Sheti Khola (river). There were four wards, a maternity suite and operating theatre plus a pharmacy/store. Outside the maternity hut was the 'first stage tree' under which ladies in early labour lounged away the hours until their pains progressed. Inside the wards were the patients on the beds, their pots and pans and blankets (and sometimes live chickens) under the beds, their relatives between the beds, and their drying meat festooned from the roof above the beds. Ward rounds were interesting. By the time I reached Pokhara, the plan was well advanced to upgrade this to a modern building with state-of-the-art medical facilities, but sadly, it never came to pass. The only alternative for patients in the early 70s was the 'Soldiers' Board' – originally a clinic for Gurkhas, which had morphed into the local government hospital. It was no real choice as all the surgery and midwifery were sited at the Shining, which meant we were very popular – and very busy.

Every morning, *Chaukidar*[27] Timothy handed out male and female numbers and a semblance of queues began their long wait for consultations. In spring and autumn it was a pleasant, relaxing day sitting out in the sun, but the monsoon tended to dampen everyone's spirits. I soon noticed that all the cards were written with English numerals, and knowing full well that Tim's reading was pretty basic, I suggested we should change to Nepali numbers. Ruth's initial response left me feeling

[25] D & V – diarrhoea and vomiting.
[26] Ghat – the holy area by the riverside where cremations are carried out.
[27] Chaukidar – caretaker.

I had (again) committed the unforgivable sin, but a couple of weeks later the numbers were suddenly changed! I learnt my numbers very quickly after that. Not every suggestion I made worked out so well. One day Ruth was doing the ward round while I was plodding on in outpatients, but the real problem was that I was feeling far sicker than most of my patients. After vomiting in the clinic waste bucket, I told Timothy not to give out any more numbers, hoping I could finish a bit quicker than usual and escape to my bed. When Ruth returned she took greater pity on the patients than on me, reversed the decision and then went off to lunch (so she'd be ready for theatre in the afternoon) leaving me to struggle on to the bitter end. No wonder her patients loved her so much; I still had lots to learn and a stack of stamina to develop.

The other iconic character in the Shining Hospital in those days was Effie, a scraggy-looking woman with a tight bun sticking out of the back of her head at a rakish angle. Very low caste, she had the unenviable job of cleaning the toilets, which she did with enormous gusto every day. Fortunately, there were only two cubicles but the routine was long-winded and the same each time. Before she could get anywhere near the pans to scrub them, Effie hefted bucket after bucket of water ahead of her. This was because, despite being presented with a (semi-)modern water closet, most of the village patients still operated on their own village system. This dictated that you never do your 'no. 2' at the same spot as anyone else; quite a practical arrangement out in the fields, but more complex and malodorously complicated to clean in a small stall. And to make matters even harder for our poor sweeper, many patients used neither water nor loo paper (not available anyway) but stones which they dropped down the hole after use. Effie was a saint for sticking at this job for so many years, but sadly, as far as we know, she never became a saint in the true Christian sense of the word.

Before setting out to practise medicine in the hills of Nepal, there used to be certain things that it would be to one's advantage to know. I don't mean the kind of knowledge that comes from books or courses in Tropical Medicine, but ordinary, everyday facts about life in the Himalayas, and I had to learn the hard way. One of those interesting things is that a Nepali mother takes ten (not nine) months to produce her offspring, but this is a mathematical convention and not a biological wonder; most easterners count inclusively. In the children's clinic it was particularly important that I remembered this phenomenon. Faced with a child that looked exactly like a one-year-old but whose mum swore was two, I found there was no need to rush off and look up all the causes of dwarfism in the paediatric textbook. Instead, I had to go back to my language lessons and, remembering this trick of inclusive counting, listen carefully for the verb – so long as the crucial word was not omitted (which it sometimes was). Then it was easy: two *lagyo* meant beginning to be two, or anything from one year to two years old; while two *pugyo* meant arrived at two, or anything from two to three years. With the advantage of even only a basic mathematical education, I was thus able to deduce that both two *pugyo* and three *lagyo* could be applied to the same infant on the very same day of its life. After mastering this conundrum at a fairly early stage of my career, I have had time to reflect that actually this is an extremely good system. With still a very high under-fives mortality rate, it was obviously to everyone's advantage to have some method of getting a child to reach five as soon as possible.

Running a children's clinic could clearly be amusing – it is fun to have to explain that a nose that does not run is perfectly normal (although, as all Nepali children in those days had runny noses, this was generally not too well accepted). But it could also be very sad. Too often I came face to face with a tiny scrap of skin and bones with big black, velvety eyes staring so trustingly at me out of their sunken sockets. With the combination of malnutrition and dehydration from dysentery, plus probably a measles pneumonia thrown in for good measure, it was often impossible to save him. It was not that Nepalis didn't care about their children; they did very much. The problem was (and for many today, still is) a combination of poverty, ignorance, distance from the hospital, superstition and generally too many children per family. However much you loved your child, if the crops had failed, there was not enough food to feed him or her. Even if you knew about the hospital, if it was rice planting time, it was infinitely more important to plant the rice, so that the rest of the family would have food for the next year, than to neglect the fields and carry the baby to the clinic. Under those conditions we had many sad belated consultations, but there were also a few successes. Those went some way to make up for the rest, when we saw the joy on the parents' faces as they took their slightly fatter, happy, gurgling infant back to the village, rather than to our nearby river.

Patient examinations were frequently a challenge. Many times I envied my colleagues in the male clinic as the men were always happy to disrobe as far as their underpants. The women were so shy that getting them to undo even a couple of ties or buttons was a major achievement. No unmarried woman was ever allowed to expose her breasts, a cultural practice that made chest auscultation[28] difficult for me and no doubt was also complicated for her when she wanted to bathe at the local tap.

If someone said she had had abdominal pain for years and then, examining her tummy, I saw a whole lot of little round scars, looking just like cigarette burns, I could be sure she was telling the truth. This was a local variety of counter irritant therapy practised by the local healers. Amulets round the neck or offending part meant that not only had the witchdoctor been called in first but that probably my patient had no money left with which to pay her hospital bill. A fancy stone stuck onto a swollen finger was a sure indicator of a snake bite. A young girl with a very prominent streak of red powder in her hair, indicating her recently married status, I learnt to direct immediately to the antenatal clinic. And a Tibetan always had upper abdominal pain no matter what else was wrong with him or her.

I also discovered in the 'good old days' that there was one sure way to tell how long a village Nepali had been ill, even if I doubted the accuracy of the proffered history. It was to count the layers of dirt on the skin, for no sensible Nepali would ever wash a seriously ill patient – would *you,* in river-cold water? In time I became quite expert at picking up these extra little clues to diagnosis that were present in patients in this part of the world. This was really useful as forty years ago I was frequently denied many of the more standard diagnostic tools we take for granted today. Nowadays patients have showers, and doctors have all the tools of the trade, so consultations are not nearly so much fun.

Another thing I learnt was that the older generation invariably dated their diseases from 'the earthquake.' This was the catastrophic quake of 1934, but I guess that a new generation of Nepalis will soon be timing their symptoms from the more recent terrible tremors. Certainly, those who have lost limbs or suffered life-changing spinal injuries will never be able to forget 25th April 2015.

---

[28] Auscultation is the action of listening to the chest with a stethoscope.

Even today, diet is a vitally important issue for Nepali patients. This is partly due to the fact that one theory of causation of illness relates to hot and cold foods, but by that I don't mean those that are cooked and those eaten cold or raw; nor do I mean those that are spicy chilli hot and those that are bland. All foods are categorised as hot or cold and the remedy is to treat with the opposite to restore the balance. Well, I *think* that's the logic of it. To a westerner the categorisation appeared random; I could never remember which was which and so never gave the right instructions.

It was also extremely important that all patients received dietary advice. What could they eat and what couldn't they? Should they take their medicine with hot water or cold? Invariably I made the mistake of telling them it didn't matter, but it did – to them – and I suspect I destroyed the faith of many patients in my cures before they had even swallowed the first tablet. Just once, I heard Ruth resort to telling one infuriating woman that she should not eat elephant eggs. More sensibly, we used to instruct all those suffering from typhoid to drink cucumber juice – brilliant advice as it stopped them eating chillies that would surely have finished off their already damaged gut lining.

One of the things at which Nepalis excel is in giving nicknames – in fact, in giving any kind of names. This proved a nightmare in the hospital as most have at least five names. The first is a secret name given by the priest; sometimes they do not even know it themselves or, if they do, are not prepared to mention it outside of the family circle. The second one is the family place name, like first son, umpteenth daughter or youngest little one. Alternatively, they use the family relationship name and naturally this differs depending on who is talking and about whom. For example, one person's *didi*[29] is another's *bahini*[30], but that is fairly easy to understand. All cousins brought up in the same house are regarded as brothers and sisters, but if you want to be precise you can be, and sometimes have to be if you wish to sort out the intricacies of family trees in tracing contacts of communicable diseases. But if cousins tend to be indistinguishable, the same is not true of uncles. Your *mama* is your

---

[29] Didi – older sister; sometimes also used as a term of respect for an older woman.

[30] Bahini – younger sister; can also mean house-helper.

mother's older brother while your *kanchha ba* is your father's youngest brother, and there are a whole host of other uncles too in most Nepali extended families. Years ago, our mission Home Secretary, who had himself formerly worked in Africa, visited Nepal. Until someone twigged, he went around calling every lady he met *"mama"*, this being the polite appellation in many African countries but totally inappropriate in Nepal!

However complex these names may be, they are the ones usually employed, which is why I have many Nepali friends whom I know only as *amma*[31], *bhai*[32] or *bhauju*[33]. In return I was usually referred to as *Daktar*[34] *Missahib*[35] to my face, which may be better than some of my nicknames, although I would really have preferred the more informal *didi* or *bahini.* In those early days, when I was everyone's *bahini,* some of the old grannies would show their appreciation for my services (to say nothing of the difference in our ages) by addressing me as *babu,* a term of endearment usually reserved for small boys but occasionally used for others of both sexes. Before I left Nepal, more than forty years later, I was regularly being addressed as *bajai*[36], even though I had never been married and never had children, let alone grandchildren.

You may envisage the sort of difficulties we ran into time and again with all these different names. Now the official name is that which is used on official documents and, as such, it may or may not approximate to any of the above. Then, as many village Nepalis did not have any official documents in the 1970s, they dispensed too with official names. The result was that when we asked them, they made one up on the spur of the moment, being ever ready to please. But unsurprisingly, by the next visit they had forgotten the original invention and had to think up another, hence the idea of consecutive hospital records was never wholly successful.

As more and more people got official documents like citizenship papers, this problem decreased, but it precipitated another. Instead of a

---

[31] Amma – mother.
[32] Bhai – younger brother.
[33] Bhauju – sister-in-law.
[34] Daktar – doctor.
[35] Missahib – a respected female expatriate – usually a white person.
[36] Bajai – grandmother.

surname as we think of it, Nepalis use their caste or sub-caste names. As there is only a fixed number of castes, the limited combinations and permutations gave rise to confusion as we could examine half a dozen Dhan Bahadur Chhetris or Prem Kumari Thapas each day. This would not have been so critical if they had all had the same diagnosis as well as the same name (which of course they didn't) – although there was one occasion when I discovered that two antenatal patients were sharing the same card!

But of all the possible names, the most important seemed to be one's nickname. Everyone (including us expatriates) had one, although we were not always aware of it. That was possibly to our advantage for they were usually very accurate descriptions of our quirks. One of our very respected and loved colleagues was known as 'long-toothed old one' and no offence meant at all. I myself discovered that I had two nicknames. One was *'Bahuni*[37] *daktar'*, after my rather prominent, Brahmin-style nose, and the other, 'running *daktar'* because of my familial, unbreakable, but un-Eastern, habit of doing everything at the double.

After working in Nepal for a while, we all picked up this habit of giving nicknames. We had one patient who rapidly became 'Mr Mouse', because on the ward rounds the only bit of his anatomy that we could see sticking out from under the sheets was his sharp little nose. Sadly, he died from TB but 'Mrs Mouse' survived and for many years I was able to help her in her struggle to raise her son and baby daughter. In 1973 I wrote about them to my prayer-partners:

> *You'd hardly recognise Mrs Mouse and her children now. They look so fat and well. The boy goes to school and the little girl is just starting to walk. I'm sure the Lord must have a plan for that family as both mother and daughter were at death's door when we first befriended them.*

By 1974 she had completed her TB treatment and the whole family was well. During those years I was excited when on one visit to her home, she asked, "Aren't you going to sing the *geets*[38] today?" She wanted me to sing some Nepali Christian songs! In fact, I suspect I played one of the

---

[37] Bahun – Brahmin.

[38] Geet – song.

gospel tapes which they and various neighbours seemed to enjoy. I guess I probably explained the words too. I even took my mother along a couple of times and again we (the royal 'we', that is) were able to share a little more about the Lord. By Christmas that year I felt Mrs Mouse was really beginning to understand the gospel; in the middle of 1976 she so enjoyed attending a ladies' fellowship that she brought a friend the next week.

Mithu Basnet (Mrs Mouse) and family.

During the late 70s I continued to visit on and off – sometimes more off than on when I was busy or she was tied up with field work. Her son started to keep rabbits, though it took them a while to realise they were meant to breed like rabbits, but in the end I did enjoy at least one meal of rabbit curry with the family. One time I took Shyam Malla[39] with me as I wanted to pay off a loan she had in the village. His job was to complete the Nepali paperwork officially. Viewed from the perspective of today's inflation and exchange rates, it was a tiny sum but very significant for her at that time. With increased health and some help from a neighbour who worked at the local Health Post, Mithu (her real name) was able to seize every opportunity to earn some money by doing field or other casual work. This was vitally important as for her it was literally true that 'without work there is no food'. I had hoped that she would keep attending the Christian meetings but then, probably because she was working too hard, she had a relapse of her TB and stopped coming.

[39] See Chapter 7.

However, once again she recovered, and I continued to pay Pan Bahadur's school fees because I reckoned that his getting an education was the only hope for them to escape their poverty trap. He studied conscientiously until he passed eighth class, but then, in 1980, when I discovered he had been cheating me over the money for his schoolbooks, I cut him off without a penny (or rather, *paisa*[40]), and told him to find a job. Somehow he still managed to continue studying to the end of tenth class; he also apparently turned over a new leaf and eventually found a job. Someone had obviously been praying for him. Then in 1984 I heard that he had joined the Police. His 'record' (known only to me of course!) had obviously been no barrier, though I did wonder how he had got in without the help he had been expecting from the Health Post lady's husband, who was a senior police officer. Unfortunately, this man had died just at the wrong moment.

Through the late 1980s and early 90s I only visited the family on rare occasions until I heard from a friend, who lived in the same village, that she had died. I was so sad and there seemed no way of tracing her son, who had been posted away from Pokhara. But then, a few years later, in 2000 – and I can't remember how I did it – I tracked him down and found Mithu still alive, hale and hearty, just a little older than me. I also found that Pan Bahadur had managed to purchase land and build a lovely little bungalow just a few minutes' walk from where he had been raised in a tiny shack.

After that I kept in touch with them and visited the family every time I was back in Pokhara. In 2005 she was knocked down by a motorcycle and was all 'black and blue' when I saw her, but she recovered from that and the following year her son was thinking of getting work overseas. In the event, Pan Bahadur wisely took early retirement from the Police before the troubles of the Maoist era. He did not go overseas but found himself a job locally. On several occasions I met his wife and three sons – two of whom eventually managed to travel overseas. Sadly, I never met Mithu's daughter as she had married and was living the other side of the river. Before I left I shared the gospel with them again and gave them

---

[40] Paisa – the smallest Nepali coin, worth 1/100 Rupee; no longer valid currency.

bibles, but sadly, as far as I know, none of the family have ever accepted Christ.

We also treated 'Biggles', a young lad who – goodness only knows from where – had acquired an old padded leather flier's helmet. And then there was 'President Kennedy'. I'm not quite sure how he got the name – perhaps because he was completely fluent in English, but then, he was also totally mad. His chief hobby was tying little trinkets onto a tree in the hospital compound.

Many years later, I reflected on names and titles as I prepared a sermon. Jesus also had many names and all of them were important: Jesus (Saviour), telling us what work he came to do; Christ (Messiah), showing his coming had been planned well in advance; Prince of Peace, proclaiming his eternal plan; and Son of David, declaring his human ancestry; Immanuel (God with us), indicating his divine origin and encouraging us that God understands our human situation; Son of God; and Son of Man, the second Adam who came to reverse the curse of death brought into the world by the first Adam; and our older brother, showing that as we trust him we join his family and that he's there like a big brother, to hold our hand and help us along.

The Shining Hospital was a friendly sort of place – basic but welcoming, sometimes almost *too* welcoming. In its heyday it sometimes seemed that all the world and his two wives were attending our clinics. Occasionally, even this was literally true. A man with no son and heir (a serious state of affairs, as no son meant no one to perform the funeral rites for him when the time came) might bring both his first and second wives to find out what was wrong with them. There was, of course, little point in suggesting the cause might lie with him, as genes and chromosomes were an alien concept, and anyway, male pride would never have let him even consider the possibility. We duly examined both wives and just occasionally also managed to conduct a semen analysis, though explaining the results was a test of our diplomacy, especially when the laboratory technician became confused between sperm mortality and motility.

Most families did not have this problem. Rather the reverse: too many pregnancies and too many children; and too little family planning.

Sometimes, I felt that all the *suitkerries*[41] in the valley (and some from outside) waited until they heard I was on call and took it as the signal to produce their babies – and usually with complications. In one short week while Ruth was away once, I think I worked my way steadily through every obstetric problem in the book – Caesars, breech, arm prolapse, and retained placenta – although my book was not forthcoming on how to conduct a forceps delivery on the floor by candlelight.

Our operating theatre was particularly popular as it was the only one within miles (or, more accurately, for days around). At the beginning, there were no Nepali nurses so our pioneers trained their own. The exercise was a resounding success; Regina, and later Mongali, made excellent operating theatre nurses. There was just one slight problem when it came to gloves. As Pokhara never got really cold, no one ever wore gloves; thus, the concept of right and left gloves to go with right and left hands respectively was initially a puzzle to some of the staff – and, by extension, a problem for some of us surgeons.

My first anniversary of arriving in Nepal was celebrated by sewing up a ruptured uterus. It was the first time I had seen one, let alone tackled one on my own, and to this day I am convinced that the reason the patient survived was due far more to prayer than my medical expertise. The most memorable feature of this crisis was undoubtedly the four-hour haggle with nine male relatives, all of whom refused to donate a pint of blood. Eventually, with a rather watery pint of blood from a kind female *saathi*[42] dripping into her veins, I had agreed to the operation. That same year I got my Christmas dinner late after an emergency Caesarean section, while on Christmas Eve some of us had listened to carols while we embroidered back into place bits of the scalp, face and back skin of an unfortunate husband and wife team who had both been mauled by the same bear.

The operating theatre was also the venue for perhaps the worst linguistic mistake I made in those early years. During surgery a relative of the patient was always allowed to sit in – so long as s/he did not move from the sterilising drum in the corner of the theatre. This was ostensibly to see fair play. Now I had developed a system of immediately putting

[41] Suitkerrie – delivery case.
[42] Saathi – friend.

into use any new constructions or vocabulary I learnt and this generally worked well. One day, after learning a new word for 'finished', I tried it out. As Ruth was inserting the final stitches after a successful operation, I turned to the relative and said the operation was *katam.* What I hadn't picked up in my language study was that *katam* carried the implication of 'finished, dead and gone'. Ruth's explosive response left me in no doubt of this and that I myself had narrowly escaped becoming *katam.*

One day, while Ruth was away, David and I decided to swap roles: he would operate while I gave the anaesthetic. As he couldn't stop the patient bleeding and I couldn't keep the patient asleep, it was not an unmitigated success. However, it did remind us that God gives different gifts and skills to each of us, and it gives him less hassle if we stick to our own.

For many years our electricity supply was precarious and I got quite good at inserting intravenous drips by feel, but one night the *bijuli*[43] actually went right out in the middle of a Caesarean section, forcing me to stitch up by the flickering light of a torch containing well-used Indian batteries – not candles, as we were using ether as the anaesthetic! Still, I was able to retain a glimmer of humour and enough grace to whisper to God, under my mask, my thanks that he had kept it from happening during the most crucial and dangerous stage of the operation.

[43] Bijuli – electricity.

6

The Digory

Patients in the Shining Hospital

(Early 1970s)

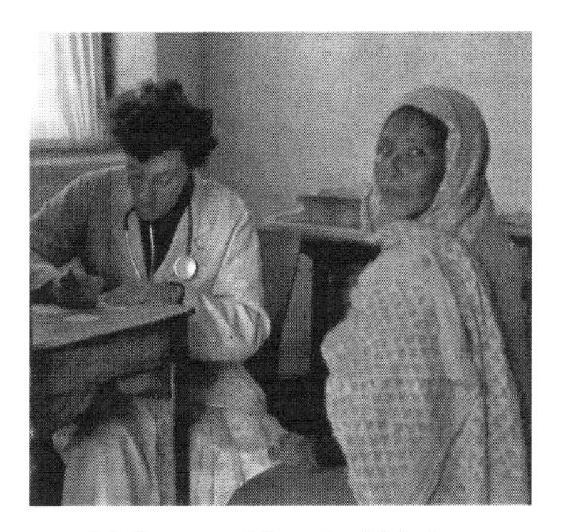

Val consulting in Shining.

IT OFTEN SEEMED TO ME that the only way of being accepted as a doctor was to apply the *digory*[44] to the offending organ (regardless of which one it was) and prescribe a *sui*[45]. Sometimes this simplistic philosophy proved too much for my relatively high-powered medical background, and I would consistently baulk at the idea of putting my stethoscope on a patient's nose. Not so, some of my senior and more easy-going colleagues. The apocryphal story is told of how one sister had applied the stethoscope to the patient's big toe, only to find he was still

[44] Digory – usually the doctor's stethoscope, the symbol of our qualifying degree.

[45] Sui – injection.

not satisfied. He wanted the other *digory,* which turned out to be the typewriter, sitting on her desk in the clinic. For a bit of peace and quiet, she picked it up and was just about to touch the patient's foot with it, when a visiting consultant walked through the door. You don't have to believe this, but I think it's true!

A few stories from the early 1970s will illustrate a typical morning of work in the Shining Hospital; they will make you laugh or cry or perhaps both, but also, I hope, help you understand why God needed to send me – and my colleagues – to Nepal.

"What, me?" said the little old grannie, from her perch on the edge of the stool, addressing no one in particular, sitting as she was with her back to me. I looked desperately around the consulting room trying to reassure myself that she was the crazy one and not I, and that there really was no one else of whom I could possibly have asked the question, "How are you today?" I suppressed an almost irresistible urge to say, "No, your great aunt Maud," as that would have achieved precisely nothing but further confusion. Subtle English humour is a total mystery to Nepali grannies, and as I could not anyway have done justice to the translation, I replied as graciously as possible under the trying circumstances, Grannie being the twentieth person in that day alone who had responded like this to my medical interrogation.

"Yes, you. Why have you come to the hospital?"

Undoubtedly in Grannie's mind, her simple answer to this, "Because I am ill," brought an end to this ridiculous conversation. But not for me; it was just the beginning of the next stage of my troubles.

Eventually, after a great deal of prodding, both physical and mental, I succeeded in getting Grannie to turn around and face me and, more importantly, to describe the exciting details surrounding the mystery of her hospital visit. It was, rather as I had suspected (seeing as I was by now cultivating the skills of both Dr Watson and Sherlock Holmes) because she was suffering from the *jhum jhums*[46] and her skin, her head, her eyes, her tongue, her urine, her tummy – in fact *all* of her – was burning. That diagnosis was easy from the history alone, but making a cursory examination to keep Grannie happy, I was soon able to despatch

[46] Jhum jhums – paraesthesia or pins and needles sensation.

her with a prescription for Vitamin B tucked into her *patuka*[47], and was able to turn my attention to the next patient in the line.

After calling twice with no visible response, I levered myself out of my chair and hauled her in, thereby also ensuring that she sat facing me on the stool. Then, in my most fluent Nepali, I said, "*Namaste*[48] *didi,* how are you?" and looking me straight in the eye, she declared, "I don't understand English." In response, I informed her that if only she would apply her ears, she would hear Nepali no matter what the colour of my skin. As I had also intimated fairly bluntly that I would appreciate some haste on her part as there were about sixty other patients still awaiting their turns, this produced the most amazing tale and for the next five minutes, at least, I was regaled with the whole of her medical and family history. Chronologically, it all seemed to date from the time her fifth child had first been fed rice (and picking that up was a major linguistic miracle for me), but the real complaint was a round, throbbing lump in her abdomen. While visions of hydatid cysts and amoebic abscesses squirmed alongside various species of worms in the depths of my memory, I asked the good lady to lie down on the couch so that I could examine her and see for myself what exotic tropical pathology this might be. Despite an ultra-careful examination of her abdomen, the only thing I could feel was her aorta pulsating against her backbone and this was because she was so thin. This probably also explains why it was a tropical phenomenon; I had never before met a patient with so little adipose tissue that I could palpate her aorta so clearly. But to persuade *didi* of the normality of this symptom – in truth, the necessity of it (without her main artery pumping away she would assuredly have been dead) – was a task that almost defeated me. At length I discovered that what she really wanted was a *sui* and without this she had absolutely no intention of budging from her seat in the consulting room. Realising I had met my match, I capitulated, and against all my better judgement, *didi* was soon happily speeding off to the injection room. Those few extra vitamins no doubt did her the world of good.

---

47 Patuka – a six-yard length of cloth that village ladies wrap around their middle and which serves as corset, purse, basket and handkerchief as needed.

48 Namaste – Nepali greeting.

And so it would go on through the morning: village women continued to struggle with that masterpiece of modern technology, the door handle, and I continued to struggle with the not-always-to-the-point conversations in my second language. There was another problem too. If I used the low form of the verb to them, I felt as though I was being rude (and to tell you the truth, I did not know it very well anyway), but when I reverted to the honorific (which, at that early stage of my language learning, I used for everyone and everything from the cat to the King – just to be sure) they did not understand me, as their own menfolk always used the low forms with them at home.

Occasionally, the monotony would be relieved by the visit of an old friend of the hospital – one of the local ladies. She, far from being strange in these semi-Western surroundings, felt with a certain justification (at least from the size of her medical records) that the hospital was hers, and she was going to make the most of it. Such customers could easily be recognised; they would sweep into the consulting room, almost before one had started to offer the invitation, followed by their brood, like a mother hen with all her baby chicks in tow. Sometimes all the five offspring were hers but that particular type would think nothing of smuggling in a couple of the neighbour's children as well. Any righteous indignation that I started to express about the ethics of bringing in six people on one number was generally swamped by her immediate and enthusiastic history-telling. She would never be satisfied until I had put the stethoscope on every single one of her screaming brats (whether they needed it or not), but on the other hand, she would never take offence when I pointed out that they would all be a lot better off for the liberal application of some soap and water. Although this sort of patient made the progress from No. 29 to No. 30 six times as long as it should have been, I was able to economise on the time spent explaining the routine to her. She knew her way around the hospital even better than I did at the beginning, and she had no intention of sitting there while I gave her instructions three times over (the norm with most of the other patients).

One of the commonest – and saddest – presentations was a badly burned child. This was invariably in the winter when the mum had laid the baby near the fire to keep it warm – and he had rolled over into the ashes. The standard treatment was to keep the blistered areas clean and dry by applying Gentian Violet (GV for short); during the cold months we always had a few of these purple-striped babies on the ward.

In the summer they were replaced by 'dried up prunes' – the kids with severe D & V with dehydration. Part of the problem was faulty logic or, perhaps more fairly, non-medical logic. It is an undeniable medical fact that if you have the trots and then you eat or drink something, you will have to run again in a very few minutes. Now you and I know (or, at least, I do) that this is largely to do with the gastrocolic reflex and that the danger of dehydration can be overcome by putting more fluids in at the top end than are coming out at the bottom end – all very simple and crude. But unfortunately, the Nepalis I treated in the early days had also worked out this equation and arrived at the totally opposite, but equally logical, conclusion: if you do not put water in at the top, no more diarrhoea will come out at the bottom. They were, of course, technically correct but it took a lot of time, patience, explanations and drips to restore these children – if it was not too late.

It was often Tibetan patients who gave us the biggest headaches. Those who learnt English excelled at it, and it seemed this was an insurance against getting ill; those who could speak neither English nor Nepali were the ones who came to our clinics. They also seemed deliberately to cause more confusion by adding their own unique calendar to the two already in use in my over-cluttered time schedule. As there was no obvious way of relating the Year of the Dragon (Tiger, Rat, Rabbit etc.) to Nepali time, let alone the international date line, there was accordingly no way of telling how long a Tibetan had been ill, how old he was or how pregnant she was. It was even sometimes a problem to determine their gender. In the 1970s most of them still dressed for the harsh Lhasa climate even when it was mid-summer in Pokhara. Male and female garb were not too dissimilar, both sexes tended to wear plaits and, being of Mongolian stock, even the macho men had little facial hair. So, one day a rather smaller than average, underweight and overclothed Tibetan was first seen by one of our doctors and admitted as a female patient with bronchitis. A short while later another of our senior doctors checked the same patient on the ward and registered him as a case of TB. The patient subsequently expired but whether from bronchitis or TB, mistaken identity or overtreatment, no one has ever let on.

In contrast to some of our ferocious-looking Khampa Tibetan patients, we used to see a large number of diminutive Brahmin brides. Married off as soon as they reached the legal age – or more usually, before that – they became frequent visitors to our female clinics; sometimes, we suspected, only because it gave them a chance to escape for a few hours from the clutches of their *sasu*[49]. Being the youngest *buhari*[50] was a tough life. One day one such sweet innocent confided in my senior colleague in a whisper that she had an itch. A few tactful questions drew out the fact that she was taking significantly less than one bath a week. With even greater tact it was suggested that two or three good washes a week in warm water would probably do her itch the world of good. On hearing that, her face immediately fell, but it was not because she was offended. No, it was, she confessed, because in her house they had no hot water. It was a tea-shop and all the heated water was in the form of tea. Would it be in order, she timidly enquired, if she used tea for her ablutions instead of plain water. I could see the tears beginning to well up in her eyes as she wanted to do as we suggested and was upset, but never for a moment did I think that Ruth would restore her smile as quickly as she did.

"Yes," she said, "you may use tea," and I nearly fell off my stool with shock.

Some patients used to take our instructions a shade too literally. Having asked one man to go "up top", meaning that he should go up to the top of the field, to the male ward, to be admitted, we discovered a considerable while later that he had never arrived on the ward. A short search revealed the poor man staring bewilderingly up at the roof of the outpatient block and muttering to himself something about crazy Western doctors who expected ill patients to climb on roofs. Much to his relief and ours, he was soon tucked up safely in bed and a more conventional form of therapy underway.

Then there was another man, to whom it had been carefully explained that he should "take [his] tablets three times a day in water". He returned after a week, complaining that he was not one whit better, but deeper questioning revealed that he had never taken his tablets. Yet before my

49 Sasu – mother-in-law (husband's mother).
50 Buhari – daughter-in-law.

colleague could administer the due amount of *gali*[51], out came his excuse. He lived on the top of a hill (like 90% of all village Nepalis) and so had found the thrice daily climb down to the river and back to take his tablets "in the water" just too much for his enfeebled state. He had, very sensibly, preferred to spend the time resting in bed. After a hasty explanation of this linguistic mix-up, he was happily off home to take his tablets with a glass of water and was soon on the way to recovery.

As well as Nepali and Tibetan patients, we also had a few world travellers turn up on our doorstep. From 1974, the one I remember best was Luigi, an Italian. He was admitted seriously ill with peritonitis. After emergency surgery he stayed with us for about two months before being transferred to Kathmandu to await repatriation. We undoubtedly saved his life, but I wonder what he did with his life after that? Had any of our faith and prayer rubbed off on him?

Most Nepali patients thought far more spiritually about their illnesses than their Western counterparts. Sometimes this was a good thing; sometimes less so. Epileptics invariably considered that their ailment was due to demon possession, and maybe sometimes it was. Either way, a visit to the Shining Hospital compound always seemed to have a beneficial effect on them. I'm sure Ruth was right when she put this down to the presence and peace of the Lord Jesus among us rather than the pills she prescribed. Christian Nepalis, I discovered, said grace before taking their medicine, something that would never have occurred to me. Of course, it was totally logical; you give thanks before you eat your food so why not before you swallow your tablets?

For many years I was General Practitioner for my expatriate colleagues. The commonest complaint was some variety of D & V, but just occasionally it all became far scarier – as when I had to operate for an ectopic pregnancy or send someone home for cancer treatment. Once, I raced all around Pokhara to try to find an oxygen cylinder, but there were none and my colleague died of pneumonia. Over the years, too, I had to medically vet new candidates; again, usually straightforward but not always so. There was one person I was sure would never survive in Nepal because of a congenital condition, but God had other ideas and she turned out to be a better missionary than I was. I myself kept

[51] Gali – a telling off.

amazingly well most of the time, although in the early days I got amoebic dysentery more times than I care to remember. Later, Giardia became popular instead, and finally I also succumbed to the blue-green algae – when I was studying Sanskrit, though I don't think that had anything to do with it. When the residue in the bottom of all my bottles of precious filtered and boiled water turned blue-green, it gave me a hint about what might be wrong! However, I avoided hepatitis, which almost everyone else had at one time; and malaria, although I didn't deserve to as I invariably forgot to take the tablets when I went to India or the *Terai*. Later, after living in Kathmandu and riding my scooter every day on the city's atmospherically polluted and bumpy potholed roads for many years, it was hardly surprising that I developed a mild form of asthma – and sciatica.

7

Exams, Etymology and English

Language study

Language study.

LINGUISTICS HAD NEVER BEEN MY FORTE: had I obtained just one less mark in French I would have failed, and had I not struggled to memorise twenty-four solid pages of Virgil's "Nisus was guard of the gate, very fierce in arms...", I might have failed Latin too, not that either language has been of any real relevance to me since 'O' level days. Based on my language skill (or lack of it), I should clearly have been rejected for overseas service, and so I had to work very hard to learn Nepali. But I do have to be honest and admit that Nepali is not such a difficult language to grasp. Unlike English, it is phonetic, its spelling is consistent and its grammar obeys its own rules. But, to be even more honest, my acquisition of the language was a matter of survival even more than of study. In the early days hardly anyone spoke English and drastic measures were needed to process the hundreds of patients yelling down both my ears at the same time.

Those measures paid off and I passed both my language examinations with distinctions; in the first year, I wrote a brilliant essay, the climax of which described how I carried home bananas *(kera)* in my gravy *(jhol)*. As in most languages, so in Nepali, similar words may have the most dissimilar meanings and the only visible difference between gravy and bag is the long 'a' at the end. This enabled me later to sympathise with those Tibetans who used to bring home *kira* (insects, not bananas) in their *jholas* (bags, not gravy). In the second year I wrote another brilliant essay but the examiner lost half of it.

But having mentioned Tibetans and Sherpas, I now want to let you into a secret: the linguistic origin of the *Yeti* (as I wittily like to think it might have been). Everyone knows from its footsteps (which is just about the only thing anybody really knows about it) that the *Yeti* is absolutely huge. So when the first Nepali came across the first *Yeti,* sometime in the year dot, he had no name for the beast, but what he did have was a descriptive term for 'so big'. Hence, when he related the scary incident to his friends that is exactly what he said – "It was *Yeti* (so big)" – with the appropriate intonation and gestures of course. And the name just stuck, for why should an economical Nepali villager waste his valuable tea-drinking time thinking up another name when the original descriptive term is perfectly adequate?

Right at the beginning, my language book had instructed me to listen for the difference between statement and question intonation, but try as I would, I could not detect any. Then, after a couple of weeks, my first language teacher left and while listening to her replacement, light suddenly dawned. She had been speaking in a monotone but he spoke naturally. After that things just got better. Shyam Malla was an innately good teacher even though he had had no training. At that time he was doing the job to earn some extra funds to complete his college course although he actually worked in the bank. He was also a mine of information on Nepali sayings, customs, festivals and basic vocabulary. He was always ready to answer my many questions. Every day he listened to me reciting the numbers from one to a hundred – a very worthwhile exercise as it meant I knew what number patient to call into the consulting room – and I could also find my way around the Nepali hymn book better than all my contemporaries. He was very good at correcting my grammar and intonation too. More excitingly, he helped me struggle through reading several simple Bible story books and then was happy to discuss the differences between Christian and Hindu beliefs. We became great friends and for a while I really thought he had understood the Good News. One day, after reading a book I had lent him, he left a little poem he had written while waiting for me to come down from the hospital:

To obtain truth for ever
He himself suffered pain and sorrow;
To show mercy to sinners
The Lord gave himself a sacrifice.

Even after I completed my two years' language study, I still kept in touch with Shyam and his family, and when his third son, Jeevan, was born in 1974, I appointed myself 'godmother'. Then in June 1976, when someone told me Shyam was in prison, I laughed; he was such an honest fellow – but it was true. He had been in charge at the airport branch of the bank when a couple of other employees had made off with a lot of the bank's money. They did it while Shyam was taking his lunch break and even though he had reported the theft as soon as he could, he was considered under suspicion and arrested. It took six months before he was released on bail and a further six months before he was declared innocent. All this time he had been suspended from work at the bank. Another six months on, an appeal was lodged, and so it was not until more than two years after the original crime had been committed that he was fully exonerated and got his job back. Such was the speed and working of the Nepali justice system in those days.

During the late 1970s and early 80s I continued to share my faith with him and once he even came to a big Nepal Christian Fellowship rally with me. On another occasion he seemed to be saying the same things as I was in responding to a very cynical young student. However, when someone asked him why he was not a Christian, he responded, "Because I like my black deeds." Perceptive but sad. During those years too, both his uncle and a nephew died unexpectedly. I found it hard to offer comfort; when someone believes in reincarnation, does that make death easier or harder to cope with, I wondered, especially as Shyam told me not to pray for him but for Biswa (the lad who had died).

Shyam Malla and family.

By the end of the 1980s, Shyam still seemed to be seeking the truth but had begun to turn to vegetarianism and increased temple-going. These are Hindu disciplines that traditionally people take up as they reach middle age, and by 1997 Shyam was already a grandfather – which made me feel old too! Over the years since then, I continued visiting the family regularly. I kept on hoping and praying – as did all my prayer partners – that Shyam would come to believe in Jesus, but it never happened. He just became more and more Hindu as the years passed, and in 2000 he took some of his family on a pilgrimage to Gadhwal/Kumaon to visit some of the holiest Hindu sites. It was not the incarnation itself that Shyam and others found hard but, I think, the uniqueness of Christ compared with the multitude of deities that most Hindus worship. By 2007 all three sons were married and working in the family snacks business, but Bindu, the daughter, was still studying; she was more of a high-flyer than her brothers!

By June 1971 I had worked my way all through the language textbooks and had a line of tape loops hanging in my hut. I knew all the standard sayings by heart but few of them were of much use in the hospital. For example: "Where is the office of the prime minister?" "In Singha Darbar." I think that stuck in my mind as it was the most difficult lesson in the first section of the book and the first completely written in Nepali script. Within this time I had also even managed to say a short prayer in Nepali at the weekly Youth Fellowship. After that first six months we had a short language school taught by senior experienced colleagues; it was punctuated for me by my daily stint in outpatients, and for Beryl by having her first child by Caesarean section. Despite this she still managed to do brilliantly – and even I did pretty well. Shortly after this we were expected to take our turn in leading Nurses' Prayers. As these happened every working day, turns came round quite often! Many expatriates just announced the hymn, asked a Nepali nurse to read the passage and maybe another to do a final prayer. Maybe they were trying to encourage the nurses? In the interests of rapid language learning, however, I adopted a different tactic. It was probably very painful for the listeners but I determined to do everything myself. It was also about this time that I began to read my bible in Nepali every day – something I continued for many years. It paid off in terms of religious vocabulary and understanding and would also often provide me with a new slant on a well-known verse.

There was strong motivation to learn Nepali as it was a mission rule that you could not take your first holiday until you had passed your first language exam. You could also not graduate to being a senior missionary without passing that all-important language exam. In the event, I never became a senior missionary – even after forty-three years – as the different categories were abolished just before I qualified. In the 70s, when work roles were more flexible, I was privileged to be able to concentrate on language learning and therefore only required to work for two hours a day in the hospital, although in practice I usually worked longer than that. Working in outpatients, where few if any patients understood more than a word or two of English, gave marvellous opportunity to use my language learning, although my vocabulary was somewhat limited to medical terminology.

One thing I learnt quickly in OPD[52] was the (linguistic) difference between burning *(polne)* and swelling *(phulne)*. The problem lay in the fact that many westerners (like me) tended to aspirate a word in order to emphasise it, but in Nepali aspirated (breathy) or 'h' sounds are different from non-aspirated ones.

Language problems work both ways and many Nepali colleagues struggled with the idiosyncrasies of English. Usually I empathised with them, but couldn't stop myself laughing the day I read that a patient had "hell burning". He was no religious nutcase but his heels were burning – yet another case of Vitamin B deficiency, and happily, he'd received the correct treatment. An equally hilarious but far more potentially serious linguistic misunderstanding had happened one day in England. In the middle of an operation, the surgeon suddenly shouted at the anaesthetist that the patient was "getting light" (meaning that the effect of his anaesthetic was wearing off) but the anaesthetist, who at that point was more deeply asleep than his patient, awoke only to hear the last word, 'light'. Immediately, he jumped up and adjusted the operating light so that it was no longer shining into the hole in the abdomen. The surgeon was by now doubly furious while the rest of us (excluding the patient as yet) were in stitches.

There are several Nepali words that are traps for the unwary foreigner. One such is *tyessai*. Literally, this means 'just because' or 'without', but without what depends entirely on the context and even then, you have to be careful. For example, if someone tells you they have come *tyessai*, they may be meaning that they have come without any reason; they are just dropping in on a friendly visit, with no ulterior motives. On the other hand, they may mean they have come without eating and therefore that it would be a good idea if you offered them a snack or, better still, a full rice meal. The solution to the conundrum was therefore not linguistic but involved developing a more truly generous Nepali-style hospitality. Oh, and before I forget, if someone leaves a restaurant *tyessai*, it means they have run off without paying the bill.

Another interesting word is *kina* or 'why', as the answer given was frequently *tyessai*. It leads to interesting conversations like...

---

[52] OPD – Outpatients Department, usually called 'outdoor' in Nepal.

"Why did you not come to the hospital yesterday (that being when I had specifically asked her to return for valid medical reasons)?"

"I didn't come yesterday." (Or, possibly, "*Tyessai.*")

This, of course, did not tell me any more than I knew already.

If then I gave her the benefit of the doubt – perhaps she had not heard me correctly – and I repeated the question, I usually got, "I just did not come yesterday."

And I know who tired first in this sort of dialogue...

But there were rare occasions when the question was answered and it always was, "I did not come to the hospital yesterday because I was ill," which, to my medical mind, was exactly why she had been asked to attend the clinic.

Another word that is less often used, possibly because it is not quite so polite, is *kunni.* It has no one exact translation but is the universal answer to the question you cannot or do not wish to answer. In broad terms it means 'I don't know' (or I can't be bothered to find out whether I know or not) and 'I don't care' combined with a fatalistic sense of 'Who knows anyway?' and 'Why bother anyhow?' And by this time, they are probably quite right too; I don't care any longer. It can be a very useful word.

Yet another lovely descriptive phrase is *bholi-parsi.* As *bholi* means 'tomorrow' and *parsi* means 'the day after tomorrow', you could be forgiven for thinking that this tidy little phrase is a neat way of saying 'in a couple of days'. It is not. Well, it can be, but in reality it far more often means anything up to one or two years (or more) or even 'never' depending on the intonation and the intention of the speaker. This sort of expression clearly underlined the haziness of happenings in Nepal. And I suppose that in a land with such a high mortality rate, it was originally wise to be cautious about the future. Sensibly, the indefinite future tense is used for just about everything except very deliberate promises and prophecies (which are fairly rare). Now, if this rather irregular indefinite future tense were as easy to master as the strictly regular definite future tense, life would be simple, albeit uncertain. The cop-out is simple. Just use the present tense and add *hola* to the end of the sentence. *Hola* comes from the indefinite future tense and can roughly be translated as 'perhaps'. This is what most normal people end up doing on most occasions, but it can be overdone. Take the time, for example, when I telephoned the electricity office to discover when the current was going to be restored and I was assured that it would come in one hour "certainly perhaps". I smiled to myself and thought that, the electricity being what it was, he was probably quite justified in using that grammatical construction, but the electricity as a subject should really have a section all of its own...

I soon discovered that there are some words in Nepali that it would be better if I avoided using – just in case I got them wrong. Thus I have never used the proper word for cheese (which is sad, as I am addicted to it) because I can never remember which of two words is 'cheese' *(chhurpi)* and which is 'loo' *(charpi)* – or 'key/lock' *(chabi)*, for that matter. So, whenever I went to the dairy I always asked for cheese in English and that is exactly what I got and no funny looks either. And that reminds me, few Nepalis distinguish between a dairy and a diary, but then Nepali diaries are funny things. The stationer always asked me if I wanted one with dates or not! Eventually I sussed it: the word also meant 'notebook'.

Now, if I wished to describe myself as a woman I had further difficulties: not the age-old village logic that anyone who wore a watch must be a man, but because of four similar words that my faulty pronunciation could not cope with. *Mahila* means 'woman' (which is fine if I get it right). *Maili* means 'second daughter' (which is not strictly true as I am an only child, although my mother did have a miscarriage before I came along). *Mailo* means 'dirty' (and usually I'm not). And *maile* is one form of 'I' or 'me' (without specifying whether it is a male or female me). Alternatives have their problems too. *Swasnimanchhe* usually means 'wife' (but I'm not married) and *stri* ('woman'), pronounced 'istri', is to me indistinguishable from *istri,* an iron.

One day I made a mistake on the ward round and my Nepali colleagues never let me forget it. I thought I had told the patient to eat a small amount – just a mouthful – but what I actually said was *ghaās* (grass) rather than *gaās.* All expatriates make these mistakes. One day a medical colleague told a mother to bring her child back *parsi,* which, you may recollect, means the day after tomorrow, but in fact she pronounced it *pharsi.* So, when the woman turned up the next day carrying a pumpkin (not the child), the doctor was perplexed, until linguistic light suddenly dawned on both of them.

Over the years my vocabulary improved and I hope I made fewer mistakes, but I cannot be sure, as the longer I lived in Nepal and the older I got, the less likely were locals to point out my *faux pas.* One of these I remember more with embarrassment; the other with mirth. I was translating for some foreign visitor in church, who was preaching on heaven and hell. She kept using these two words, so I thought I would substitute an alternative for heaven as I was fed up with using just one term – and, you've guessed, I came out with the alternative for hell instead. Fortunately, some educated member of the congregation shouted out the correct word and saved me from being excommunicated. Perhaps this experience was why, when I started teaching in Bible Colleges, I tried to be very careful and simple with my use of English and, in particular, avoided the use of double negatives. How easy it would have been to start a new heresy!

Another time, I was teaching at a ladies' seminar and speaking on Psalm 42 – how we should be thirsty to know more of God just like a wild deer longs to drink from a stream of water. The problem was I was a doctor and the word *mrigaula* (kidney) slipped out of my mouth instead of *mriga* (deer). This time I was able to correct myself, and all the ladies enjoyed the joke with me.

Many years later – as a result of my experiences in Nepal – I discovered two new English words or, to be more precise, two new usages for a couple of old words. 'Volunteered' always used to be grammatically active and something I did of my own free will and desire. In Nepal I found it could also have a passive use, meaning that someone else decided what I should do without bothering to tell me. For example, one year INF was volunteered by the government to contribute to their leprosy budget, discussed it, agreed it and included it in their red book (which I think is a bit like the British chancellor's red briefcase) and only after all that did we find out about it. 'Disappeared' also always used to be an intransitive verb which referred to those times when I hid from something I wished to avoid. However, during the decade of the Maoist insurgency it also acquired a transitive and causative use. Both the Maoists and the Nepal army or police caused people to disappear – they 'disappeared' (i.e. 'executed') them. But unlike when I hid, these people rarely reappeared.

Despite my innate lack of linguistic skill, I found that I really enjoyed Nepali language learning and in time succeeded in becoming reasonably fluent, even more so than some of my colleagues who did not have the advantage of working in the challenging hospital environment. That situation certainly provided me with a higher motivation than I had ever had at school, for in the 70s doing medical work without speaking Nepali was almost impossible. Then many years later, and for a rather weird reason, I spent almost a decade doing further Nepali (and Sanskrit) study, and then research into Nepali proverbs.

8

Tundikhel 111

Life in Pohkara (and Kathmandu)

Top: WRH doctors' residence. Bottom left: Compound 'mud' hut. Bottom right: Bazaar bungalow.

MY FIRST HOME IN POKHARA was a mud, bamboo and thatched hut with a four-inch gap between the walls and the roof. There was a magnificent view of Fishtail Mountain, if only I could have seen it through the plastic windows. There was no lock on the door but in those days there were no robbers (they came later – with progress!) Running (cold) water was just thirty seconds' sprint away at the tap; and the loo was also thirty seconds away in the opposite direction. There was, initially, no *bijuli* in my hut, just a spluttering kerosene lamp; but as we invariably retired early, this was no great discomfort. I wasn't lonely as a colleague shared the other half of the hut and in the roof I knew there must be many of my eight-legged 'friends', and on one occasion a bat came to join the party.

Culture shock was not in itself a shock, but there were so many little things to remember: take off your shoes before going into a house or shop; whatever you do, don't sit with the men; remember to boil all your water; don't clean your teeth under the tap (not that my house had a tap); always give or receive things with your right hand (the left hand is what you use for dirty jobs); don't refer to the cat as 'pussy' as that is apparently a vulgarity in Nepali. There were also several strange Nepali actions that shocked me at first: seeing a woman discover a doorknob; experiencing a man spitting over me and out of the bus window; finding a boy dressed as a girl with long plaits to deceive the gods; and hearing about a girl kept and worshipped as a "living goddess".

However, in my first year in Nepal I had many medical shocks – conditions or complications that were only found in out-of-date textbooks, the ones I had never read: catastrophic haemorrhages after childbirth; burnt and charred babies; men with bellies so swollen from bowel blockages that they looked like pregnant women... So many patients came too late – due to lack of money, superstition, ignorance, distance from the hospital, being busy with essential fieldwork, or simply because their husbands did not allow them to come. In contrast, I never had an electric shock in those days; rather, I remember lighting a candle to check whether the electric light filament was glowing or not!

I also soon discovered that I needed several extra possessions, most of which I had not packed in my 29 pieces of luggage. One was a large black umbrella with a long-pointed end. Not only was this essential protection against the sun or the monsoon deluges but it was invaluable for chasing away buffaloes, cows and dogs and as a support to prevent me slipping into the mud. It was useless for dealing with snakes, for which a forked stick was recommended. But the two most important bits of kit proved to be a sense of humour and the special spiritual equipment God gives to us so that we can survive – and more than survive – in an environment where his rivals are all around. I slowly recognised that "the weapons we fight with ... [which] have divine power to demolish strongholds", mentioned in 2 Cor. 10:4, are very important equipment in a land where gods (and goddesses) other than Jesus were always being worshipped and appeased. Gradually, I began to trust God even in the little things of each day and find time (not easy to achieve) between hospital work and language study to pray more. Even today, I'm still working on this.

About six months after I had arrived in Nepal, we had some special visitors in Pokhara, invited by our mission director. They were Michael and Jeanne Harper from Fountain Trust. Apparently in around 1968/9 there had been some amazing happenings in the mission and especially among the patients in Green Pastures. Many had been healed – even from leprosy – by an outpouring of God's Holy Spirit. The Christians – both Nepali and expatriate – had also had a new spiritual experience, which they described as being filled with an abundance of the Spirit. This was something I had not met before but when I learnt of it, I wanted it too. I needed it. And my prayers were answered during a joint meeting held in our multipurpose dining room. It was exciting – and offbeat. One verse from Jeremiah 1 stuck in my mind: "Then the Lord reached out ... and touched my mouth and said to me, 'I have put my words in your mouth.'"[53] My lip swelled up – almost certainly an allergic swelling, but it did seem a strange coincidence; and then I received the gift of tongues. A short while later I was able to share my Christian faith with a young American Peace Corps girl called Mary, who said she trusted Jesus at that time. Not long afterwards I visited her in the village where she worked, somewhere near Kolma. I was young and zealous but not very tactful; I tried to distribute some Christian tracts among the schoolkids and nearly got lynched for it. Then, around 1974, someone told me Mary had been to a Buddhist meditation course and started taking drugs, both very common in those days. However, the good thing was that some Christian friends in Kathmandu had met her. After that I never heard from her again, although I often wonder what happened to her.

Another thing I discovered was that most Nepalis are fatalistic. This is probably a direct outcome of Hindu *karma:* you are what you were born and you can't change it; you just have to go along with it. This almost certainly helped them to cope with many of the problems life

---

[53] Verse 9.

threw in their direction, but it usually meant that any initiative to change or improve their lot was not even considered. It also made development work difficult in the early days, but the possibility that there just might be something better made the very different and positive teaching of Christianity particularly attractive, especially to low castes and 'lepers', many of whom gained hope and were radically transformed by Jesus.

Linked perhaps with this attitude was a very useful little phrase – *ke garne!* It meant literally 'What to do!?' It was what everyone said when they didn't know what to do. It was what we said when things got on top of us. I used it a lot – when patients lived too far away to come daily for treatment and yet weren't ill enough to merit us putting an extra mat on the ward floor for them; when patients didn't return for the rest of their treatment until months later, when sometimes it was too late to save their lives; when I was faced with a medical situation I'd never seen before; when sick World Travellers turned up on our doorstep; when a colleague's dog developed rabies; even when just going shopping was a nightmare of new shops, sights, sounds and smells; when it was so cold at night that I needed a hot water bottle while at midday I sweated in my tropical kit; when I came down with the inevitable D & V attack; when the cows got onto the compound and ran riot; when to reach the church was one hour's walk through the pouring rain and muddy fields; and when I could see so much need all around me and yet there were laws that said I shouldn't speak openly of God and his love. In fact, there was always an answer to all these problems, and I found it in Isaiah 58:9: "Then you will call, and the LORD will answer..." It was very reassuring to realise that God knew it all and was in control.

For the first couple of years in Nepal, my priority was to learn the language, work in OPD and theatre, and just do what I was told. I had no other responsibilities, which meant I was free to spend some time in the bazaar and visit patients or friends. Phrases I picked up included "When are you coming to visit us again?" a query from Gita's husband; and "Come in... eat some tea," an invitation from my friend in the Gurung Teashop. I was thrilled to have these contacts and tried my best to share my Christian faith, and follow through with repeat visits, but I fear I didn't do it too well. For a real treat in those days, a few of us would visit Excuse Me's little restaurant. She was so nicknamed because that was just about all the English she knew and she prefaced every conversation with the phrase. But her *momos*[54] were delicious – and they were a lot easier to eat with the fingers than a fried egg 'over light', which was standard guest fare in many homes. One day, visiting friends at the Hyangja Tibetan Camp, we were presented with six boiled eggs each – easier than fried ones to consume, but by the sixth it was all getting a bit too much of a good thing. Still, they were a lot better than the salty Tibetan 'tea' (made with rancid butter) that came with them. Even thinking of it as soup rather than tea doesn't help it go down. And the most diabolical thing about it was that the Tibetans kept it in huge thermos flasks from which they repeatedly filled up one's glass. I had to be very vigilant to prevent this happening.

Pokhara was a small town (actually in 1970 it was still an overgrown village) set on a hill. The Shining Hospital was at the top end, on the old parade ground, and Green Pastures more than halfway down. The Air Ground and Phewa *Tal* (lake) were at the bottom end. There was just one road and it was not all tarmacked. The compound where I first lived was just below the hospital and above the Sheti River adjacent to one of the funeral *ghats.* The reason the mission was allowed to use that site was because no one else wanted it. Who, after all, would want to live on ground infested by evil spirits? But our stalwart pioneers had prayed and the spirits departed; and long before I arrived, it had become very peaceful and safe. Outside the compound was a buffalo pool and when the buffaloes were not bathing, it sported an amazing reflection of Fishtail Mountain.

Inside the compound was where most of the single missionaries – and the Nepali nurses – lived. Almost all our houses were mud and thatch but a few had been upgraded to cement structures with tin roofs. There was also a small prayer hut and a communal dining room, used not only for dining but for almost every other joint activity in the mission. Above it was a loft in which we stored our empty drums and trunks, and this was where the rats held their football matches each week. Kick-off invariably coincided with our English language fellowship on Sunday evenings. This rather colonial setup continued for many years, but when the Shining closed, the nurses' hostel became our mission office. Much later INF/Nepal took over the whole compound and, among other activities,

[54] Momos – small steamed dumplings.

used part of it for a small drug rehab centre. Perhaps the most exciting change, however, was when the dining room – the site of so many encounters with God over the years – became the home of Santwana Church.

In the 1970s the only shops in the bazaar sold (very) basic provisions or household requisites: rice, lentils, salt, sugar, oil, matches, kerosene, rubber *chappals*[55] and lengths of material. There were tailors' stalls to get your clothes made and gold shops for those who could afford jewellery. Vegetables and fruit were strictly seasonal, except for onions and bananas – and, of course, chillies! It was many years before the first ready-made fancy goods shop arrived; and when it did, it was such a novelty that we all had to go and visit it. Nowadays Pokhara is more and more like a Western town: too much traffic and no parking places, posh restaurants and huge supermarkets with fixed prices. Gone is the old-world charm of a lazy bazaar, bargaining and chatting with shopkeepers.

When it rained the main bazaar turned into a river and some of the side alleys into waterfalls. Walking uphill meant the water flow kept my *chappals* securely on my feet; going downhill was more of a challenge. One day, during a particularly heavy storm, I was riding my motorbike down the hill and needed to put my foot down, but the water was almost up to the footrests. One *chappal* was immediately swept away and onto the bridge, where its most likely fate was to be washed overboard into the Sheti Gorge. But, being the thrifty missionary that I was, I parked the bike and went looking for my *chappal.* Amazingly, I found it resting precariously against one of the bridge girders. Very carefully – so as not to knock it over the edge – I reached out and retrieved it. I was not so lucky the day I lost a *chappal* in a river while out trekking. The result was that I had to walk barefoot the last half hour up the hill to the road before I could buy a replacement – or rather a new pair, as the shop refused to sell me just one! One year, at that same Mahendra Pul (bridge) in Pokhara, a lady cutting firewood on the slope of the gorge was not as fortunate as my sandal. She slipped and fell into the gorge. People heard her crying out for help for several days but no one was ever able to find or rescue her.

---

[55] Chappals – rubber flip-flops.

Electricity had arrived before me but it was AC – alternating current – sometimes on and sometimes (more often) not on. Coca Cola had also arrived, and in 1974 it was the only thing to be found in shop fridges in Pokhara bazaar; it got lukewarm when the *bijuli* went off but, unlike most other things, didn't perish when that happened. Most of the time, therefore, we depended on kerosene lamps (and even kerosene fridges). There were three species of lamp. The basic one had a simple wick and if the glass was clean you could just about read by it. The Aladdin Lamp had a fancy wick and long thin glass chimney. It gave a much brighter light but was rather temperamental and had a tendency to go up in smoke, blackening not only the glass but the whole room as well. The pressure lamp was the one favoured by real pioneers. It gave a really bright light but needed to be pumped up regularly, and for wimps like me, the thought of it exploding in my face meant I stuck with types one or two – or just went to bed early. Matches to light these contraptions were available in the bazaar, but they were what we called *kaccha*[56]. There was a joke that went around the mission. A junior missionary was watching a senior missionary light a lamp. She struck the first match from a new box and lit the lamp. Then she threw the box away. The junior was horrified by this waste and asked why. "Oh, I got the (one and only) good match first time."

Over the years the electricity supply slowly got better, but then, as more and more people kept tapping into the grid, it got a whole lot worse. By the time I left Nepal, daily twelve-hour power cuts (known as 'load shedding') were common during the dry season in Kathmandu. In the UK I had never heard of a 'zero watt' light bulb, but then, when zero volts and zero amps are coming out of the socket, I suppose it's just the thing to use. Lack of *bijuli* I found far more frustrating than lack of running water, and it has also had far wider adverse effects on the country – on the crime rate, development, literacy and even the church. If you're like me, getting on a bit, just try reading a small print bible without any glasses by the light of one flickering candle and you will soon know what I mean – and be able to sympathise with a large proportion of older Nepali Christians.

---

[56] Kaccha – crude, imperfect.

For outside illumination, village Nepalis used burning branches, but we used torches with Indian batteries. Using these shed new light on 2 Corinthians 5:7 – "for we walk by faith, not by sight"[57] – as they shone very little actual light on our paths.

As the only running water was in the Sheti Gorge just below the compound, or from an outside tap, we all kept a drum of water on our verandas. This was for washing; drinking water, duly boiled, was carefully stored inside in bottles or jugs. There was a German family living in the bazaar and one day one of their children fell into the water drum. The water came up to his chin, but happily, he was rescued quickly. When his dad found him, he asked, "Why didn't you drink the water to lower the level?" and the reply came back, "But you told us never to drink unboiled water."

You will be unsurprised to learn that Pickford's do not have a branch in Nepal. It's beginning to change but until recently if you wanted to move house you found the new house and then did the packing and the transporting yourself. I was fortunate to arrive in Nepal with some experience in the trade: I had once shifted flat in Liverpool on my little Honda 50 – but at that time I did not have any furniture to move, and that makes a big difference! In Nepal I have moved many times – sometimes with the assistance of a mission vehicle or truck, and always with some helpers. One lot of friends reported back, having carried some very heavy boxes for me, "Aunty does have an awful *lot* of books!" My requirements were always modest – important, as INF had a conservative rent ceiling. I wanted a decent kitchen with a sink and draining board, an inside bathroom/toilet, mosquito netting, somewhere for my motorcycle, doorways wide enough to get my desk inside, reasonable *bijūli,* a good water supply in the area, and to be relatively near to the church I currently attended. The time I moved just a short distance down the lane, I dispensed with vehicles and hired a couple of sturdy porters. My bed, wardrobe, cupboards, trunks and drums all walked off down the road and round the corner, and smaller things I carted round on the back of my pushbike. Three hours and thirty trips later I was in. The total cost of the move was £1.50 and nothing was broken. The only thing left to do was to cleanse the place, and by that I don't mean clean it. My

---

[57] ESV.

bahini[58], Priscilla, and I removed all the *puja* accoutrements and the little *yagya* or altar in the garden; and then in the evening the house group came around to pray and rededicate the house to our God. It was some time later, when I got around to attacking the garden, that I discovered some of the plants with pretty leaves were actually hashish. I soon replaced those with rosella (patwa).

At the very beginning I lived on the mission compound – a state of affairs I considered rather old-fashioned, but it was convenient for on call in the hospital. Later I was able to move into the bazaar but not until we had arranged a phone connection – so I could still be called from my bed in the middle of the night. INF was one of the first to acquire a telephone in Pokhara. Our number was Tundikhel 111; not that many people used it. When the extension was put into my house, for reasons known only to Nepal Telecom, it was allocated the same number as the hospital, which meant that we were the only two people in Pokhara who could not contact each other! Eventually, we found a way around this: lift receiver – ask for 111 – immediately put down the receiver – wait for it to ring and then stop ringing (implying that the extension had picked it up) – immediately re-lift the receiver – start talking!

Over the years I moved many times in Pokhara and even three times in Kathmandu. One time it was mainly to escape a neighbour with a screaming son and a barking dog, but also to obtain a better water supply. Sometimes the landlord would repaint the house for a new tenant. That was usually a good thing but one time the workmen applied water-soluble silver paint over the pre-existing months of dust to the grills on the windows. This only came to my notice a while later, during a ladies' tea party; I saw one of the children standing outside the window and looking at her hands in horror. The solution was smelly: to wash the grills with kerosene. Perhaps, after all, I should just have waited patiently for the monsoon to do the job for me. In the final move in Pokhara, I got a very friendly landlord who even allowed an elderly lady (from Kunahar church) to live for free in a room at the bottom of the garden. She had a *lato*[59] (mentally challenged) son who sometimes came and made faces at me through the window.

---

[58] Bahini – in this context it means house-helper.
[59] Lato – idiot, half-wit.

Pokhara (or *Tal*) means 'lake' in Nepali and there were three main lakes in the area: Phewa *Tal* (the biggest), Rupa *Tal* and Begnas *Tal.* It was around the north shore of Phewa *Tal* that the tourist trade developed, and in the 1970s this area became a favourite haunt of hippies. At first there were just a few shacks and we could easily find a quiet spot for a swim on a day off, although more usually we took a dugout canoe to a small bay on the other side. Then the tourists started to do the same in increasing numbers, but in the early 70s I recollect that an American boy was drowned while swimming, and there were other rumours of boats capsizing. Serendipity perhaps, but we did just wonder whether this had anything to do with the Hindu goddess in the temple on the island, who was perhaps angry because of the tourists or the Japanese who were sponsoring the building of a Buddhist temple on a nearby hill! Then in winter 1974/5 there was a real crisis: the Fewa dam burst, releasing a huge amount of water from the lake, such that the island ceased to be an island. Fortunately, there was no great flooding, but the Pokhara electricity became non-existent and the beauty of the lake was lost. Ironically, the government had just minted a new 5 *paisa* coin with an impression of the dam on it signifying progress!

In the 'good old days', real missionary ladies had real missionary buns – and I know why. There were no hairdressers. There were still no hairdressers in Pokhara bazaar in the 1970s and this was a problem for me. I had given up long hair because it was a hassle in the UK; now short hair was a problem in Nepal. Fortunately, some of my colleagues were able to cut hair and Vera was even willing to give me a perm – problem solved for several years until one day I desperately needed a cut and perm and no one with the right skills was around. By this time I was working at Gandaki Zonal Hospital (GZH) and my Nepali colleague Dr Yamuna, maybe with mixed motives, informed me, "You don't need to go to Kathmandu to get your hair done as someone has opened a salon in Pokhara." This sounded wonderful – until I found the place... in an old-style Nepali house, with no running water and dubious electricity. However, I was encouraged to see that the lovely Lusu's had someone with a perm half in and so I ventured to ask if she could do me too immediately. "Yes," she said, "if you bring your own curlers as I've only got one set."

That should have rung a warning bell but instead I rushed home for the curlers and still felt confident even when I had to squat on the floor while the hairdresser turned on the tap of the plastic bucket above my head and a little boy held the dirty water bucket approximately in place underneath. For some reason I don't think I ever found out, she mixed my perm lotion with some of hers and, surprisingly, all was proceeding well until she ran out of curlers. The solution was to take a few off the other lady, but then, just as we got to the neutralising stage, the electricity went off. That was no problem for the rinse under the bucket, but candle power was obviously not going to work the hairdryer, so I stuck my helmet on, negotiated a reduced payment and went home to set my own hair. Later others followed in my footsteps and Lusu gradually acquired a respectable chair, running water and reasonable electricity – and a bible.

In the bazaar we all employed a *bahini* to help in the house. This I considered as a remnant of colonialism, despite the fact that Nepal had never been colonised. Eventually, I reconciled myself to the fact that it gave employment to someone, and so I decided to think of my series of house-helpers – Pushpa, Priscilla, Bhim Kumari, Tika, Jun Maya, Sarita and others – as living and versatile varieties of hoover plus washing machine cum dishwasher with the added personal extra. Although I was hardly ever in when they were on duty, the system worked well as most were literate enough to interpret my written instructions.

A couple of times the system broke down – probably more my fault than theirs. One time I had just returned from the UK and asked Bhim Kumari to bake me a cake: "You do remember how to do it, don't you?" She assured me she did but, when it came to it, could not decide whether it was the white powder or the yellow powder she should use to make it rise. She made the wrong choice and I discovered that cake made with custard powder is disgusting. The other time was when I asked her to make a cheese and onion quiche and a plum pie – for my visitors that night. By the time Diane had arrived (the other, Gaynor, had taken sick), I was also feeling unwell and did not notice that there was only one pie in the kitchen. Diane nearly broke a tooth on a plum stone in the cheese and onion quiche. Another time, Tika managed to leave the kitchen tap on for five hours and so effectively drained the whole tank of water. I was not pleased. Maybe it was her way of speeding up my sanctification, but I was a slow learner.

When I first employed her, Tika had a lopsided smile due to the loss of one important front tooth, but one year I gave her a Christmas gift that enabled her to restore her beauty through dental treatment. Tika had become a Christian, I believe through Beryl unexpectedly staying in her house one night. She had a husband called Gom, who originally came to church with her, and two children, but later Gom veered away from the 'straight and narrow' and Tika was effectively left on her own. I think she went to Butwal for a while, but then, some years later, she went overseas to work in Cyprus and, as far as I recall, I only saw her once again after that.

Left to right: Pushpa; Priscilla; Tika; Bhim Kumari; Jun Maya.

Most *bahinis* were very good at cleaning the floor and up to their eye level (usually slightly below my eye level) but not so good at noticing cobwebs above their heads – but that was a small price to pay for getting (most of) my housework done for me. Traditionally, village Nepalis used to wash up outside (with ashes) under a tap and leave everything to drain, so the Western system was a mystery to them. In the really early days, I was therefore instructed to teach my *bahini* not to use the tea-towel as an all-purpose cloth and especially not as a handkerchief. To my knowledge none of them did, but then, I wasn't there most of the time.

When I lived in Bagh Bazaar, near the Shining Hospital and later the INF office, my *bahini* for most of the time was Priscilla. Her husband was Daniel, and no, I don't have my names and testaments mixed up. As you might have guessed, the family were Christians and originally from Darjeeling. In the 90s they struggled to look after their son's two children – Praju and Jupak – as he was rather irresponsible. The children turned out pretty well and both went overseas to work. Their daughter Pushpa (who also worked for me for a while) was a hard worker, married to Luka, an INF paramedic. He was the son of Yacob and Rebecca, two of the original Nepali pioneers who walked into Pokhara.

Later, when I lived on the GZH compound in Ramghat, Bhim Kumari – she of the custard powder and plum and cheese pie – was my *bahini.* She also was the *peon* in our Gynae clinic and the wife of the pastor of the church I subsequently attended in Kunahar. Over the years I developed a deep relationship with the whole family. They had four daughters (although sadly, one died in her late teens) and, belatedly, two sons, who were, in my opinion, more trouble than twice as many daughters. Originally, they came from a hill village in Lamjung, but Rikhman had joined the Indian army and was away for a while. When he returned he married Bhim Kumari, who was only thirteen at the time – not an unusual occurrence in those days in the villages. At some point he was given a Christian tract and this eventually led to him accepting Christ. He was the first believer in his village and he used to walk several hours into Pokhara most weeks to get fellowship. Eventually, the family shifted to Pokhara, but at first life was not so easy. Rikhman had taken to heart, perhaps too literally, the story of the rich young ruler who was instructed to sell everything and give his wealth away. Rikhman did just that: he gave everything to the church and then he and his wife struggled to bring up their family. It was therefore about that time that Bhim Kumari started working in the hospital, and for me. Later, things improved for them: Rikhman became pastor of the new little church in Kunahar and they managed to build a house adjacent, where they spent many happy years.

I kept in close touch with them even after I moved to Kathmandu in the late 1990s, but then one day when they came to visit me in Gongabu (Kathmandu) I realised that what had been a very happy marriage was somehow going wrong. Bhim Kumari accused Rikhman of having a 'lady love' and he accused her of mental delusions. At that time I didn't know who was right, but I tried to help by getting them to talk the matter through with an older, mature Christian couple from Ramghat church. Sadly, over the next few years, things went from bad to worse and ultimately Rikhman ran off with a young woman half his age, also from their village in Lamjung. Bhim Kumari was devastated and confided in me that on more than one occasion she had stood overlooking the Sheti

Gorge and contemplated jumping off. In time she began to cope; she still had the church and her daughters and sons-in-law for support. Bindu and her husband Bijay, however, went to work in Israel, but Sarbada's husband Bimal became the pastor of Kunahar Church. Deependra, the older boy, started – but did not complete – Bible College and the younger one, Imman, spent some time in Doha. Rikhman, to the disgust of his daughters and their husbands, subsequently fathered another three girls despite the fact that he was over seventy-five when he started this second family.

In Kathmandu, too, my *bahini,* Jun Maya, was from the church I attended. Her husband, Dil, had found my house for me, and at first he seemed a nice enough guy, but later on I realised he tended to leave his wife to do most of the work and earn all the money, while he ate more than his fair share of the food. One time he ate a whole packet of special diabetic biscuits I had bought for Jun Maya! Originally, I lived in Gongabu (in the north) and she stayed close by, but when I moved to Jawalakhel (in the south) it meant she had to commute across town. This was inconvenient for her, but also for me as whenever there was a demonstration or strike she did not turn up. Dil eventually got a job overseas but was back within a fortnight; I assume he had discovered how hard migrants were expected to work! Jun Maya was with me for more than ten years and then left to join Dil in trying to set up a small restaurant in Narayanghat[60]. After that I lost contact with her and never did discover if the project was a success. For the last few years I was in Nepal in Kathmandu, I employed a series of different *bahinis,* Sarita being the last. Between Jun Maya and Sarita, there were two *bahinis* who gave me some trouble. I felt bad about terminating the contract of one as I knew she struggled financially but she was, in my estimation, lazy and inefficient, and I needed the work done. The other I had to sack because I could not condone her solving her money problems by removing, on two separate occasions, 100-rupee notes from Dot's pocket and from mine. (Remember Dot, who helped me buy supplies to take to Nepal in 1970.)

---

[60] Narayanghat is a major town on the Terai, south of the midpoint of a line joining Kathmandu and Pokhara.

I tried to be friends with the families of my *bahinis,* including their children and grandchildren. Praju and Jupak (Priscilla's grandchildren) once declared, "Doctor Aunty brought a mouse to my birthday party," and then at Christmas I turned up with a frog and a snake. I hasten to add that all these were toys, but real live animals were also an integral part of life in Nepal.

9

Toad Hall

My colleagues and other animals

Wildlife in Nepal.

EVERYONE KNOWS THE BRITISH have a – well, *British* – sense of humour. As the majority of expatriates in our international mission have usually been Brits, one of our original mud huts was called Buckingham Palace, though I doubt if the Queen has ever actually had to lie in bed holding an umbrella to avoid a leaking roof. Watership Down was predictably where Hilda Rabbitt lived, while for a time I lived at Toad Hall, sharing this accommodation with a family of those amphibians who came and went through a hole in the bathroom rather than using the front door. One of my residences was a moated house – or that's what it felt like when it rained, and the road outside was really the bed of a stream; another was situated in the appropriately named Mud Lane. Even the first house I rented, many years later in Kathmandu, I called Quagmire Cottage. The next one I contemplated naming Monkey House as it was situated just behind the zoo. Later when we started to worry about the possibility of a big earthquake (and the zoo walls collapsing) I remembered the tigers and hoped it would not turn out to be Tiger Tops instead. Ratty also used to frequent one house I lived in, though with the help of a handyman friend I managed to confine him to the roof. He clearly did not appreciate this restriction and spent many evenings having raucous parties with his friends directly over my head. I suspect he was related to the large footballing family who lived above our mission sitting room.

At the time I arrived, almost all of the INF team lived on the compound just below the hospital. It was a bit like living in a doctors' residence except that not all my colleagues were medics and so conversation had to be censored – a bit! Fortunately, we had communal meals, as I would never have had time to cook in between on call and language study. Breakfast was a pretty close approximation to a Western breakfast – with some kind of cereal and bread and sometimes 'eggy bread' (French toast) for a treat. I was always happy when there was some porridge left over as I could then eat this cold for lunch when I could not face the *daal-bhat*[61]. The evening meal was also semi-Western – often buffalo stew (tough as old hide) followed by Jit's 'bomb' (stodgy pudding). Jit was the Nepali cook, who always came to work in shorts, an apron and a pair of wellington boots. His scones were his other speciality, which we got for elevenses; they were as hard as rocks. I had arrived in Nepal a few months after Dr Pat O'Hanlon, our founder, had retired and the regime had already begun to be somewhat less colonial, although we still used a little bell to summon Jit and his bomb when we'd chewed our way through the buffalo hide. I was told that because Pat, our pioneer founder, used to pray over the portions she served out, no one had ever been allowed to complain if they got too much or too little. Also, if anyone had any water left in their glass at the end of the meal, they had been required to take it to their hut and use it for cleaning their teeth; throwing away drinking water had been a cardinal sin.

---

[61] Daal-bhat – lentils and rice.

Before the electricity improved and before we could afford fridges, we used to keep our boiled water cool in big earthen pots called *gargros.* One day a non-medical colleague noticed that the water from her *gargro* was gradually turning yellowish. At first she paid no great attention – one learns to put up with a lot worse things than discoloured water – until one day she upturned the *gargro* for the last dregs and out tumbled a dead rat. Yes, I thought that too!

Until we moved out of mud huts and into concrete boxes, there was little we could do to stop rodent invasions. We did set traps from time to time but as a method of population control it was not very efficient. You can only catch one rat (and maybe one finger) at one time in one trap, so you either have to set lots of traps (which makes it far more likely that you lose lots of fingers than catch a rat) or spend the whole night emptying and resetting one trap (and you are even more likely to trap your fingers when you are half asleep). The alternative – the way to commit rodent mass murder – sounds safe and simple, but isn't. Warfarin was often not available, and so we had to use a poison that drives the little creatures mad with thirst before they die. In theory, after consuming the poison the rats were meant to rush out of the house to the nearest water and conveniently die out of olfactory range. In practice they always managed to find some water near at hand before returning to their nests in the roof above my head. There they died in peace in the bosom of their families (whom they warned not to take my poison) and decayed slowly and odiferously over the next ten days.

There were other ways of ridding myself of rodents. I could drown them, but as rats can swim the container needed steep sides and I needed a pair of artery forceps to hold them under the water – not nice. I once caught a *chichindra* (a kind of shrew) by slamming a drawer shut on its long snout, but this doesn't work with rats or when a whole family of squeaking shrews have taken up residence in the wall of your house. Other memorable occasions when I managed to catch them included suffocating one in a plastic bag, beating another with a hammer and drowning yet another in a tin of *ghiu*[62]. The last method was not so good as Betty N, a Canadian nurse, with whom I worked in Ghorahi, then

---

[62] Ghiu – clarified butter.

insisted on throwing out the *ghiu;* what a waste! So, why didn't I keep a cat? Simple: cats don't like *chichindras* and I don't like cats.

One last interesting thought about rats. I found I needn't waste good cheese in the trap: stale crusts were just as effective – and rats even seem to like soap!

Cows are sacred animals for Hindus, so if tourists want to eat beef in Nepal, they have to ask for 'filet'. Bit of a cop-out, if you ask me. I also discovered that it was OK to throw stones at cows so long as you didn't harm them. You could also shout at them when they trampled all over your carefully planted garden, and the correct word to use was *'hut'.* However, if your vehicle knocked down and killed a cow the traditional penalty was more severe than if you killed a human pedestrian. I found it paid, therefore, to be wary when driving at night; cows used to love to sleep in the middle of the road – without lights.

Second cousins twice removed to cows are the water buffaloes. They have certain intimate problems and one is a tendency to uterine prolapse, an ailment that I was told they shared with Brahmin women who wore *patukas.* Ruth Watson had educated me in both conditions, and in the female clinic I felt confident to insert pessaries. Not so when I was faced with a buffalo in the field at Green Pastures. One hour later, my best sari full of little grass seeds and the buffalo still uncaught, I gave up – probably wise, as Ruth had never explained to me exactly how to insert the deck quoit.

Buffaloes seem prone to gynaecological problems and I had an O & G[63] diploma. One day, on my way home from church, a neighbour hailed me to help her buffalo who had just given birth but not produced the afterbirth. I was, of course, again wearing my best sari. Gritting my teeth, I immersed my arm to the hilt (shoulder) and bit by bit removed the placenta. The buffalo recovered – and so did I, but that brought to an end my forays into veterinary medicine.

Buffaloes are large and lumbering brutes, simple but not sacred, and love nothing better than to wallow in muddy puddles – but just occasionally they go on the rampage. I quickly learnt that if I ever heard the word *marchha*[64] I needed to unfurl my umbrella (something they hate)

---

[63] O & G – obstetrics and gynaecology.

[64] Marchha – it kills.

and jump onto the nearest wall – or even, *in extremis*, down the nearest cliff. A buffalo gore can be a nasty injury. In the hospital I had learnt that not all surgical emergencies were surgical emergencies; they just thought they were. When, however, a lady gored by her own buffalo was carried in, with the best part of her small bowel, covered with bits of grass and mud, festooned all around her figure, I recognised this as a true surgical emergency. And buffaloes have one other party trick. Another patient found out the hard way that it was not advisable to bend down while facing away from, but in front of, his buffalo. A horn up the back passage leaves the doctor with some fascinating and long-winded surgery – and the patient literally with a pain in his a***.

And this reminds me of one bit of very sensible advice I was given. Always – repeat, *always* – when out trekking in the hills, walk on the inside of the path, so that if you have to jump out of the way of a buffalo, goat, or a mule carrying a large and very wide load, you have the chance of jumping up the bank and surviving. If anyone has to go over the cliff, let it be them.

There is a Nepali proverb that says that a barking dog does not bite. I'm not really sure that it's true; and as I have seen someone die of rabies (not a nice experience), I think it's wise to be cautious in the presence of any Nepali canine. I confess I don't like dogs; in fact, I'm downright scared of them – and with good reason. It's not a phobia as with spiders but a genuine fear of what they might do, and a couple of times one *has* done it to me.

The first time was when I was young, enthusiastic, conscientious and stupid. I was determined to carry on with the leprosy survey in Baglung alone when my Nepali colleague was off sick. All the village children warned me not to go anywhere near a certain house, and proved the dog there was vicious by showing me their scars. But I thought I knew better, although I did take the precaution of hailing the lady of the house from behind the safety of the compound wall. Assured that the dog was tied up inside the house, I ventured onto the veranda, but was immediately attacked by not one but two massive hounds. One dug its teeth into my calf and only the fact that I was wearing a sari prevented this from being a really nasty bite. I learnt the hard way that it's always sensible to listen to good advice. The only redeeming factor in this incident was that as the dogs had bitten every child in the village and both dogs and children were all still alive, there was clearly no danger of rabies and no need for injections.

The other time was when I was much older and should have been much wiser – not that it would have made the slightest bit of difference. One evening I was walking back from a fellowship meeting with friends. As they went one way, I went the other, and the next thing I knew was a pain in my bum. The brute had appeared out of nowhere and bitten my buttock.

There's another saying that a dog's bark is worse than his bite and in general this one is true. Few dogs bite but they all bark – and sometimes continuously all night. Only dead dogs don't bark. I once had a dead dog thrown at me, but I never discovered whether this was a deliberate insult or the work of the village idiot. Another time I discovered a decaying canine corpse in my garden, and as neither the dog nor the smell was likely to go away on its own, I had to pay the outrageous sum of five rupees to get the hospital's *lato peon* to drag it away. Again, I never found out whether the dog had chosen to expire in a pleasant environment or whether someone didn't like me very much. Maybe it was the attraction of my garden, as sometime later another dog got itself trapped in the barbed wire fence and (understandably) whined pitifully all night until someone braver than me released it in the morning. Yet another – this time a real bitch – used my veranda as her lover's lane, and the next morning I had the unpleasant task of sluicing away the blood and smell myself.

Apart from a short visit to the Chitwan National Park, I cannot claim to have encountered any of the larger and more ferocious wildlife of Nepal like rhinos, crocodiles and tigers. One of my friends lived for a time in a fairly remote village, and inevitably sometimes had to visit the loo in the middle of the night. One time, between her going and coming from the outside privy, a leopard whisked in and ate her pet dog which was chained up nearby. She was lucky; more than once I've heard of leopards snatching unfortunate women who went out to the fields to answer a call of nature in the middle of the night. This just goes to prove how important it is to promote latrine building in any community health programme.

After my father died suddenly in December 1973, my mother felt unable to face Christmas 1974 on her own and bravely decided to visit me in Nepal. Two things stand out from that time. One was the day we went to visit Swayambhu, a famous Buddhist shrine set on the top of a hill, and where there were more monkeys in residence than idols. We had barely set the box of sandwiches on the grass when the monkeys descended and grabbed almost all our lunch. And – because I am a slow learner – when I tossed it to my mother, I lost a tangerine in the same way. The other thing doesn't concern animals at all. Mother had repeatedly complained about locals spitting in Nepal, and worried that they would hit her, but I kept reassuring her that they were so practised in the art that this would never happen. But, once my mother was safely back in Britain, I was to eat my words. I was riding my bike innocently up the bazaar in Pokhara when a gob of sputum came flying out of a top floor window and landed on my lapel. Yuk! I'm pretty sure I never told mum about this.

Even many years after I had graduated from a village style hut to a town house, I had one interesting experience. I was sitting in my house, minding my own business and chatting to a friend, when into the living room hopped a large white rabbit! Like Alice, I was a bit confused, but instead of offering us tea, he hopped away again – back to the downstairs flat, though what he had been doing there I have no idea.

Finally, no section on wildlife would be complete without some mention of snakes. I don't like snakes any more than I like spiders but at least the fear is rational. Unlike spiders they have a front end and a back end and you can be pretty certain which way they are likely to travel – but, when they do move, it's best to move faster. I bought a pair of Wellington boots to wear when snake-hunting, but the snakes didn't understand the rules of the game; I never saw a snake when wearing my boots. Most (but not all) snakes in Nepal are non-poisonous, but most people didn't know this and, when bitten, applied a tourniquet – just in case. A little knowledge, however, is dangerous, and all too often we had to take the limb off simply because no one had taken the tourniquet off.

10

Fleas ad INF

Long-legged beasties

One of the many species of spider in Nepal.

NEPALI SPIDERS (ALL 175 SPECIES OF THEM) and insects deserve a chapter to themselves.

You have probably by now picked up that I am afraid of spiders. 30.5% of the world population share this phobia – so I've read. I know it's not rational and although some are quite large – well, *ginormous* to me, like six inches across – I don't think any of them are poisonous. I am truly, *truly* grateful that God did not send me where there are tarantulas. At least no patient of mine ever presented with a spider bite, but I had several who came with an interesting itchy rash on their abdomen, which they had self-diagnosed as where a spider had urinated on them during the night. Just the thought of it gives me the creeps. Even writing about arachnids leaves me a bit weak at the knees, and if a colleague had not prayed for me, I doubt if I would have lasted in Nepal more than the first six months. But that prayer was answered and I survived in Nepal for forty-three years. However, every time I encountered one, I still needed to claim courage from God, although after that I was able to dispose of them myself without help. Maybe I should have prayed that I might get to like spiders, but I could never have brought myself to say amen to such a prayer. In other areas, however, I have found it is important to ask God for precisely what I need. He may already know but I have a feeling he really does like to be asked.

Nepali spiders may not be poisonous but *juicylo kiras* (or furry caterpillars) can cause really serious trouble. If you touch one – or sit on one by mistake – you will be itching for days. That's bad enough, but if you get one of the hairs in your eye and it's not removed quickly, you can lose the sight of that eye. I know because in two mission families one of the children had that happen. And some years when the moths evolve from these monsters they swarm, but if you kill them the powder can equally cause blindness.

One of the houses I lived in was nicknamed the Ant Heap, and for good reason. One day I walked into my bedroom to find that the whole of the wall adjacent to my bed was black and moving. It was a solid mass of tiny ants. The first few times this happened I attempted genocide with a spray gun, but it was no use; the population living in the walls was just too big. Not only was it futile but the fumes almost killed me, so I gave up the unequal struggle and in future left the room until the swarm had gone away.

Ants also like kitchens, and their espionage network informs them immediately when just one crumb has been dropped. Many times have I watched their manoeuvres! Despite carefully emptying the scraps from my meal into the waste bin and rinsing the dishes, within nanoseconds a full battalion of ants would appear marching along the window ledge from their camp inside the wall. They used to leap across the (1 mm) chasm to the draining board, skirt the edge of that, abseil down one of its legs, race across the plain cement work towards the waste bin and then form an assault phalanx up the steep green overhang of the bin in order to finally to reach their target. It always reminded me of that verse in the Bible, "Go to the ant, you sluggard; consider its ways and be wise."[65] I'm not sure I've got a lot wiser, though I did discover an interesting fact: when ants suffered from night starvation and there was nothing in my waste bin, they ate my rubber *chappals,* leaving them honeycombed and looking like blue gruyere cheese.

And while we are still in the kitchen with the creepy-crawlies, I must mention cockroaches and weevils. I never had much trouble with the former, though several friends suffered a lot. Wikipedia says they are tough and hard to kill, and considering that they are omnivores and can live for two weeks without a head, getting rid of an infestation was inevitably a major undertaking. *Sitophilus granaries* (or weevils by another name), on the other hand, are faddier about their food. They used to flourish in the flour bin during the damp days of the monsoon, but it was only when my pancakes showed just too many little black dots that I knew it was time to re-sieve the flour and dry it out in the sun. Sadly, this only extracted the mature ones, so I had to put up with eating extra protein in the form of baby weevils until they grew big enough to not fall through the holes in my sieve. Pancakes taste so much better in the winter!

You've no doubt heard quoted the 18th century proverb, 'You have to eat a peck of dirt before you die,' but did you know that a peck is the weight of anything in a two-gallon container? Seems like quite a lot of dirt or weevils – or perhaps, locusts – you have to eat before you are allowed to expire from the activity. I have never (to my knowledge) eaten locusts and have no desire to try, but some of our real Nepal pioneers did. Once when they were visiting a Nepali friend in a remote village, they arrived tired and hungry at dusk, and so were relieved to smell the meal cooking. Darkness had fallen by the time the food was served and the only illumination was one small, smoky oil lamp. They could not see what they were eating but pronounced the crisp crunchy treat with the rice very tasty. The next morning, when faced with the same menu in the harsh reality of broad daylight, they found fried locusts significantly less

[65] Prov. 6:6.

appealing – which all goes to show that John the Baptist must surely have been someone quite special!

Out walking in the villages and staying in *bhattis*[66], I encountered several other ghoulies and ghosties and long-legged beasties that I wished I hadn't. Just once I had a tick but fortunately never got typhus. I am 'flea positive' which means I am a sensitive individual with a sensitive skin, which fleas tend to take advantage of. There are human fleas and animal fleas, but both prefer me to any other meal. 'Flea negative' people, in case you're wondering, are thick-skinned insensitive individuals who think people like me make far too much fuss about a tiny little insect bite. But like the gnat that can make an elephant cry (according to a Nepali proverb), so too a flea can inflict agony far in excess of its size. I know because I once got bitten 500 times by 25 fleas in 10 days and survived to tell the tale. The diabolical thing about fleas is that without infrared eyesight, it's impossible to catch them during the hours of Nepali darkness. However, I discovered that if I lived through the night, the way to get rid of them was with a damp bar of soap – very efficient but unpleasant to wash with afterwards.

Bed bugs, however, are guerrilla fighters and they used to attack without being noticed and then retreat into their bunkers for the hours of daylight. But if I did notice them, they were easy to kill at night even by the light of a Chinese torch with failing Indian batteries. I always knew if I was winning as the characteristic smell increased with every bloody carcase smeared on the sheets, wall or my pyjamas.

One of my medical colleagues claimed that finding he had lice was a badge of honour. It meant he had got sympathetically close to his patients. I never had lice and I got close to my patients too – except when I thought they had fleas!

The funniest insects I made the acquaintance of were the May bugs. These are armour-plated beetles with wings – aerodynamically ridiculous flying tanks. After a noisy and miraculous take-off, their engines usually fail immediately and they crash straight back onto the runway. If, by another miracle, they manage to remain airborne for longer than a few seconds, they crash elsewhere – like just inside your sitting-room. When they do that it's easy to pick them up and throw them back out through

---

[66] Bhatti – small wayside inn, sometimes house of ill repute.

the window. One balmy evening I learnt another trick. I was enjoying a time of fellowship and prayer with a group of Nepali Christian believers, but the poor light, oppressive heat and the May bugs were distracting me. Then I noticed that in the centre of our circle the flickering kerosene lamp had been placed in the middle of a bowl of water. Strange… I watched, paying more attention to this than the Bible message or prayer requests. May bug after May bug, attracted by the light, zoomed unsteadily towards it, smashed into the glass, lost power and crashed directly into the moat below – medieval but effective!

This chapter would not be complete without a mention of the ubiquitous mosquitoes. Whereas bed bugs crept up on me unawares and fleas jumped on me when I was not expecting them, mosquitoes announced their arrival like fighter squadrons, buzzing around my face while deciding which targets they should bomb. I always used a mosquito net, even long after all my friends had discarded theirs in favour of window netting or electric vaporisers. Underneath the net I felt safe as if I was in an air raid shelter; I could hear the planes overhead but knew they could not reach me. Only when my beautiful fifty-plus-year-old nylon mosquito net started to disintegrate did I know it was time to retire.

11

Red A.L.E.R.T.

Leprosy and TB control

(Mid to late 1970s)

Green Pastures Leprosy Hospital (1970s).

I HAD ONLY BEEN IN NEPAL for a couple of years when rumours started to go around the bazaar: "The Shining Hospital is packing up and going home." A shopkeeper even asked me, "When are you going?" As I had thought the Lord had called me to Nepal for lifelong service, this was a bit disturbing. My first years in Nepal had been pretty much as I had expected them to be: working as a busy GP-obstetrician-surgeon in the Shining Hospital. At the time, I thought I was overworked (and underpaid) – and I probably was – but it was a happy time. I learnt a lot and made many friends. I delivered hundreds of babies and cured thousands of patients. Then several very significant events changed all that and led to a decade of uncertainty and challenge for the mission organization and for me personally.

The first thing that had happened was that there was a new health plan for the country – in itself a good thing, but not so good as His Majesty's Government of Nepal (HMG/N) in its wisdom had decided that Pokhara did not need two hospitals. The Shining was to be phased out and the Soldier's Board to be upgraded. In 1972/3 no one knew what this would mean for INF mission personnel. Would we be able to stay and help – maybe in building and staffing the new government hospital? Would we be allowed to move farther west and open a small hospital in Jajarkot? Would we be able to continue or expand our small village dispensaries? Nor did we know what the future of Green Pastures Leprosy Hospital would be. However, when the local people objected and petitioned the King, he decreed that INF should work together with the government – and in those days if the King said, "Jump!" you jumped, even if the bar was well above your head! Nowadays there's no king to say, "Jump!" but there are umpteen general hospitals (and even a teaching hospital) in Pokhara. At the time, I was tempted to think that God had sidelined us or even let us down – after twenty-five years of faithful medical service to the people of Pokhara and around. Now I understand that INF was spared the responsibility for running what would have been an increasingly expensive modern hospital. Instead we were able to concentrate on TB and leprosy work – and provide care for the poorest of the poor and needy.

By mid-1974, after many months of uncertainty, the merger of Shining Hospital with the Soldiers' Board (later Gandaki Zonal Hospital or GZH) was confirmed, and so I had begun to reconsider my own future and had applied for a Public Health diploma course. This was because I had (what was in retrospect) a misconstrued vision of myself as a pioneer village medic, but my seniors, being far wiser than I was, decided to let me find this out for myself. In 1973 I had spent a short time in Beni, a small village to the north-west of Pokhara, but I didn't discover the truth at that time; in fact, the experience had only increased my desire to get into 'real' developing world medicine.

INF had started three village dispensaries. Baglung was the first and, depending on how fast you walked and how hot the sun was, it was 1½ to 2½ days' trek north-west of Pokhara. Beni was a couple of hours farther on and Sikha (closed by the time I went to Beni) yet another couple of hours farther on, up what was justifiably called the *mahabhir* (the great hill). Beni itself was set between the Myagdi and the Kali Gandaki rivers and so boasted three bridges and, in those days, had just four shops, where you could buy everything essential to survive and nothing else. Medical life there was much lower key than in the Shining and, without electricity, nothing much happened in the evenings. Prithi, a Shining Hospital trained nurse, helped us in the dispensary, while his wife Elisheba (together with a local village girl called Mongala Devi) helped us in the kitchen. Prithi, being the man, was the 'doctor' and I was demoted – much to his and my amusement.

Prithi and Elisheba, both former Green Pastures leprosy patients, were the only Christian believers in Beni, but they made the most of all opportunities to speak of the Lord to their friends and also to many of the patients and their relatives who used to stay for a while in the lower part of their house until the patients were well enough to return home. This also gave us chances to speak to them, sing for them or visit later. On Sundays we had a short service and invited any patients and relatives or neighbours to join us – and some did.

Prithi, Elisheba and family.

I recollect a couple of things about living and working in Beni. I wasn't stretched medically and obviously could not offer operative deliveries other than forceps and, perhaps because of that, I realised anew how vitally important antenatal care was; I even gave a promotional speech about it – in Nepali – in the bazaar. The second thing was about the house where we lived. It backed onto a Hindu temple – not the site I would ideally have chosen! It therefore gave us a grandstand view of the gory *Desai* sacrifices in our back garden. These provided us with a new understanding of the Old Testament sacrifices, but also left a dark and oppressive atmosphere – because they did not take into consideration the light that Jesus brought into the world, when he offered himself as the final ultimate sacrifice for us.

Concurrently with all this, the mission was planning to work alongside the government in leprosy control, conducting surveys throughout the west of the country. INF medics had treated leprosy patients from the beginning of our work, but in 1957, empathising with the great suffering of many 'lepers' and realising the need was greater than could be provided by outpatient care in a small general hospital, two stalwart pioneer nursing sisters, Eileen and Betty B, had established Green Pastures Leprosarium (later Hospital). It was situated in an uninhabited area, where there had once been an old leprosarium, to the south-east of Pokhara bazaar. This was because officials stipulated that it had to be at least a couple of miles from other dwellings. Ironically, over the many years since then, a whole new village, Nayagaon, has grown up adjacent to it and the area is now a suburb of Pokhara town. Perhaps that speaks for the fresh understanding of the disease and declining stigma surrounding leprosy?

By the early 1970s both HMG/N and INF had realised that clinical care alone was not going to eradicate leprosy. More specific public health measures were needed. This was the beginning of the Leprosy Control Project (LCP), and the first project in which the mission had worked closely with the government. Thus, in 1974, back once again in Pokhara, I was roped in to help with the training of the first group of paramedics held at Green Pastures, and my job was to teach them about eye diseases. In those days I lived up to my nickname of 'running doctor' as I raced down to Green Pastures for the lectures and then raced back to the Shining for the clinic, just before the patients rioted because the doctor had not turned up. Then in 1975, although the formal agreement was not signed until the following year, I started supervising some of the early surveys in the west. During that time I was based in the little town of Baglung but travelled, with a Nepali 'chaperone' and several young Nepali paramedics, through many of the *panchayats* of Baglung and Myagdi Districts.

Supervising young Nepali lads was a new role for me. I could cope with the medical side OK but found myself constantly saying, "Use your handkerchief, wash your socks, don't spit..." However, they all worked hard and achieved a lot. In those days most village people regarded leprosy as a curse of the gods and were mortally scared of it. 'Lepers' (the equivalent derogatory term in Nepali is *'kori'*) were frequently shunned and many sufferers were pushed out of their homes into caves or shacks in the forest. This had happened to Prithi and his brother Nandi before someone from INF discovered them and brought them to Green Pastures. In such an unpopular context I reckon the paramedics were brave to tackle the surveys. It was not an easy job but they managed to unearth many new cases of leprosy and get patients onto treatment and headed towards a more hopeful future. They also put a lot of effort into trying to convince the people that leprosy was just a disease caused by a bacterium, but it must have been hard for Hindu lads who had been brought up with that same superstition. In contrast, Maili, my chaperone, was a Christian who was aware of God's love for those suffering from leprosy. In between the surveys, I did Bible studies with her and taught English to the paramedics. In one test one of them wrote that "Jesus was a dependable angel". I'm so glad that actually he is much more than that! Of the original four lads – Krishna, Badri, Ashok and Him Prasad – who worked with me, at least one (Krishna) later became a Christian.

When we reached Baglung 'town' in our survey, the paramedics came up against an apparently insoluble problem. Bazaar women and girls adamantly refused to be examined by the young men, but looking only at exposed hands, feet and faces was unlikely to reveal any early lesions. Then God provided help for me in an unusual way. Kathmandu University went on strike and so Radha, a Christian nursing student from the town, was at home and free, and so able to assist me with the survey among the women.

The next major happening was that in early 1976, while I was on home leave, Dr Ruth Watson was unexpectedly diagnosed with a brain tumour. She was rushed home for surgery but never recovered sufficiently to go back to Pokhara. So, instead of studying Public Health, I returned hurriedly to Nepal to fill the gap in the Shining left by Ruth – not that anyone could ever really have done that! It was a sad time but now I realise that Ruth would perhaps have found the next few years – with the closure of the Shining as a hospital – just too traumatic. For all of us it was a bereavement almost equal to that of losing Ruth herself.

The third strategic change also occurred that year. At the end of 1976, the Shining Hospital closed and the 50-bed GZH opened. A couple of new doctors arrived to take over the Shining clinic work. In that same year, despite other organisations having their contracts terminated, we got a new formal agreement signed with HMG/N for involvement in leprosy control in the whole of the west of the country. (Subsequently this was limited to the West and Mid-West while a Dutch organisation took over the Far West.) Green Pastures in Pokhara was to be the base, the referral hospital and training centre. Subsidiary centres were to be established in Baglung, in the West, and Ghorahi (and later Surkhet) in the Far West. I was free to attend a Leprosy Training in A.L.E.R.T.[67] in Ethiopia and then move on to a new role.

For six weeks I exchanged the Himalayan 'roof of the world' with the 'roof of Africa', and experienced a bit of life under a communist regime – a tank guarding the supermarket! It was a doctors' course and contained a concentrated mixture of high-powered and simple knowledge and procedures relating to the diagnosis and treatment of leprosy, followed by a short visit in the rural area. In Ethiopia the clinics were held to coincide with the weekly markets but, as I pointed out to our tutors, this would never work in western Nepal, as the nearest we had was an annual fair! After a couple of weeks of extra ophthalmology experience, it was back to the grindstone in Nepal. I'd learnt a lot, seen a little of the countryside and had sampled the local cuisine: 'wot' (a hot, spicy, curry-like dish made from meat or eggs) served with 'injira' (a kind of bread reminiscent of two-foot-diameter discs of sour sponge rubber), and followed by 'bunna' (very black, very strong and very sweet coffee)!

On my return, I went to Ghorahi, a small town in the western *Terai,* to work with the INF team, developing the TB and leprosy clinic and supervising the surveys in several Mid-Western districts. In all honesty, I think the following two-year stint in the back of beyond got pioneering out of my system, probably to the great relief of my colleagues.

In 1973 Ghorahi had been INF's first big step south and west onto the *Terai.* In those days that area was still called Far West and it certainly felt far away both to those venturing out and those back in Pokhara. Logistical problems with supplies and a serious accident marked the beginnings of the work in Ghorahi as apparently inauspicious. In the following years illness in the INF team, a refused visa and persecution for the few Nepali believers might also have been interpreted as mistaken guidance. But no, the team persevered, and prayed – and unravelled

[67] A.L.E.R.T. – All Africa Leprosy Rehabilitation and Training Centre.

government bureaucracy to make leprosy (and later, TB) control effective. By the late 1970's, when I arrived, the new East-West Highway was under construction and before long we were able to travel by Mission Land Rover west to Nepalgunj or east back to Pokhara through billowing clouds of dust.

We lived in a house on the edge of Ghorahi bazaar, near to the hospital and just above the river. At the beginning we had no running water and no electricity. I remember Mal Kumari (our Tharu[68] helper) – her teeth went before her – carrying all our water up from the well (fortunately very close by) and myself lying prostrate before the kerosene fridge, willing its wick to turn blue and keep the vaccines cool. Our kitchen boasted an unusually smoky 'smokeless *chulo*[69]' and the walls were home to a brood of squeaky *chichindras.* Then in 1978 the electricity came and life was never the same again. Next door, the landlord's family lived in the 'big house' where the whole setup was strangely medieval. The *Karindar* (the steward) did all the work while *Baba* (the patriarch) strode around as lord of the manor and his rich young Brahmin sons commuted in and out from Kathmandu, India or their other estate farther south in Deokhuri.

I was Regional Leprosy Officer between 1977 and 1979 and my duties covered clinical work, training and record-keeping. My particular contribution was to colour-code the register and help design the multitudinous reporting forms. My mission colleagues were Betty B, Betty N and Peter. Initially there were only a handful of Christians among the Nepali staff – Martha and Datta Ram (and his wife, Keoli), all ex Green Pastures patients, who worked in the clinic, and Martha's eldest son, Bedi, who was the TB/leprosy assistant. Among the paramedics, only Dhan Raj was a Christian to start with, but much later (after my time there) Nar Bahadur and his wife Seeta also believed. Just a small group of us met to worship in our house, but slowly, a few local people began to show interest and gradually came to believe. It was several years, however, before that fellowship became the church in Ghorahi.

We reorganised the clinic, giving the senior paramedics more responsibility and freeing the sister to spend more time caring for the

---

[68] Tharu – a tribe that lives on the Terai.

[69] Chulo – wood-burning village stove.

inpatients, of which we usually averaged about two per bed. We also launched an attack on the TB and leprosy defaulters in the surrounding Dang District. Some returned for further treatment but others the team reported as 'having died'. A few months later one or two of these 'dead' patients trickled back to the clinic and I had to create a new category in the register – not Returnees but Resurrections!

Much of my time was taken up with establishing the leprosy follow-up programme for the northern hill areas of Rolpa and Rukum – training the government health post staff while also allocating some of our own project staff to improve the patient regularity and care. Some patients had to walk for a week to reach their nearest health post and even longer if they needed to visit our referral centre. At times it felt as if we were fighting a losing battle as patients defaulted because of the distance or stigma or problems at local health posts. If they did come many arrived with horrendous ulcers on their feet from walking along rough mountain tracks with inadequate shoes to protect their insensitive feet.

Regina.

During this time I also had two particularly memorable field trips, on both of which I was accompanied by Regina, an ex-Shining Hospital nurse. The first tour was to Rolpa and Rukum, districts to the north of Ghorahi, but we travelled by a circuitous route. Our first stop (after walking five hours to the airport in Tulsipur) was in Nepalgunj. It was hot. Very hot. There are only two things I remember: drinking innumerable glasses of coffee, tea, squash, Coke and water; and then lovely evenings of fellowship with some of the believers on the development land at Khajura. When one evening I discovered I was the visiting speaker, it seemed natural to reflect on water – ordinary and spiritual. Then we flew to Chauljahari and started walking. It was there, after we met up with the paramedic teams, who were having difficulty persuading the villagers to be examined, that we also met the fleas.[70] Surviving that encounter (just) we pressed on to Musikot for a training course and Rukumkot, and then began our return through Rolpa, first stop being Thabang, a village where the only crop they grew was hashish. I have one rather sad memory of that: a young lad with severe osteomyelitis whom the family refused to take to hospital; I dread to think what happened to him. In Libang we joined forces with Bedi, who had planned a meeting with the Christians in the Jangkot area. This was one of those close fellowships with seventeen of us crammed into one small, hot and smoky room. When the Kotgaun contingent arrived just as the meeting was finishing, Bedi started all over again while I confess I fell asleep.

After a short break back in Ghorahi – just enough time to apply gallons of calamine lotion and let the flea bites heal, we were off again, this time to Jumla via Kathmandu. When we arrived in Kathmandu, I felt a little like Jesus' disciples with their 7 loaves and few small fishes, for I was faced with the prospect of having to treat 400 leprosy patients with less than a tenth of the needed medicines. But the Lord provided; just a quarter of an hour before the offices shut we got some and then the rest came at 11pm! That encouraged me to believe that he would also fix it so we could get our 45kg of medicines onto the restricted allowance plane. Everyone else was dumping excess baggage all over the airport but somehow we were eventually able to take all our stuff with us. Then followed 5 hectic days, treating 186 patients, visiting officials, lecturing at the college, teaching the hospital staff and just enjoying the cool stream outside our back door. During those days I functioned as doctor, sister, nurse, dresser, messenger, sweeper, washerwoman, hairdresser and administrator. It was a highly successful trip.

Other experiences of travel around Ghorahi were rather different. Peter, Betty N and I decided one day to take the LCP Land Rover and visit some Nepali friends. The first obstacle was a swollen river. After waiting for that to subside, we crossed and met the next obstacle: a couple of big cracks in the road. We filled those in using our bare hands and the old UK number plate as shovels, and set off again. The final obstacle – a huge crater (five by fifteen feet) caused by water erosion – proved insurmountable. We turned around and went back to Ghorahi.

---

[70] See Chapter 10.

That experience reminded me of Isaiah 40:4: "Every valley shall be raised up, every mountain and hill made low; the rough ground shall become level, the rugged places a plain." Much work still remained to be done to make the road system in Nepal efficient; similarly, a huge amount of preparation is needed before people are able to find the way to Christ. Some of us medics also used to joke that that verse referred to the healing of the lumps and ulcers that disfigured a leprosy patient's skin surface.

1977 was the INF's twenty-fifth anniversary of working in Nepal but it was also a time when we began to assess the effects of the leprosy surveys to date. Although surveys were currently the 'in' thing, there was some feeling in the mission that scattered clinics might be more efficient and economical – and more caring. We also began to plan for further outreach into the Far West. Surkhet was already functioning and Jumla, in the remote north-west, was identified as the next centre to be opened. Then in 1979 our senior leprosy specialist and I met with Dr Mali (Head of the Nepal National Leprosy Control Project) and agreed that consolidation of what had already been achieved was vital. This fitted well with our mission perspective. A long-term interaction with patients and staff would surely provide better patient care and facilitate Christian witness much more readily than the quick in-out effects of the surveys.

But by then my own time in the Leprosy Control Project was at an end.

12

So Many Hats and Only One Head

Shining Community Health and TB Centre

(Late 1970s and early 1980s)

Baidam clinic.

BY EARLY 1979 I WAS BACK in Pokhara, co-ordinating what work was left in the Shining and planning for a new future for that as well as for myself. God had plenty of surprises in store for me. The next few years were difficult ones. What had been Pokhara's first and only real hospital slowly evolved into just a glorified health post. Gone was the drama of difficult surgery, the excitement of saving the lives of mothers and babies. At the time, retraining the nurses to be diagnostic paramedics who could run the clinics very efficiently did not compete with the earlier thrills of hospital medicine. Only later did I accept the gains. In those days I hated going to the bazaar. Instead of being greeted with a smile and, "You delivered my baby!" I got dirty looks and, "Why have you stopped loving us?" There was just one week when it was different...

In September 1979 the staff of the Gandaki Zonal Hospital donned black arm bands and declared a 'go slow'. At first we took little notice, but then, despite drastic measures by the Civil Surgeon, they announced strike action, locked the theatre and walked away with the keys. From the patients' point of view, it mattered little that many of their grievances were legitimate. Pokhara was suddenly left with no emergency service. At the request of one of the doctors, the Shining stepped "once more, unto the breach, dear friends..."

The Acting Nursing Co-ordinator was immediately recalled from a shopping spree in the bazaar and the former theatre nurse from a day off with her family. Cleaning the old theatre and locating instruments not used for over a year took until dusk. Friday morning brought us our first *suitkerrie* in need of an urgent Caesarean section. Our adrenaline levels rose to meet the challenge but, more importantly, we experienced God's presence with us. In the middle of the operation, we discovered that some absolutely essential forceps were missing – we had already handed them over to GZH – but somehow we coped, with God's help. The electricity was off but the sun was out until the last few minutes, when we had plenty of willing torchbearers. And God added one extra special blessing for this family. The mother had lost twelve of her thirteen children and the one surviving child was a 'mere' girl, so when we delivered her of a healthy little boy, the family's joy knew no bounds. On Sunday our next Caesar came from a bazaar family well known to us. They were absolutely thrilled, proclaiming, "Weren't we lucky to have our baby during the strike!"

Literally overnight our reopened wards filled up with delighted patients and as we delivered a handsome selection of exclusively male babies, our popularity rating in the bazaar rose to dizzy heights unknown for the previous couple of years. Meanwhile we had accumulated one dislocated hip, two gangrenes, three broken collar bones and at least four broken arms and legs. I was not so happy with those, but fortunately the GZH orthopaedic surgeon came up to Shining and to my rescue.

For seven amazing days the nursing staff were fantastic, despite a few groans at the idea of night duty after eighteen months of sound sleep. Then one week later, when we had run out of beds, surgical gloves, staff to put on the duty rota, and energy, it was all over. But for me, the emotional exhaustion of once again having to say no to patients and send them to GZH was far more draining than the physical weariness had been.

The foundation stone for the 150-bed extension for GZH was laid in 1979 and happily there were no more strikes, but then it took the best part of another ten years for it to morph into the 200-bed Western Regional Hospital (WRH). Somewhat more quickly, between 1979 and 1981/2, the Shining Hospital evolved into the Shining Community Health and TB Centre (SCHTBC) and I stayed with it until 1983.

I became the Medical Co-ordinator of this hotchpotch of different functions. Instead of inpatients we established a Day Care Ward, mainly for sick children. Instead of surgical drama we did just a few minor operations. Instead of curative care we emphasised community health and ran a series of clinics to supplement the increasingly efficient contribution of the Gandaki Zonal Hospital. On the *Tundikhel* site we had under-fives, male chests, gynaecology, antenatal and general women's clinics, which were staffed by our nurses and paramedics – on the whole very efficiently – with only the problems being referred to me. The TB clinic, established in 1975, moved to the lower site, where the laboratory used to be, and well away from vulnerable mothers and children, and now had its own day care unit. For many years two nursing sisters had run an MCH[71] clinic at Tirsapatti, in the middle of the bazaar. This continued to thrive. We added one weekly mobile clinic in Dungasaon (the other end of Pokhara Bazaar) and later opened two new clinics in Kunahar and in Baidam (near the lake – and the tourists). It seemed increasingly that our future would be community health outreach and TB treatment and control, although we also began to think of seconding more personnel to GZH.

Our former nurses took to their new roles with enthusiasm. Some specialised in TB and became the backbone of the Pokhara TB clinic and its associated health education work headed by Jean, our former Matron. During these years we were fortunate to have a retired chest specialist join us short-term to help develop the TB work. Dr Black ran a basic training for the TB paramedics and my job was to work with him; it included interpretation of his lectures and publishing the resulting handbook. The majority of the former hospital staff, however, turned

---

[71] MCH – maternal and child health.

their hand to maternity and child health. For these MCH Nepali staff too, in 1980, there was a Child Health training, this time run by a friend of mine, Dr Pat Wakeham, who had had extensive experience in both India and Afghanistan. Once again my skills in interpreting and publishing were called into play.

One other spin-off from all this metamorphosis was the work in the Tibetan Camps. In Pokhara there were three camps: Hyangja at the north end, about half an hour's walk from the Shining; Simalchaur in the middle of the town; and Chhorepatan at the south end, near where the road to Tansen and the border starts to climb out of the valley. The fourth was at Kotre Khola, about an hour's drive east along the Kathmandu road. For several years two colleagues ran clinics and trained some of the Tibetans in basic health care and TB.

These refugee camps had been established to settle those who had fled from Tibet after the Communist takeover in the early 50s. One such Tibetan was Tenzing. She had an amazing story to tell.

Tenzing and family.

In the days when she was growing up in Lhasa, it seems that her father had had a bible. How he came by it, she didn't know, but it had obviously made a deep impression on her. Her journey south had been long and traumatic and her first husband had died *en route,* but then she settled in Pokhara. She became a Christian believer – and was baptized in the lake. This also was amazing and courageous as the Tibetan community at that time – unlike the supposedly peace-loving Buddha they followed – had zero tolerance towards anyone who tried to leave Buddhism. For many years Tenzing remained the only faithful Tibetan believer in Pokhara, and several of us from INF used to visit her regularly. Although her Nepali was never brilliant, we could communicate and encourage her while also enjoying her home-cooked *momos.* Tenzing had two sons but, to my knowledge, neither of them has followed their mother in accepting Christ. Both emigrated to Germany, where John managed to get some training and was able to send support back to his mum. After a couple of visits, Tenzing herself went to live with him there – economically a good move but I am not sure how much fellowship she has found.

Thus, the majority of the former Shining Hospital staff found new and challenging roles, and many became talented paramedics. The cleaners, *peons* and *chaukidar* also kept their jobs. It had been a peaceful changeover. A couple of staff, however, gave us some problems. At the end of the strike week, I had to calm down one who was known to suffer from periodic manic attacks. She was brandishing a big stone in one hand and an *arsi*[72] in the other. On another occasion a more senior staff colleague, sadly from a church family in which some members regularly had episodes of mental instability, went berserk for a short while. When he threatened me I managed to lock myself in the office/ consulting room but it was over an hour before he quietened down and I was able to escape.

Earlier generations of missionaries had always – or so it seemed from their biographies – been paragons of spirituality and versatility; they could turn their hands to just about anything, and usually did. St Paul, perhaps facing similar overload, once said, "I have ... been all these things to all sorts of men that by every possible means I might win some to God. I do all this for the sake of the Gospel: I want to play my part in it properly."[73] No one could legitimately write like this about me, but over the years I did wear a succession of very different hats, not all of them medical: hairdresser, funeral director, hearse driver, chauffeur, florist, electrician, plumber's mate, optician's assistant, cook, gardener, vet, secretary, bookkeeper, author, publisher, teacher, to mention just a few.

In the middle of 1981 I mentioned this in a letter to my friends and I heard later that someone really believed that I wore numerous different

---

[72] Nepali curved all-purpose knife.

[73] 1 Cor. 9:22-23 (PHILLIPS).

physical hats! I had written something along the lines that I used to begin the day with an ordinary Christian hat and then exchange it for a paper one for an hour's administration before the clinics started. At 8am I took my five medical hats off the peg and headed for the Shining Clinics, where I alternated them in rapid succession: supervisor of general clinics, supervisor of TB clinic, doctor to mission personnel, general practitioner to tourists, and clinical teacher of visiting medical students. For a brief fifteen minutes at 10am, I threw the whole lot in the air and went for a cup of coffee. In the afternoon I used to hide under my planning hood until I needed the medical hats again at 4pm to check on the children in the day care unit and look at the lab and X-ray results, but when I was doing annual or pre-home leave medicals, I wore my mission doctor *topi*[74]. For sorting out equipment orders I needed my thinking cap, but exchanged it for my editor's cap when working on the handbooks. I donned a missionary bonnet for prayer meetings, and when I needed to head off down the bazaar I strapped on my bright green crash helmet in case I fell off my moped. On Sundays the end of my sari, draped over my head, took the place of my many hats and fulfilled the Nepali church requirement in those days. Each night, at the end of each long day, found me of course wearing my night cap.

Happily, most of the calls in those days were during the day and not at night, but they were still challenging:

"Johnny's swallowed a coin. Please come and see him." That was Mission Health, and Johnny was accident-prone.

"Tourist dead in front of my office – help!" Increasing numbers of tourists visiting Pokhara were an opportunity but sometimes also a problem.

"For fostering – one baby of a mother who recently died from TB." Dad couldn't cope and neither could we. There were just as many social problems in the TB clinic as medical ones, but this one, if I remember rightly, had a happy ending as the baby was adopted by a Christian family.

"Respected doctor, we have a patient in labour – bleeding badly and needs Caesarean section. Theatre has been informed. Please come. Signed: staff nurse, Mat." This was from GZH and I needed to run fast.

[74] Topi – Nepali man's hat.

I may not have measured up to St Paul's standards but at least I was working for the same God as Peter, who said, "Cast all your anxiety on him because he cares for you."[75]

Just occasionally I managed to get a full day off and there was one extended weekend I simply cannot forget. Gaynor and I opted to spend it quietly at Lakeside. On Saturday it poured with rain, but we were determined to sell our supply of Christian literature to the second-hand tourist bookshops, and so we nobly plodded on through the mud. Suddenly, a voice hailed us from inside a gift shop. We retraced our soggy footsteps and came face to face with the speaker – a long-haired non-English world traveller, holding a copy of the Watchtower in his hand. He asked us if we were Christians as he needed help to explain that Jehovah's Witnesses were a heretical sect. We spent the next hour sitting on the shop floor talking with the young Nepali shopkeeper, who turned out to be a slightly mixed up Christian. Finally, we agreed to a trade-off: he gave me the Watchtowers (to burn) and I promised to send him some more suitable (Renewal) magazines via a mission friend from church. We also challenged him to get rid of the batiks of Hindu gods he was selling. On the following Friday I heard that Pradip no longer had any Hindu batiks in his shop. This story has an even happier ending as Pradip (aka Phil) and his whole family became deeply committed as Christians and, later, leaders in the church.

By Monday, however, I was back at work and busy all day. Returning from a visit in the bazaar, at 7.30 in the evening, I nearly ran over a man (whom I recognized as one of the members of Bagh Bazaar church) on the corner of the road. He was doubled up with pain and groaning. He'd been to the hospital but had not obtained the medicines because he had no money. *What to do?* I also had no money (on me). However, I reckoned I could get the drugs on credit at a friend's medical hall, so I left him to stagger on home while I fetched the drugs for him. The bill came to 88 rupees (about £2), or the best part of two day's wages for a man like him; no wonder he had not been able to buy them himself. This story also had a happy ending as Jit Bahadur was much better and in church the following Saturday. His wife said that if I hadn't met him on the road that evening he would have died – maybe an exaggeration, but

[75] 1 Pet. 5:7.

then, maybe not... And how many other people, I wonder, never got that kind of help when they needed it? Or – more worrying to me – how many people have I not helped when I should have done?

Then at the end of 1982, after twelve years of on-and-off involvement in the Shining, I was ready for the next big change. In the event, it was both a relief and a loss to let it go, but the fact that some new doctors were coming to take over made it easier.

By the end of the 70s I had already become a member of the mission leadership team as well as having responsibility for all these jobs. And then, I'm not quite sure how or why, I found I was in charge of organising and ordering the new equipment for GZHEP, the Gandaki Zonal Hospital Extension Project.[76]

[76] See Chapter 16.

13

No. 11 Jeep

Trekking in the Himalayan foothills

Trekking in Nepal.
Left: Nepali Hulak (postbox). Right: Porters with dokos (baskets).

BEFORE YOU JOIN ME AT GZH for the next stage of my career, I want us to take a break out of Pokhara and go trekking in the hills and brave the buses along the mountain roads.

Even today, the most reliable form of transport in the remote hills is the No. 11 Jeep – a euphemism for those sturdy pairs of muscular legs possessed by all local-grown Nepalis. This vehicle can go almost anywhere and its speed too is often quite remarkable. In my mid-thirties (when I was young and energetic), I thought I had done well to walk from Baglung to Pokhara in one day, until I met the young Nepali lad who completed a far greater distance in significantly less than half my time. What really squashed my ego and made me feel decrepit was the fact that he did it only a year after having had a fractured femur pinned and plated. But trekking in the hills is not just a matter of fitness.

Distances in the hills were sensibly measured by time rather than miles or kilometres. The basic unit was the *kos,* which is approximately that distance which could be walked in one hour (but no one ever clarified whether this was a young man's hour or an old woman's hour). Two *kos* was one *hulak.* Now, a *hulak* is a post office, which means, theoretically, that every two hours I could have stopped to post a letter home. Practically, however, I found that postboxes from which letters were likely to be collected were far more spread out than that, so it was simpler, quicker and more reliable to take my letters home and deliver them personally.

I also learnt to my cost never to ask a village man how far it was to my destination. On the one hand, he might look at me with distain as an overweight non-hillsman (hillswoman!) and assume I could only walk at a fraction of his speed. Multiplying his own estimated time (likely to be highly inaccurate anyway) by a factor of anything from two to four, he might declare it would take me, say, six hours. If I dared to carry on after that discouragement, I might find it was actually an easy two-hour stroll. On the other hand, he might look at my well-covered Western frame with a slight tinge of jealousy and over-enthusiastically divide his own estimated time by two, so that six hours and two very sore feet later I would stumble into the next village. There are also three very good reasons why it was even less advisable to ask a village woman this same question. One, women usually had no idea how fast they walked; two, they didn't wear watches; and three, they might have misunderstood the question and told me how many children they had had (which was usually in double figures).

No matter how long a time it took me to arrive by foot, I could always get there more quickly by language. When speaking about their journeys, Nepalis colloquially say they have arrived at the next village as soon as they have left the last one.

In the 1970s, when I was young and fit and enthusiastic, I went on many treks – several times to and from Baglung or Beni, and even to Kathmandu and the Annapurna Sanctuary for holidays. Later I trekked with Rejina for leprosy surveys out west and went on holiday with her in the east, but all these treks had several things in common: I always managed to climb the steepest bit of the trail at midday in the glaring sun and heat. No matter what time I set out, it was always the same. Survival dictated strategy. Every time I found a water tap or stream I dunked my head underneath and then soaked my big black umbrella, and those manoeuvres kept me cool for about the next ten minutes. If the trek was overnight, we often stayed in a *bhatti,* which, according to the dictionary, was a house of ill repute where travellers could buy *rakshi*[77] and a companion for the night. Of course, I never did either of those things, but there were always plenty of minute companions very willing to share my *gundri*[78] and sleeping bag. It goes without saying that there were also no bathrooms or toilets; I washed in a stream and went behind a tree. When my route took me via a place called Tatopani (meaning hot water), although it was a bit sulphurous, it was fun to have a dip in the spa – until I heard some of the rumours. Apparently, women would come there to have an abortion as the water was sort of antiseptic. On longer tours I found that hanging out my washing on the umbrella was a good idea. Only once did I carry all my own paraphernalia on my own back; every other time I took a *bhurria*[79]. These porters were amazing in the amounts they could carry, but sadly, professional porters had a somewhat decreased life expectancy, presumably something to do with over-straining the heart. Before roads were developed, however, everyone had to walk and carry. Just imagine carrying a sick child (or, worse still, a *suitkerrie*) for maybe a whole day to reach the nearest doctor.

All sorts of weird and interesting things used to happen on trek. In Takum, which, at the time I first visited, was a very remote and undeveloped but extraordinarily beautiful little hill village, I met the village elders in their library. I don't recollect there being any books in the library – not surprising as few people in the area could read – but I do remember a picture of man's first walk on the moon stuck onto the wall; a bizarre choice as the village elders had just assured me that the sun went round the earth.

In 1989 I went to Burtibang in early June, and it was a big error of judgement. The run-up to the trek was fraught with difficulties: a mysterious bug that left me less than energetic; and an early start to the monsoon. Everyone knows that the rains start on 15th June, but by the

[77] Rakshi – locally made alcoholic drink.
[78] Gundri – mat made from woven straw.
[79] Bhurria – porter.

6th (when I was due to leave) it had already been pouring continuously for a couple of weeks. I was therefore banking on RNAC (Royal Nepal Airlines Corporation aka Really Nothing Absolutely Certain) cancelling our flight to Balewa so that I could cancel the trek without losing face. They didn't, but it was only when we arrived at the airport by tractor (during a taxi strike) that we discovered this conclusively – although the flight was delayed by three hours. A non-medical colleague and I spent the first night in Baglung and very early the next morning tackled the big hill, but by the time we had climbed for 5 hours up and slithered 5 hours down, our knees were like jelly and our feet burning – with blisters. We eventually made it to Burtibang and back, and I don't think the rain ever gave up.

Colleagues have had even more exciting encounters while trekking. Most of us in INF were medics of one sort or another; not so, Keith, a horticulturalist, but of course the local people did not know that. One day, at a small hotel stop, a large Tibetan Khamba noticed Keith. "Doctor-sahib, please examine my son." When no amount of explanation that he was not a doctor would satisfy the man (who was twice Keith's size), my friend hit on an ingenious solution. "OK, but he is very dirty; before I examine him, you must take him down to the river and wash him." And while the Tibetans were at the river, Keith made his getaway.

My most memorable experience was as scary but in a different sort of way. I was returning from Jomson on my own with just a porter for companionship. We stopped at Kalo Pani for the night, where we bunked down upstairs in a large two-story shed. In the middle of the night, something jumped onto my bed and I screamed (understandably). This woke the porter who declared it was a *bhut.* At that time my language was so deficient I had no idea what he was saying. I thought perhaps this was another word for *biralo* (cat) but he kept insisting it was a *bhut.* Only later did I discover that a *bhut* was an evil spirit, which perhaps explained the undue amount of darkness and fear I had felt. It seems that we must have upset the *jankri*[80] in whose house we were staying.

80 Jankri – witchdoctor or spirit doctor.

14

Bugger, Bugger, Bugger

Buses, taxis, planes and trains

Typical Nepali bus.

IF YOU ARE NOT OFFENDED BY the title of this chapter, and are still reading, let me explain. Small boys toting for custom as their taxis plied up and down Pokhara bazaar would lean out of the window screaming, "Bugger, Bugger, Bugger," that being what the top end of Pokhara bazaar was called. I vaguely remember being told it actually meant 'meat market', though my dictionary says it's a 'sandy place'. Both would fit. The rather prudish mission community renamed it Bagh Bazaar and the name stuck – except with the taxi boys.

A taxi in Pokhara in the 1970s – and still for the most part today, even in Kathmandu – is a small Toyota saloon with threadbare tyres, dodgy brakes, broken doors, jammed windows, worn-out upholstery and a horn stuck together with Sellotape. This was the vehicle into which the driver used to squash seven or eight passengers as well as himself and the little boy who solicited trade for him. It was not so bad going up the hill to Bagar but freewheeling all the way down could be a tad scary. The biggest change since those days is sadly not the introduction of MOTs[81] but rather that the numbers of passengers carried has decreased while the fare has increased – both quite dramatically.

In towns – except for Nepalgunj, where they still thought they were in the Victorian era and used horses and carriages – I found that taxis were the best way of getting somewhere on time. That was before I had my own wheels. Buses, admittedly, are cheaper but they keep stopping, are slower and don't always go where you want to go.

But with an increasing number of roads now snaking their way into the hills, for most people, buses are the preferred – and most economical – way to travel. All the roads are B roads (B for bad). Each year the monsoon washes away many hillsides and takes great chunks of road with it. Better not to travel between June and September. Better, in my opinion, not to travel by bus *at all,* but many times I had no option but to take a night bus to reach Kathmandu, Nepalgunj or Surkhet for my work. How I hated those journeys!

I have rarely seen a new bus on a Nepali road but they must be born sometime, although, like the rest of the population, they do tend to age quite quickly. How they keep going at all is a minor miracle. The major miracle is that although road accidents have become commoner, I have only been involved in three. One was not even a proper accident as the only thing damaged was the offside front side-light of the bus (and possibly the ego of the bus driver). Another was when the bus knocked a child down and the driver then drove off at top speed to the nearest police station to avoid being lynched by the local community. The third was the most spectacular. The night bus would almost certainly have gone over the cliff had it not crashed into another vehicle, and this was probably because, like me, the driver had fallen asleep. But happily, my guardian angel had not dozed on duty.

One of the main reasons why I have always hated bus travel is rather embarrassing. Most journeys take at least six hours, which is a lot longer than my bladder capacity. Buses usually had one scheduled rice-eating

---

81 MOT – Ministry of Transport (vehicle test).

stop and, with a bit of luck, I could find the facilities: a hole in the ground (usually with a rickety privacy shield) at the back of the restaurant. All other stops were invariably in the middle of a village full of over-inquisitive children or by the roadside just where there were no bushes. Searching for a suitable spot back down the road we had just travelled left me with a good – or rather, bad – chance of the bus leaving without me. Don't laugh: it happened to Nepali friends of mine. If I was really desperate, the solution was to walk on a little, unfurl my umbrella, close my eyes and squat, pretending that because I could not see anyone, no one could see me either. Since the 1980s things have improved enormously; nowadays there are many more restaurants – and all with respectable restrooms.

I am short but not skinny. So... I usually had enough room for my legs on a Nepali bus, but being one of three people on a standard two-seater bench, I discovered, could feel a bit squashed after a while. Once (and I'm so glad it was only once) I travelled with a group of women who had never been on a bus before. They were unanimously and unitedly travel sick. One vomited all over my feet while trying to reach the window and another narrowly missed doing it down my neck. I'm never travel sick. No, that's a lie; I was once, and I found it was the quickest and easiest way ever to get a window seat.

But a window seat can be a mixed blessing. Most times I was unlucky with them. In the winter time (when it's really cold at 5am), my seat was always the one by the window that under no circumstances whatsoever would either close or stay closed; in the summer time (when the temperatures are in the nineties) mine was always the seat by the window that was permanently jammed shut. The alternative was to book an aisle seat, but it was a toss-up which was worse, for aisle seats had their disadvantages too. It usually turned out to be just half a seat next to the only obese Nepali on the bus, and from which I was repeatedly shaken off as we hit each bend. I was regularly trampled on by the conductor, used by standing passengers as a ledge to dump their large bags and incontinent babies, or attacked by the goats and chickens trying to take over my foot-space. Long-distance (night) buses had armrests, presumably so that passengers could safely doze off without the danger of falling out of their seats. You've guessed! I once got the seat with the broken armrest, and so was forced to share the aisle with a family of tomatoes that rolled out of a fellow traveller's bag every time we went around a bend. Twelve hours of this – the jagged stump of the armrest boring its way into my right buttock – was not the perfect way to end a holiday!

Hardly a bus journey went by without some sort of technical hitch, usually a puncture – or two, or even three! For this sort of emergency, they usually had a spare tyre (but often not two) and always a jerry can of water for when the engine overheated on the hills. They also came equipped with a crowbar, which was handy when they needed to prise a rock out from between the double wheels or lever the vehicle back into a vertical position. During the monsoon season we also suffered from 'fallen nature' incidents. Torrential rain invariably brought down mud and rocks onto stretches of the road (physical landslides), causing kilometres of traffic backups. Delays were then lengthened even further by selfish drivers all vying to get past the blockage first!

One (daytime) journey from Kathmandu sticks in my memory. Approaching Pokhara, but happily well past the places where there's a huge drop to the river on one side of the road, we came across a recent accident – a private car upturned in the rice field and a group of Sri Lankans standing nearby, clearly not seriously injured. Our bus agreed to give them a lift and I was able to chat to them (in English) and reassure them, even sharing some of my faith with them even though they were Buddhists. Their leader was a large and – dare I say it – rather neurotic gentleman, who was convinced he was far more damaged than he was, and when he discovered that I was a doctor, well... he insisted that I go with them to the hospital (GZH) for a check-up and that I should stay with them overnight at their posh hotel (just in case of need).

Ordinary Nepalis always arrived at the bus station at the very last minute and never boarded until they had finished drinking their tea and said their lengthy goodbyes. Most ordinary Nepali buses therefore never used to depart on time, or at least not before every seat was overfilled and there were at least another half dozen passengers perched on *moras*[82] in the aisle. Nowadays most long-distance buses do stick approximately to their schedules although they only become non-stop expresses after they have dropped off the local passengers along the first ten kilometres

[82] Mora – small stool made from bamboo.

and stop being expresses for the last ten kilometres for the same exercise, to generate a little extra pocket money for the crew.

Night buses were the worst of the worst – unless you actually enjoyed being trapped in a rickety metal box full of noisy, smoky night owls for ten hours during the time one normally takes one's beauty sleep. Nepali passengers invariably quietly snoozed from boarding until mid-journey. Then, after gorging themselves on huge plates of rice, instead of falling back into deep post-prandial slumber, they indulged in a raucous sing-song or shouted conversations. The driver also took this as his cue to turn his radio on full blast. I can't sleep semi-upright, but even a short nap was impossible under such conditions. The only good thing was that the driver also could surely not fall asleep amid all this noise. That was a very comforting (if not very peaceful) thought as we careered around the edge of a precipice more generously known as the road.

Once, with a colleague, I took the bus back down those 1,200 Z-bends I had first travelled in 1970, to attend a Community Health Conference in Tansen. When I had foolishly agreed to carry back a borrowed 20-litre metal petrol can, I had overlooked the fact that it was near the end of the monsoon, when landslides have an annoying habit of blocking the roads. Even by the time we arrived at the bus station in Pokhara, I was regretting my generosity. By the time we reached the first landslide, I was regretting my stupidity, and by the time we got to the big landslide which totally blocked the highway, I was regretting travelling at all. I'm just too naïve – and I never learn.

Many years later I visited Tansen again – on a different errand. It was a long and tedious trip and I could have wished the driver was as old and careful a driver as I am, but we got there safely enough and I completed my teaching. Ideally, I would have preferred to teleport back, but as that was not an option, I booked on the regular minibus. Initially, I was very reassured by the driver. Down the hill and along the plains to Narayanghat he drove with remarkable restraint. Then we stopped for rice. Well, *most* of us ate rice; what the driver had is questionable, for after that he drove like a man possessed, his foot hard on the accelerator and overtaking on almost every blind bend (of which there were hundreds). From the moment he took off until we arrived back safely in Kathmandu some four hours later, a former colleague who was visiting and I never stopped praying, and that was probably the only reason why we *did* get back safely.

Joshua, one of the Bagh Bazaar church leaders, once told me how God had looked after him and his family on a bus trip. He'd pre-booked them on the 6am minibus from Kathmandu to Pokhara but when they arrived at the bus station, they found the seats had been double-booked. The man apologised and said they would have to go on the 7am bus. They were understandably a bit annoyed – until, that is, a couple of hours later, when they passed the site where the 6am bus had gone over the edge of the road, with significant loss of life and serious injuries.

Once or twice I was forced to use alternative forms of transport when buses were not available. One was a peanut lorry – but more of that later.[83] The other was a tractor, because we had to cross the Rapti River and buses don't swim. Regina and I were visiting some friends and that was the only way (at that time) to reach them – other than braving the elephants, crocodiles and rhinoceroses by walking through the Chitwan forest. We joined about forty other stoical passengers along with all their personal luggage, plus sacks of provisions, bits of a bicycle, and a goat with diarrhoea. At the river all the men had to get off to lighten the load and make sure we didn't sink. All but one happily removed their trousers and waded across. Just one poor soul stayed shivering on the bank – but whether he was more afraid of the cold water or the crocodiles I never found out. Eventually, someone helped him across, but it was not long before we were bogged down again. This time even the women and children – and the goat with diarrhoea – had to get off. It then took so much time and effort for the men to dig the tractor out of the sandbank that our next stop was to eat rice in the nearby village. By the time we arrived at the end of the 'road', therefore, it was pitch dark. There was no thought of walking on to our friends, so we took a public bath under the tap and settled in for the night. After just one short day with Prithi and Elisheba (remember them from my time in Beni), it looked as though our return trip would be thoroughly boring – until we were almost in sight of the main road. The tractor in front of ours took the final sharp bend at the wrong angle and tipped over right in the middle of the track. We laughed as all the passengers slowly rolled off into the ditch, but the

[83] See Chapter 19.

next hour was not so funny as we had to wait while they unloaded all the sacks of grain, righted the tractor and then reloaded the sacks. Only then could the convoy set off again.

Although few and far between, planes came to Nepal before buses, trucks and tractors; thus, simple village people who had watched the small aeroplanes flying overhead were totally baffled when they encountered their first car. I was told on utterly reliable authority that as they watched with fascination and mystification a car being offloaded from the belly of a plane, one woman explained it for them: "The plane has had a baby." In actual fact, I believe the first car that was born in the Kathmandu Valley arrived somewhat differently – carried on the shoulders of porters, across the hills from India.

Travelling by plane is certainly far more pleasant than by bus, but it's expensive, and as planes need somewhere flat to land, their destinations are limited. In the beginning most of the airports in Nepal were air-grounds – fairly flat plots of grassy (not tarmacked) ground. In Pokhara they used to blow a whistle when a plane was expected, which meant that all the people walking across the ground (it was a short cut to Green Pastures) plus the local cows and buffaloes had to get off the pitch.

Buses regularly transported peculiar passengers with bizarre luggage but, understandably, pilots were less keen to do so. I was once asked to certify that a mentally disturbed tourist was safe to fly. After chasing her around the airport buildings I managed to inject a sedative and hastily wrote out a certificate to say that she would be OK for a couple of hours (until the sedative wore off). As the plane took off, and my responsibility was ended, I breathed a huge sigh of relief and went home. At crack of dawn the following day I was none too pleased to be awoken by one of the members of that tourist group – wanting another certificate. Apparently, the plane had got halfway to Kathmandu when it was discovered that one of the local passengers had with him a pressure lamp full of kerosene and so the pilot had felt obliged to return to the safety of Pokhara. This time I couldn't catch my patient but issued the certificate anyway as I reckoned that the real madman on that flight had already been exposed.

Many times I spent longer waiting in the airport than in the air. Usually that was because of bad weather, bad planes (a technical fault) or just bad management, but sometimes it was because of arguments over excess baggage. One time I had to fight really hard to get my tins of Dapsone[84] on the plane with me; without medicines there would have been no point in my going to Jumla to run the leprosy clinic. However, the check-in clerk saw that as the solution, neither I nor my tins should go. Eventually – goodness knows how, but perhaps God did – I went, the tins went, and snuggled down among them, a tin of peanut butter also went, to help me survive the week in Jumla.

Fighting for the Dapsone was really fighting for the rights of my leprosy patients. I felt no guilt whatsoever. Not so when it came to the bed-roll. Although I had only just got back from the UK, there was an urgent need for me to go to Ghorahi to relieve a colleague and this entailed first travelling to Pokhara, picking up some clothes and then getting down to Bhairawa to catch the shuttle to Tulispur the next day. All went remarkably well until I reached the airport. There were no seats left but they put me on the waiting list – not a hopeful sign. Every quarter of an hour I enquired about the state of play and eventually, perhaps to shut me up, I was rewarded with the 20th seat on a 19-seat Twin Otter – but, they said, my bed-roll could not go with me. That was not a major disaster, but the fact that it was not labelled *was* (it wasn't even mine). I fought hard to get it marked so that it would eventually catch up with me, but the man at the check-in desk misunderstood; and after a lot of discussion, he tagged and loaded it. I felt bad but there was no time to explain; all I could do was pray it would not hinder the plane staying in the sky. My prayer was answered. I disembarked (plus bed-roll) and found the Mission Land Rover waiting (as arranged) to take me the final two hours to Ghorahi. But this was the end of the monsoon; as we rounded the corner to the last river, we saw a huge bore wave bearing down on us. Like us, the driver wanted to get home that night, so he put his foot down and roared across to the far bank. Thirty seconds later and we would have been stuck there all night – if not washed away in the flood. God was obviously still looking after us.

Rail travel, in case you were wondering, is not an option. There are only two stations in Nepal and unless you are a raw product travelling to the factory in Janakpur, or a cigarette coming out of there, the train

---

[84] Dapsone – one of the early medicines used for leprosy.

would not be of much use to you. But travel on Indian rail added an interesting dimension to several of my holidays in India.

15

Luna-cy

Cycles and motorcycles

Val on Luna moped.

IT IS MY CONSIDERED OPINION that there are a lot of lunatics on Nepali roads, but I was never one of them. Nor were the drivers employed by INF. The ideal method of long-distance travel was therefore by mission vehicle. I found it had many advantages: no need to start at the crack of dawn; convenient comfort stops on request; and I was usually delivered right to the door at my destination. Just once I remember we had a problem: two punctures but only one spare tyre. The solution was to send our nursing colleague off with two strange men in a passing truck to get some help – something I wouldn't recommend in England these days.

The real solution to the transport problem is, without doubt, a personal vehicle. The first one I had was a pushbike, which was great for whizzing around Pokhara or popping out to Lamachaur where I ran a weekly clinic for the boys at the boarding school. No good at all for anything farther afield, like my visits to Lumle Agricultural Centre to teach family planning to the ex-soldiers. Anyway, apart from that, in the early days I never left the Pokhara Valley; I was far too busy in the hospital.

Regularly, all the nuts and bolts would rattle loose on my pedal-cycle, and occasionally the chain would dislodge itself and I would end up pushing it home. That's the one big advantage of a pushbike over any other form of transport: it's fairly easy to push. Of course, I also had more than my fair share of punctures, especially as its tyres wore thin. Finally, it expired from an aneurysm when the man in the cycle shop pumped it up so vigorously that the worn tyre just swelled and burst in front of my very eyes. This gave me cause to remember my great aunt Phoebe who must have suffered a lot when her aortic aneurysm did the same: it burst and killed her.

Sometimes when away from Pokhara I used to borrow a bicycle, and possibly the most embarrassing moment of my whole life happened while I was riding a bike in Kathmandu. I was wearing a maxi-length Indian cotton wrap-around skirt and you can guess what happened. The loose end caught in the wheel, wound itself around the hub, and left me firmly anchored to the bike but sitting in the middle of the road and unable to extricate myself without disrobing. Along came a group of gallant Nepali youths to rescue a maiden in distress. I never even heard them laugh – well, not while I was still within earshot.

Another time I borrowed a friend's bike, unaware that it had a continental-style brake, so every time I back-pedalled I came to an abrupt halt. I didn't do that again. But one time I did hire a bike to join some friends on a ride to Chobar Gorge. This time I checked the brakes (normal British-style ones) before I set off but not while riding the bike. That was a mistake, as I soon found out while descending through the rice fields. They were so fierce that I almost flew over the handlebars at the slightest touch. Except, therefore, for one steep uphill stretch, I pushed the bike most of the way there. Returning down the same steep hill, I nearly ended up in the river and wished heartily that I had brought my crash-hat with me, while I suspect that my friends were wishing they had not brought me with them.

In my second or third year in Nepal, I acquired a driving licence and although that wasn't the same as acquiring a drivable vehicle, it was a major achievement and a step in the right direction. It was also ridiculously easy. There was no test; all I did was show the man in the office my British driving licence and tell him I had to hurry back to the hospital in case there was an obstetric emergency. Perhaps his wife was about to deliver a baby for I got the precious document almost immediately. Others were not so lucky. Keith was asked what he'd do if he had a puncture in the middle of nowhere and no spare wheel. I thought his answer, "I'd pray and then wait and see what help God brought along," was pretty sensible, but apparently, he was meant to have stuffed the tyre with grass. Others have been asked to identify road signs. There used to be one that looked as though it meant 'Beware: bananas crossing ahead' although it was actually a warning about boats. I can't say I've ever encountered either a banana or a boat blocking a Nepali road in all my forty-plus years there.

In the days when the monarchy was still very much absolute, there was one crucial 'you get your licence or you don't get your licence' question. Several of my friends were asked to imagine themselves as a policeman on point duty and say in what order they would let traffic through at a crossroads, although the examiner never used to explain that the context was the middle of a war. The politically correct answer was: 1. the King, so he can then direct his troops; 2. the army, so they can do what the King orders; 3. the fire engine, as there's a whole village on fire; and 4. the ambulance, as, after all, it only contains half a dozen battle casualties. Nowadays, there is a formal written test, from which I suspect this question has been omitted, followed by a practical test in which motorcyclists are expected to display a high degree of skill in slalom riding. This is eminently sensible as that is how everyone rides their motorbikes.

Armed with my new driving licence and some knowledge about eye diseases, for the duration of the leprosy paramedical training, only I was allowed to drive a Mission Land Rover. I used to take it from the top end of the bazaar to Green Pastures at the other end of the valley, but I am sure that this privilege was purely so that I would be back from my lecture in time for outpatients at the Shining Hospital. Some years later I was again trusted with a mission vehicle but that was the last time. After driving a group of nurses home from a party, I put the Land Rover into a ditch and couldn't get it out. The worst part, however, came the next day when I had to confess to the vehicle department, but I guess the exercise was Christian character building.

In the early 70s Ruth imported a Honda motorbike. After the technical guys had restored the wires eaten by the rats while it had languished in customs, I taught her how to ride it, drawing on my vast experience in Liverpool. Funny how God always manages to make use of all the skills he's allowed us to gain along the way!

Sometime in the early 1980s I bought my own first motorbike. It was a Luna and was actually a moped. That action might best be described as Luna-cy! Once I got it started, it would wheeze its way up the hills and then coast down them at a top speed of around 20mph with a following wind, but mostly it was a great improvement on the pushbike. However, before I could get it started I had to register and tax it, a task far harder than pedal-starting it. In the early days I guess no one really quite knew how to go about it, especially in Pokhara where there were so few motorbikes and even fewer four-wheelers. But registered it had to be – like all dogs, jackals (!) and radios.

At the Office of the Inspector of Police, I had to complete a registration form in, I think, quintuplicate, visit the bank to pay the fee and then deliver the form back, hoping the official was still at his desk, only to discover that he would not hand over the registration documents until I had taxed the bike. That entailed visiting the tax office, filling in more forms, re-visiting the bank, collecting a tax book hot off the press from the printers and remembering to buy a stamp before heading back for the needed signature. Finally, the Police gave me the registration 'blue book', which in my case turned out to be pink. All that then remained was to get my own number plates painted in the bazaar.

Over the years I discovered that renewing a driving licence and registering, taxing and, later, also insuring a vehicle were all gradually streamlined and computerised as the motorcycle population of Nepal exploded, but perhaps because of work overload, efficiency was still not guaranteed. The final time I renewed my licence, the man pressed the wrong button on his computer and registered me as coming from the

British Virgin Islands. He charged me 100 rupees to correct it and as my mobile phone was also stolen, that final memory of the tax office is not altogether a happy one.

There were also one or two apparently simple and self-explanatory traffic rules that I had to relearn when driving in Nepal. One was flashing headlights. In the UK this is a traditionally polite British way of saying, "After you," but in Nepal drivers flash their headlights to warn others that they are going first, regardless. The other is the use of the right indicator. In the UK, as everyone knows, it means 'I am turning right' or 'I am overtaking on the right'. It's not so simple in Nepal. It certainly can mean that I am turning right but it can also be used to indicate to a following vehicle that it is safe for them to overtake you. The logic of this continues to escape me. All I can advise is that if you ever drive in Nepal, you remember these two rules. They are neither simple nor self-explanatory. They are vitally important!

After some years I upgraded from my blue Luna to an almost new one-man (i.e. one-woman) Honda. When its former owner and I went to the office to transfer ownership, I was a bit peeved to have to fork out 40 rupees (more than £1 at the time) to a professional writer to provide us with a certificate of transfer fully attested with thumb prints. I really loved this little yellow bike and kept it for twelve years. And, oh, the bliss of being able to kick (not pedal) start it!

I did fall off it once but it wasn't my fault. It was pitch dark and the rain was pelting down so I could see precious little to start with, so when a vehicle with a very bright un-dipped headlight approached, I could see nothing at all. Instinctively, I swerved to the left and ended upside down in a wet and muddy ditch, although happily still all in one piece. After that I reflected on the experience: was my assailant a motorbike (narrow like me so I would have been safe to remain on the road), a small tractor (narrow at the front and wide at the back, so I was safer in the ditch), a truck with only an offside headlight (so again I would have been OK staying on the road) or a truck with only a nearside headlight (so again I would definitely have been better off in my muddy ditch)?

Since those days I have owned three other motorbikes – scooters, actually. The first two-stroke (blue and white) one I loved. In 1998 I even rode it to India and back, thereby proving to all my friends that I was totally mad as they had already suspected. And many times I commuted the 200 km between Kathmandu and Pokhara. Others disputed this, but I reckoned it was far safer than going by bus. Riding my bike, it was up to me to drive carefully and my fate was not in the hands of a bus driver who might – or might not – have been sober and wide awake. That first Honda was a faithful friend and I only parted from it when it got too old to climb a certain steep hill – a favourite short-cut of mine – in Kathmandu. As the powers that be had decided two-stroke machines should be banned (not that it had the least effect on the pollution levels), it was followed by a four-stroke silvery coloured one with a host of stupid design faults. That also served me well but again eventually gave up on the hills. The last scooter was a bright red Mahindra, which was still going strong when I myself gave up on the hills and retired to the UK. I sold it to my landlord.

16

I Saw Beds Walking

Equipping the Western Regional Hospital

(Late 1970s and early 1980s)

'Walking' beds.

THE KING'S DIRECTIVE HAD BEEN that INF should work with the government to develop the small Soldiers' Board hospital, first into the 50-bed Gandaki Zonal Hospital (GZH) and eventually into the major 200-bed Western Regional Hospital (WRH). This gave us over a decade of hassles and headaches, hard work and heartache. The German funding we had been promised for the upgrading of the Shining Hospital had to be reallocated to this project and INF needed to renegotiate its own involvement to fulfil its responsibility to the donors. We ended up with a voice (although I'm not really sure we had a vote) on the Construction Board, and I was given the job of Equipment Consultant, but in Pokhara in the 1970s and 80s this was not a matter of poring over glossy catalogues, placing orders and then sitting back to wait for the goods to roll in by themselves. It was far more 'interesting'!

I'm not sure that I had any initial qualifications but along the way I discovered or developed several basic survival skills. First was the ability to drink three bottles of Coke one after the other. I was not a lover of the drink to start with and since then I have not been able to face a single bottle. My solid build saved me more than once when the workmen dropped a cupboard and later a compressor on top of me. As my mother would have told you, I have always been pig-headed, but my stubbornness in sticking up for my specifications when bazaar traders tried to persuade me otherwise definitely stood me in good stead. I've always liked making endless lists, although nowadays they are not for equipment but purely as aids to my aging memory. I developed a large measure of tact, something I definitely didn't have before, to deal with senior officials who wanted me to buy the most inappropriate items – like expensive copper buckets for sand and cigarette ends. At the time I also had a disregard for dust; although at the time I did not stifle in the atmosphere of the hospital construction site, this, combined with many years living in Kathmandu, has subsequently had long-term effects on my lung capacity. But perhaps the most important of my qualifications were a knack of making money go twice as far as it usually does, a basic knowledge of what is needed inside a hospital, and a desire to see the medical services in Pokhara upgraded. As there was no one else in INF who met these qualifications any better than I did, I got the job.

"Budget 4,000,000/-; Funds 3,000,000/-; Shortfall 1,000,000/-." The task would have been a lot easier had there been unlimited funds available – but there weren't! One of my jobs, therefore, was to raise funds and that is one of the many things I am not very good at. During my home leave in 1983/4, I spent more time with my mother than doing mission deputation; stuck behind her typewriter, I repeatedly pruned the lists until they balanced the budget. Then when funds became available, I was able to place the orders and wait for a steady stream of forceps and fridges, scissors and scalpels, kidney dishes, sterilisers, oxygen cylinders and a dental drill to arrive in Pokhara. One unexpected bonus of working in Nepal was receiving a special Christmas present one year. With Christmas Day just another ordinary working day, a letter granting us funds was delivered on that very day.

The budget, as well as appropriate technology, demanded that all the basic furniture should be made locally and in many cases this meant drawing the designs myself, followed by innumerable visits to the wood and iron works to check on their progress. Deliveries also were unusual. I decided that instead of loading the beds onto a truck – which would have damaged their nice new shiny white paint – I would employ porters to carry them from the factory to the hospital, about a mile away. 85 beds therefore walked through the bazaar on two men's heads, and the rest of the stuff jogged its way down on 100 tractors or was piled by me and my merry men (some unemployed local young men) into the mission Land Rover. Over 4,900 metres of assorted cloth also went that way. I brought one dustbin from Kathmandu on the top of a bus, but the others followed more sedately in a truck. Carrying fifteen kilogramme scales and weights on a motorbike was another of my accomplishments. All this inevitably meant a high degree of contact with a number of bazaar tradesmen. I spent a lot of time chatting and drinking tea with them, which led to good relationships and an improved understanding of the GZH Extension Project and INF's involvement in it. I am sure our honesty in all these business dealings was a witness even if I was rarely able to explain more specifically why we behaved like this. But just once – and that was only during an extra visit made because the Nepali auditor had demanded extra documents – was I able to chat about the true meaning of Christmas.

Using this local industry saved a lot of money which was then available to import the more specialised equipment from overseas. However, my biggest headache was then the holdup over the granting of customs exemption for goods from India and overseas. After more than eighteen months' preparatory work by at least half a dozen other people in the Mission, it still took seven personal visits to the Health Department and four to Customs plus lots of prayer by everyone before the papers were eventually granted. At last expensive anaesthetic equipment and other items arrived safely and, happily, the mattresses had not been chewed by rats.

Although the next stage buildings were under construction, there were innumerable delays, and the equipment started to arrive before the rooms were ready for it. I had to store it somewhere in the meantime, but this meant I was continually moving and stacking so many beds, benches, blood pressure machines, buckets, blankets and the like, that I almost lost count. Keeping track of everything was such a huge task that I had to employ a storekeeper-cum-caretaker to ensure that all the stuff stayed where I had put it. The other half of his job description was to paint 'GZH' and serial numbers onto almost all the items to ensure that later on they still remained where they were placed in the new buildings. Also, because of the delays, the rats took a fancy to the new stored pillows, but apart from one overseas consignment there was little damage to the equipment, and as that had happened *en route,* amazingly I got some compensation. However, my task was not easy to complete because people kept adding extra items to my lists, and one essential order – it would be the obstetrics and gynaecology instruments! – had apparently been totally overlooked in Germany.

Another part of my responsibility was to be a member of the Construction Board. Initially I considered this a real privilege, but I soon discovered that being a board member also meant being a bored member. Meetings seemed to happen 'out of the blue', or at least notification always came (to me) at the very last minute. I dared not be late even though the meeting proper never started until the *thulo manchhe*[85] arrived, usually an hour after me. The good thing was that coffee was always served; the bad thing was that all the discussion was in Nepali, so I could not afford to doze. There was one big difference from Western style committee meetings and that was that votes were never taken – so that no one would ever lose face by voting in opposition. The result was that the meetings dragged on and on until consensus was reached. Immediately this occurred, however, the minute secretary wrote it in the book, and the minutes were read and passed around for signature. No matter how hard I tried to understand what I was signing, I could never be wholly sure it was something I agreed with, and even when I knew I disagreed, I could still do nothing about it.

By 1979 the first stage of the project was complete and the 50-bed hospital started to function. INF began to second clinical staff and I think the first two people to work there were an anaesthetist and a theatre sister. Then, as the 70s turned into the 80s, I started to think of returning to my own first love, obstetrics, and began by adding to my equipment

---

[85] Thulo manchhe – important person (lit. big man).

duties occasional locum trips to the hospital. It was exciting to experience once again some medical – obstetric – drama but it also meant that I could tangibly demonstrate before the patients that Shining and GZH really were working together and so help them to accept the new situation.

At first I visited only occasionally and then once a week to help Drs Hira Dongal and Jyoti Rana. I wasn't an official member of the team but this did give me the chance to get to know many of the medical and nursing staff and understand how the HMG/N system worked. I began to empathise with the doctors as I saw first-hand the difficulties they faced. At that time I was still working in the Shining Clinics and so was in a unique position to see things from both sides – and sometimes also a third, funny side. As a generalist at Shining, I occasionally referred a patient for specialist care and then saw the same patient as a specialist myself in GZH. Often patients wanting a second opinion got the first from me in Shining and then the second (same) opinion from me in GZH. The government hospital had just a few drugs and tests available free for poor patients, but no pharmacy and no poor fund to help those who could not afford bazaar prices. The free medicines never lasted long and the supply was often abused. Government doctors who cared – like my O & G colleagues – really struggled.

The official 'inauguration' happened before the new inpatient block was finished. The hold-up was partly due to the construction company, who, among other not-so-good things, diverted some of their time to building a small Hindu temple in the hospital grounds – having almost certainly diverted some of our project money (without our knowledge of course) to do this. Delay was also due to red tape – and I don't mean the bit that the King cut on the big day. Nevertheless, the King and Queen visited in January 1985. The red carpet was 40 metres of 36-inch-wide red cotton cloth, unceremoniously stuck to the tarmac with Sellotape and Elastoplast. On 22nd January, HRH King Birendra and the Crown Prince (but not the Queen as she had toothache!) 'inspected' GZH – and to prove it, both national and daily papers published a photograph of them and me together. His majesty was "very impressed" with our "nice, clean hospital" – and so he should have been after all our hard work. The next day the Queen did come and I escorted her around the new buildings, giving a non-stop running commentary to prevent the Medical

Superintendent usurping our opportunity as he had done with the King. I also have a photo of the Queen and myself (wearing my best red sari), but both photos are worthless now Nepal has become a republic.

In November 1985 the new wards were still not functioning, and I had time to reflect on the building projects that Ezra and Nehemiah had been commissioned to carry out. They too had experienced a long delay in the middle of their work, and so I began to see the length of time in a new light. Their delays and opposition were clearly because they were involved in carrying out God's will, and while our hospital project was by no means in the same category as the Temple and city walls, we still believed that God had led us into it. That certainty made learning to handle delicate relationships and replying to official letters just a little bit easier. As in those far-off Old Testament days, God had himself been with us in all our plans and negotiations; and he had provided us with the right team members, having all the necessary practical and diplomatic gifts. Towards the end, especially, we saw clear evidence of that when Mida, an accountant from the Philippines, joined the team to sort out the finances. The auditor came exactly on time and was so helpful. And then precisely two weeks later, all the Construction Board problems were thrashed out during a marathon two-and-a-half days of meetings with all involved parties being present (usually at least one important person was missing when we met). Final settlement was confirmed in writing on the last evening, balancing the precious documents on the boot of the contractor's car and then on the hotel bed of the architect/consultant. Then, as the new INF Agreement with HMG/N was signed in December 1985, we recognized that we had, like Ezra and Nehemiah, experienced "the good hand of our God on us"[86].

Eventually, by June 1986, the hospital extension was almost ready to be opened, but first HMG/N had to grant their part of the budget. Then the cabinet had to agree the hospital could change its name to the Western Regional Hospital – a little controversial as although it was designated as a 200-bed hospital, at that time only three of the four new wards (150 beds) were completed. Only after the name change could the press officially gazette (publish) the constitution of the new Hospital Management Board, but the board could also only be agreed after the

---

[86] Ezra 8:18 (ESV).

INF/GZH Agreement was ratified by the King. All this was all supposed to happen within a couple of weeks. If it had it would have been a miracle of major proportions. In fact, it took considerably longer before our prayers were answered and the new board was set up. But eventually it was, and it met and settled the bye-laws. It advertised for and appointed new staff, and then at last we could arrange for the patients to be transferred to the new buildings; and the new theatre and other new departments opened for use, but that was only in 1987.

Those extra months of delay in 1986 were not easy but this time it was Habakkuk who encouraged me. *Though the extension does not open and there are scant supplies in the stores, though the name is not changed and the board not yet convened, though there are few doctors in the clinics and so few nurses on the wards, yet will I rejoice in the Lord.*[87]

Some of the last things I added to the hospital were some lovely Nepali scenic pictures which also had Bible texts on them (in small print). Initially, no one commented, and I dared to hope they would stay put. However, sadly, after only six weeks I was instructed to remove these posters, although, to my great amusement and joy, all eighty of them rapidly took their scripture text messages into the homes of hospital staff from all levels of the medical hierarchy. At this same time (and probably as a result) two senior doctors asked for New Testaments.

In November 1986 rumours began to circulate that the opening was imminent, and by January 1987 everything was happening at once. An urgent meeting of INF representatives and the Regional Director was called, and during that, two earthquakes occurred. When the first (minor physical earth tremor) hit, the Medical Superintendent, who had once experienced a bad one, dashed outside and left the rest of us sitting staring at his empty chair. When he returned, the second (metaphorical) one hit. After informing us that INF would no longer to be represented on the Management Board, Dr. Shrestha said the hospital should open in three to four days. Scarcely convincing him that three to four weeks was the minimum, we escaped to draw up plans for the impossible. Thus, in three frantic weeks, prior to the 13th All Nepal Medical Conference being held for the very first time in Pokhara, we found ourselves scrubbing wards, shifting the old theatre light to its new home, preparing sterile

[87] cp. Hab. 3:17-18.

packs of instruments, putting up pictures, trying out light switches and taps, evacuating a swarm of bees from the new male surgical toilets, checking inventories and (fortunately with the help of the student nurses) making up a hundred beds.

The name was changed overnight and on Monday, 9th February the new Development Board had its first meeting – a five-hour marathon endured by most of the members plus INF's Executive Director and advisory representative. Basic agreement was reached regarding a scale of fees and the employment of new laundry staff. Suddenly, the move was on. On Tuesday the inventories were checked with the ward staff, and at 8.30am on Wednesday, 11th February 1987, the keys were handed over and the first patient wheeled over to the new Surgical Ward. The Western Regional Hospital was at last a reality. However, because of all the delays, the old 50-bed block, which had been in use from 1979, was already in need of renovation. In due course a team from the INF Technical Services Department completed this to a very high standard. INF also began to further develop pharmacy, physiotherapy, housekeeping and maintenance – those departments we had initiated – as these were not normally part of a government hospital at that time.

During those last few weeks, I had been staying at Green Pastures because I had found the stress of clinical work on top of finalising the equipment just too much, especially as for the previous six months I had been almost single-handed in the O & G department. However, after the opening, and feeling refreshed, I returned to WRH, looking forward to a further period of clinical involvement. What I did not then know was that within a couple of months, my responsibilities would take a very different turn.

Special Occasions

ABOVE: Left: MB ChB Graduation 1967. Right: MA Graduation 2008.
BELOW: Top left: Devkota Award 2010.
Top right: OBE Presentation 1996 with Terry and Mollie Spinks and Alison Craven.
Bottom left: The King and I. Bottom right: The Queen and I.

Nepal

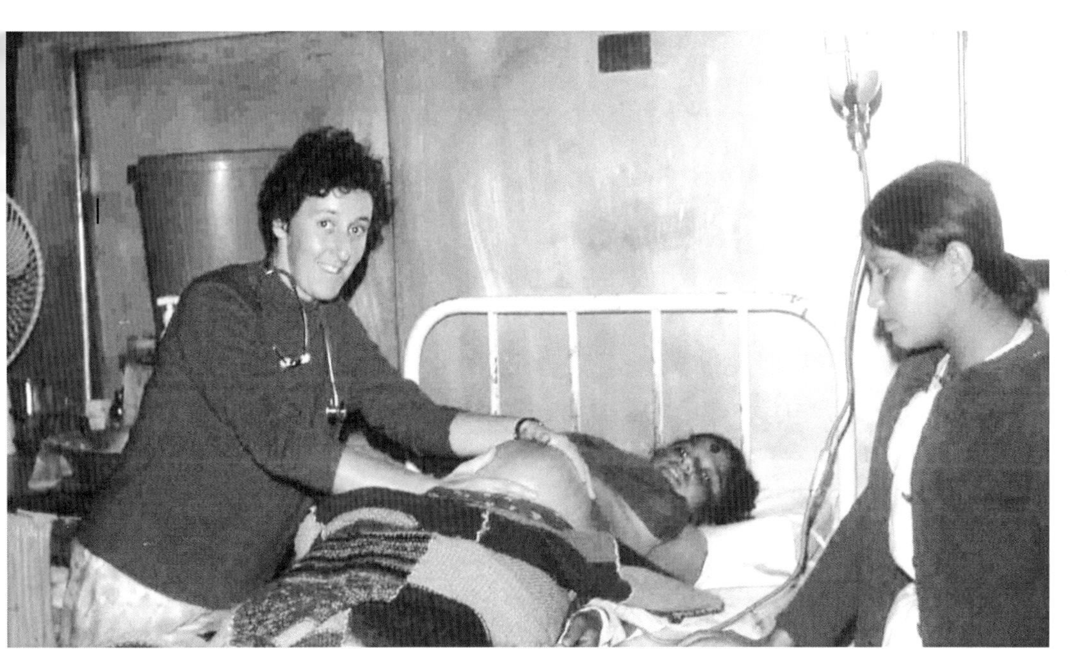

The Shining Hospital, Pokhara (1970s)

ABOVE: Maternity.

BELOW: Top left: Ward. Mid left: Outpatients – dressing area. Bottom left: Operating theatre.
Top right: General view from cattle grid. Bottom right: General view from Kaski hill.

Pokhara

ABOVE: Fishtail Mountain from Green Pastures.
BELOW: Top left: Welcome Arch. Mid left: Old-style general store. Bottom left: Sheti River Gorge.
Top right: Pokhara from Serangkot Hill. Mid right: Pokhara Bazaar in 1980s. Bottom right: Phewa Tal.

Leprosy Work

ABOVE: Left: Patients in Ghorahi. Right: Leprosy survey.
BELOW: Left: Green Pastures patients.
Top right: Ward in Surkhet. Middle right: Leprosy paramedicals. Bottom right: Outpatients in Jumla.

Community Health and TB Work

ABOVE: Left: Animal health. Right: TB microscopy.
BELOW: Top left: Child health. Top middle upper: Water tap stand. Top middle lower: Chest X-ray.
Top right: TB examination. Bottom left: Health education. Bottom right: Literacy class.

Trekking

Transport

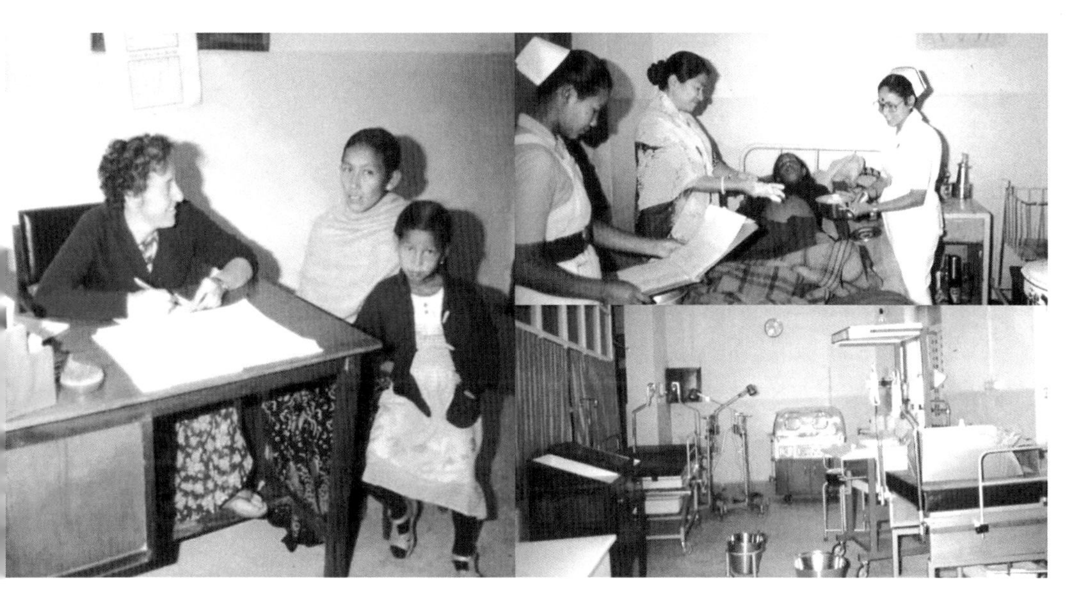

Gandaki Zonal – Western Region Hospital, Pokhara (1980s)

ABOVE: Left: OPD. Top right: Ward. Bottom right: Maternity.
BELOW: Top: 50-bed GZH. Bottom left: 150-bed WRH. Bottom right: WRH (view from nearby hill).

Kathmandu

ABOVE: Left: Valley Agriculture. Right: Martyr Memorial Arch.
BELOW: Top left to top right: Buddhanath Stupa; Pashupatinath; Asantole; Chobar Gorge.
Middle left: Hanuman Dhoka. Middle right: Tri-Chandra College.
Bottom left: Darbar Square, Patan. Bottom right: Potters in Bhaktapur.

INF Centres

ABOVE: Top: Burtibang. Bottom left: Baglung. Bottom right: Ghorari.
BELOW: Top left: Nepalganj. Top right: Jumla. Bottom left: Takum. Bottom right: Surkhet.

Nepali Churches

ABOVE: Left: Baptism in river (1970s). Right: Easter Rally (1990s).
BELOW: Top: Ramghat Church (then and now). Middle: Bagh Bazaar Church (1980s-90s).
Bottom left: Kunahar Church construction. Bottom centre top: Kunahar congregation (1990s).
Bottom centre bottom: Ashish ladies. Bottom right: Ashish Church (2000).

Bible Yatra Nepal (BaYaN)

ABOVE: Top: Church seminars. Bottom: Diaspora seminars (India & Qatar).

BELOW: Top left: First two trainees. Top middle: Oldest student. Top right: Making the video.
Middle left: Early seminar. Middle centre and right: Training Centre seminars. Bottom: Training of trainers.

Diaspora

ABOVE: Nepalese Migrant Unity Network (NeMUN).
BELOW: Top left: At the airport. Top middle: Porter in India. Top right: Malaysian factory.
Middle left: Jordan. Centre: Oman. Middle right: UK.
Bottom left: Malaysia. Bottom middle: Qatar. Bottom right: UAE.

17

I Heard Babies Crying

Obstetrician in GZH and WRH

(Early and mid 1980s)

Mother and baby in GZH.

IN JANUARY 1984 I HAD MOVED to Ramghat and soon began working full-time in the GZH O & G department. Later I was given a doctor's quarter on the hospital compound, adjacent to my new colleagues, Dr Yamuna and Dr Chandra Sobha – and later Dr Kusum Thapa. Apart from its leaky roof and initial lack of a kitchen, plus the rats, frogs, ants and cows that also regarded it as their home, this small bungalow was ideal for me and also for the hospital *peons* as it was far easier for them to call me from there in an emergency. The new outpatient department eventually opened on my birthday that year and then about four very happy, but very busy, years followed.

When I first started at GZH, the clinics were small and we were not so busy. It took time for patients to gain confidence in the new hospital, and so I had plenty of spare time to continue my equipment ordering. But soon our popularity increased and so did the numbers attending the gynaecological and antenatal clinics. Increasingly, too, the patients were becoming more sophisticated, but there were still plenty of jungly ladies to keep us amused. One day a patient appeared dressed in a purple sari, blue petticoat, red blouse, and green *khasto*[88].

Many of their problems were the same as I had encountered years before in the Shining. Many of the patients were no clearer about their obstetric histories; one lady told me she had five or six children. Another said her last period was in *Pous* (Dec/Jan) but her periods stopped in *Mongsir* (Nov/Dec)! Several used to struggle with the doorknob and almost everyone had a problem with our bathroom scales. Many tried to sit on them, others stood back to front, and in every case their sari draped itself over the bit I needed to see. Eventually, I solved most of these problems by drawing around the *peon's* feet with a black marker to show how they were to stand.

I discovered that the commonest Gynae symptom was white discharge, but it proved very hard to treat as a small amount is perfectly normal and needed as lubricant – but then, how small is small? Once again I met many women who were miserable as they had had no children; one day, again I operated on two wives of the same man, and when I asked one of them whether she was the *jethi*[89] or the *kanchhi*[90] she replied, "Middle." More and more we tried to ask about and investigate their husbands, but it was an uphill task. Surely the chances of getting pregnant when your husband is a night bus driver must be significantly reduced! On the other hand, theoretically the one who said her husband didn't do any work at all (I think that meant he was a farmer) should have had a greatly increased chance. Perhaps the saddest experience in the Gynae clinic was on Christmas Day, 1984. My day started with a tearful couple arriving on my doorstep, requesting an abortion – how ironic on Christ's birthday! But joy came in the afternoon, when I was able to explain the whole thrilling Christmas story to one of my happier antenatal patients. In the end I concluded that

[88] Khasto – ladies' shawl.
[89] Jethi – oldest (or older) – in this case, first wife.
[90] Kanchhi – youngest (or younger) – in this case, third wife.

running a Gynae clinic was very simple: almost all my patients had either too many or too few children, or too heavy or too scanty periods.

In Nepali there are several words used for menstruation. The one I really prefer is *mahinwari* or 'monthly'. It has no bad connotations. *Rajaswala* ('one who is bleeding') plus *nachune* ('don't touch'), *para sarne* ('move away') and *panchhanu* ('shun') all hark back to the traditional culture and understanding that a woman is unclean and untouchable during her monthly bleeds. In fact, there still exists, especially in remote parts of western Nepal, the dreadful custom of *Chhaupadi.* It is usual for a young girl to be separated from the family when she has her first period, but with *Chhaupadi* this 'sitting apart' occurs for about five days every single month during the fertile period of a woman's life. This means that a woman is forced to leave her home and sit in a shack in the forest for a total of around six years of her life. As if this were not bad enough, the shacks are so poorly constructed that snakes can easily get in and many women have died this way. I shudder every time I think of this custom and remember with thankfulness the story in Luke 8 of how Jesus allowed the woman with a longstanding menstrual problem to touch him and be healed.

By the time I left WRH, the antenatal clinic had risen to a hundred and fifty attendees two days a week. These ANC[91] days were totally chaotic, and so Vera's help in organising the ladies was invaluable. That's the same Vera who was good at organising (perming) my hair in the past. Sometimes I would be called to an emergency and have to leave the clinic while I performed a Caesarean section. The best way to handle this was to tell the ladies left in the queue what had happened, as that seemed to help them cope with the extra-long wait. On other occasions the clinic well overran our lunch hour. Again, I found that the best way to manage that was to walk outside to the line of waiting ladies with my sandwiches in my hand and inform them that unless I ate *now,* my hunger would make me angry with them all. They invariably laughed and put up with the delay. One patient in particular understood. I had treated Sonam, a Tibetan from Chhorepatan Camp, for an intra-uterine death. She had nearly died from exsanguination, but we had managed to save her life and she remained extraordinarily grateful. Every time she turned up at

[91] ANC – antenatal clinic.

the OPD for a check-up or with some other problem, she would come laden with bottles of Fanta, not just for me but for my colleague and for our *peon,* Bhim Kumari. Especially at times like Christmas, I also used to visit Sonam at home in the camp; she so enjoyed hearing the Advent story. My visits continued, somewhat irregularly, right up until I left Nepal, but her situation became sadder as the years passed. Her husband died of liver failure from alcoholism and one of her sons also became an alcoholic. From being relatively well off running a Tibetan trinkets stall, both at the camp and Lakeside, she lost everything and had to take employment at the local Himalayan Museum, for which she was paid a pittance. Right up to the end, I continued to share the gospel with her, but language made it hard and I was never sure she really understood.

Sonam.

One of the other patients I came to know well was Rashmi. She was very different from many of the women I treated: slightly older than most in the antenatal clinic and vastly more educated; both she and her husband, Ram Gopal, were college lecturers at the Prithvi Narayan Campus. Many years ago, before there were any roads in Nepal, Newar business families had spread out from Kathmandu and established a network of trading centres across the country. Pokhara was at the junction of the route west from Kathmandu and the north-south route from Baglung to Tansen. Kunahar was the small trading bazaar in the early days before the modern town of Pokhara centred around Mahendra Pul came into being. Ram Gopal was a grandson of the Kunahar *Sau*[92] and Rashmi a granddaughter of the Baglung *Baidya*[93].

The families had been known to INF since almost the beginning of our work in Pokhara. Ruth Watson had delivered Ram Gopal by forceps in their house in Kunahar, as in the early 1950s there was no bridge

[92] Sau – big businessman
[93] Baidya – Ayurvedic or herbal doctor.

suitable to carry a *suitkerrie* across to the new Shining Hospital. In due course, during my time in GZH, I delivered Rashmi's daughter, Abuni, by Caesarean section and her son, Bibudh, by forceps – like his father. I appointed myself as their 'godmother' and even arranged birthday parties for them – a thing unknown at that time in Pokhara. Each year, too, I tried to share Christmas and the message of Jesus' birth with the whole family. When they missed my showing of the 'Treasures of the Snow' video, due to a misunderstanding, I was very upset – I reckon the kids would have loved it and, who knows, the visual message might have sunk in better than anything I ever said. Both children were very bright, especially Bibudh, who eventually majored in English and Journalism at college. As a ten-year-old he had already started writing poems, one of which included the line, "East or West, Dr Aunt is my best!" When I was studying a course on World Mission, I interviewed their parents (Ram Gopal and Rashmi) for one of my assignments, and at the time, this opened the way for further discussion on our respective beliefs and practices – but sadly, nothing more, although Bibudh did ask me one time some theological questions about redemption. In January 2007 I was honoured to be invited to their Silver Wedding party; and even now, I am still in touch with this family, though I missed the weddings of both of my 'godchildren'.

Ram Gopal, Rashmi and family.

Work on the wards of GZH (later WRH) was also challenging. It was fortunate I understood both Nepali and English as the nurses tended to use both – intertwined: "Bed number 2-*ma bhayeko* patient serious *chha.*" Their record-keeping too was a test of my ingenuity; vital facts were sometimes omitted, and spelling sometimes humorous ("antinatal" instead of "antenatal"). I recollect one memorable week when I was utterly frustrated. On Monday every baby I examined was freezing cold (but then, so was I), the examination gloves were lost, and the nurses forgot to show me one patient (only discovered the next day). And, had I not enquired, they would never have mentioned that they thought the new patient was a breech. The one redeeming feature was that they had remembered I was allergic to Dettol and left it out of the hand-rinsing bowl. My hands were probably not as sterile as they might have been but at least they weren't covered with itchy vesicles. Three minor operations, two deaths, a drip, an abnormal baby, a special forceps delivery, a breech and a couple of ward rounds followed, but then by Tuesday things were improving.

There was always a shortage of nurses, and not enough equipment to go round, in contrast to the excess patients littered over the floor. Before the new buildings were completed (and even for some time afterwards) there were chronic shortages in the hospital – sheets, gowns, and gloves, not to mention water and electricity; although when the *bijuli* was on, I once noticed that at least one socket in the old hospital building was glowing white hot. Although most of the staff tried hard to give a good service to their patients despite all the deficiencies, there were a few who clearly did not care – an attitude that all too often went along with fatalistic beliefs. Some auxiliaries did not to turn up for their duties, and a few nurses took more than an hour to call in the extra staff needed for an emergency Caesar. My medical colleagues decamped to their private clinics every evening for a couple of hours or were occasionally sent off on family planning camps or just transferred without replacements, and sometimes I found this almost overwhelming. On the other hand, I found I also learnt from the forbearance of some of my Nepali colleagues – to make do with what I had, to mend things and mend them again instead of bemoaning the fact that I could not get hold of a new one. Of course, there was always the danger that this attitude could turn into apathy and inactivity. Sometimes, too, their responses were a challenge to me. Whenever a patient did something which I found particularly annoying, one national colleague used to comment, "She's so funny!" It was undoubtedly just a turn of phrase and not meant literally, but it made me stop and think about my own reactions in these cases.

I didn't have a private clinic but occasionally I was asked to treat posh 'private' style patients. One had a rather intimate gynaecological problem that required daily treatments, and so I duly visited her each day. While I never received any fees, I never refused the substantial snacks she provided. I remember this well although I cannot recall her name and it is probably because it was at exactly the time when our allowances had been cut – the only time it ever happened in forty-three years. God sometimes works in rather strange ways to provide for us! He works in other strange ways too. Her husband – and later, the daughter-in-law – both asked me for "a book", meaning a New Testament.

There was another challenge too in working in the government hospital. It was a Hindu environment with mostly Hindu colleagues, although even in the 1980s there were already a few Christian nurses working there. When one day a patient died on the operating table, I summoned up courage and told the theatre staff (uniformly Hindu or Buddhist) that since I was only human I should ask God's help before each operation. Happily, they agreed with me. After that I always tried to pray with each patient before operating and only ever once did one refuse. Some even later expressed their appreciation for my prayers.

But then one time I became more than usually aware of the spiritual battle going on... Binimaya had come to the hospital to have her baby – a simple occurrence that most women did with no fuss, doctors or sterility in the buffalo shed behind their village homes. But now I had told her that she needed an operation. This she accepted; if the doctor said her baby was lying the wrong way round and would never pop out on its own, then it was so. It was just that operations were so expensive and frightening – and there was that cold, nagging fear that up until then she had shared with no one...

The following morning a fearful Binimaya was wheeled into theatre and greeted by two apparitions in green. Theatre nurse Ute and I pushed down our masks and smiled reassuringly at her. Then I put my hand over the baby in her tummy and explained that we would like to pray with her.

"Dear Father God, thank you for bringing Binimaya to us. Give us your skill and may her baby be born strong and healthy. And may our little sister know your peace today. In the name of Jesus Christ. Amen."

As Ute, our German theatre sister, wheeled in the instrument trolley, I listened to the baby's heart and pronounced it "OK". The operation started and I was soon able to tell Binimaya the happy news that she had a big, bouncing baby boy. Normally such an announcement meant the remainder of the operation went very smoothly as the mother relaxed. But this time a tearful Binimaya watched me hand the baby to Ute and then groaned. We were puzzled; we were used to the rejection of a girl but never of a boy. So, why was Binimaya upset?

Once the Hindu staff had left, we turned to Binimaya, who by then was lying, uncomfortable and miserable, on the hard, narrow trolley. I put my arm around her and asked gently, "Why didn't you want a boy?" At that, her face crumpled and the whole sad story tumbled out. She explained that having a boy meant the curse was coming true. A seer had predicted everything: she would have a boy, he would give her a lot of trouble and then he would die. These awful words had been etched indelibly into her mind and now their fulfilment was overwhelming her.

I smiled thoughtfully and said, "Little sister, don't you remember that before your operation we prayed for you in the name of the Living God? It is true that what the seer predicted began to be fulfilled. The baby is a boy. He did give you a lot of trouble. And, he would have died had we not operated."

I watched as a glimmer of understanding and hope filtered into Binimaya's mind, and then continued:

"Remember, we asked Jesus to help us and he did. He has broken the power of that curse. Now you and your baby are free. I believe he will live."

About a week later, mother and baby were discharged fit and well.

However, a few days on it seemed that the Enemy tried to get his own back... It was a hot and sticky night after a hard and stressful day. Outside, apart from the buzzing of insects, all was quiet. I was in bed; no babies were being born that evening. Then suddenly, I stirred and through my sleep-filled eyes squinted at the dim light refracted through the nylon mesh of the mosquito net. I held my breath. No sound came – no ring, no knock, no urgent shout – so it was not, after all, the night-watchman who had awoken me. My pulse started to slow and I began to relax under the thin cotton sheet, knowing that for once I did not have to jump out of bed and rush to the delivery room.

By then sleep had departed and in its place my mind was filled with a garbled Bible quotation, "...the full armour of God ... helmet of salvation ... sword of the Spirit..."[94] My first thought was that I should sit up and read the passage, but it was the middle of the night, I was tired and the electricity was probably off. Instead I lay back, and as I did the darkness became thicker. I could smell it; I could feel it – and it was evil. The darkness hurt but disobedience always does, for when at last I tried to sit up, I couldn't. My arms and legs seemed clamped to the bed. I couldn't even lift my head; that too was held in a vice-like grip. And as I tried to cry out, all that came was a silent puff of air returned from vocal cords that were as paralysed as the rest of me. I was scared – *really* scared. Desperately willing every muscle into action, I tried again but still nothing happened. No sound emerged. And the darkness hurt even more. Panicking now, I strained and with increasing desperation managed at last to cry aloud, "jesus – Jesus – JEsus – JESus – JESUs – JESUS!" At first it came out only as a hoarse whisper, but as I continued, the walls of my bedroom finally reverberated with that sacred Name and the darkness no longer hurt.

This was perhaps the most momentous lesson the Lord ever taught me, but I was a slow learner and regularly made mistakes or missed opportunities. Take my relationship with the senior sister Sarada, for example. One day she told me off; I don't remember what for but clearly it was something a Christian should not have done. Another time, she shared with me a dream she had had, but unlike Joseph or Daniel I blew that too and missed the chance to share the gospel with her. But just occasionally I managed to get things right. As I got to know more of the medical and nursing staff, that gave me an opportunity to invite them in to watch various videos like 'The Hiding Place', 'The Birth of Jesus' and 'Treasures of the Snow', with its clear message of love and forgiveness in Jesus. One doctor even asked to read the book after that. In those days, also, the hard work and conscientiousness of all the INF secondees was much appreciated and we were definitely missed when we took a holiday.

Over the years it has never ceased to amaze me what things people will bring into the hospital with them. In the Shining, if we had allowed it (which of course we didn't), we'd have had cows attached to patients' big toes for some special religious rite. We did have dogs wandering in and birds flying about from time to time – that was the nature of our

---

[94] Eph. 6:13-17.

'open-style' wards, but I assumed it would be different in WRH. Not so; one day I discovered a bird in a bedside locker – apparently a present for the patient's grandson.

In those days (and, I suspect, still now) the delivery room was the busiest place in the hospital, and not just in the daytime – strange how so many babies put in their appearance in the middle of the night! It was also the most chaotic, although not every pregnant woman made it there in time. More than one baby was delivered on the drive outside casualty, but that was much easier to cope with than a retained placenta in the right room when the lights were off. Despite the problems, most patients were truly grateful, although one mother ran away without her stillborn baby and placenta, leaving me to wonder who the father had been! Delivering babies can be a 'bloody' business and so the hospital provided plastic aprons for us. After a while, finding them useless (as leaning forward during a forceps delivery, my sari always ended up in a pool of blood), I discarded the aprons in favour of a pair of waterproof motorcycle trousers. This was such a success that my colleagues took to borrowing them when they were on duty.

No doubt you've heard the saying, "It's hard to get blood out of a stone." A couple of stories provided a new twist on that. The motto of the Nepal Red Cross Blood Bank service was 'The Gift of Blood is the Gift of Life' but in 1983 the blood bank had not been established as the electricity was too erratic. Instead, they maintained a list of potential donors in case of urgent need. At the top of the list were the hospital *peons* until it was discovered that they were selling their blood rather too often. Many of the others on the list just refused to give when asked. I had to laugh when a man asked me whether I recommended human or bottled blood for his relative's transfusion. Then one day, while volunteering to give blood to the daughter of one of the local Nepali Christian families, I gained intimate personal experience of the service...

Although I knew my blood group, the technician naturally felt happier checking it first for his record. That was fine with me – so long as he used a new lancet and not the 'used at least once before' one lying on his desk. His confidence boosted by proving that my blood group was still 'O' Positive, exactly as it has always been, he proceeded to the actual X matching; and with the use of a brand-new plastic disposable syringe and needle, our relationship blossomed, the required amount of blood was soon taken and only a small bruise left behind. The technician then vanished for a while, leaving me alone in his office with the opportunity to transfer all the discarded bits of cotton wool and broken glass from the floor to the wastepaper basket (no sharps bins in those days). A few minutes later, having satisfied himself that my blood *'milled'* (i.e. was compatible), he set about removing 500ml of it, this time using a needle I had thoughtfully provided for him. He too seemed mutually relieved at having a needle which fulfilled all the prerequisites (new, sharp and sterile) with which to stab a fellow member of the medical profession. 1 *mana* (pint) of blood later, but without the cuppa I had hinted at, I carried my own blood to the patient and reinserted her drip. Sadly, the girl died a few days later, but not before receiving three pints of blood from three different members of the church. I still wonder how challenged those who witnessed our giving our blood willingly and freely may have been. Although this time it was unfortunately not the gift of life for her, I hoped that in the future such actions would give us opportunities not only to save human lives but also to speak about the gift of life that we have each received through the blood of Jesus. That happened at least once. After giving one of my Caesars a pint of my own blood I was also able to explain why I had given it.

My second story shows me in a much worse light. I had blown my top yet again... One of my patients was literally dying for want of an urgent blood transfusion, but her high caste Brahmin husband was adamant that he was not donating any of his blood, even though it was his baby she had just delivered. It was his attitude as much as his action that had infuriated me. Maybe I had been a bit aggressive in my request, but then, Bishnumaya was deathly pale and gasping with air hunger, desperately trying to hang onto life – and he had protested that he was too weak. I had zero sympathy and excess anger. I told him bluntly, but with a genuine desire to shock him into some kind of selfless giving, "If you don't give, your wife will die," and he had replied quite calmly, "In that case, I will get another wife." No wonder I was incandescently irate! I lost it. I don't remember what I said but it wasn't nice. Then I turned and stormed out of the ward; there was nothing more I could do.

As I walked along the corridor, I began to feel deeply ashamed of my behaviour and a thought started to run through my head. *What was the use of my being in Nepal anyway? I was a lousy doctor, unworthy to be a missionary, an abject failure even as an ordinary Christian.* I assumed this was the voice of the Lord chastening me, and with tears beginning to sting my eyes, I bowed my head and started to pray, "I'm sorry, Lord..." Then suddenly the Lord *did* speak, but not in those words. He spoke softly, gently and authoritatively. "You just tell Satan, 'The only reason you wouldn't have lost *your* temper is because you don't care whether that woman lives or dies.'" And so I did.

Although these years at GZH were some of the happiest of my time in Nepal, many times I felt really frustrated – sometimes because patients or their relatives refused to take advice or accept my treatment, and sometimes because my colleagues could not always be relied on to be there to work the on call rota. During my last year in GZH/WRH, one colleague left to have a baby, another developed TB and the third spent most of a three-month period in training, holiday or family planning camps rather than actually working in the hospital. The times when they were missing often seemed to coincide with a Christian festival, like Christmas, or an INF Conference, like the one in 1985. That year I realised afresh that being on call was the primary part of my ministry at that time. It was not always easy to accept, but did lead to my discovering three things. One, that missing a fellowship I had looked forward to did not mean missing the blessing the Lord wanted to give me. He was quite able to deliver it in a very different way! Two, that just sometimes my colleagues came back in time – once, it was even a day early – and were ready to cover for me. And three, that being a missionary was often hard work, but just being a Christian was sometimes even harder!

Sometime during these years, I made a resolution to have a weekly day of fasting. No big deal – Nepalis regularly fast – but it did seem that every Friday after that the clinics were busier than usual and there were more emergency operations. Unfortunately, hypoglycaemia tended to make me rather irritable, and I began to wonder if St Luke had ever fasted – but then, there were no Caesareans in his day. After one operation, the *peon* served up hot sweet tea as usual, but it was not until I was wiping the biscuit crumbs off my fingers that I remembered... *Had I really upset the Lord?* Perhaps not with the tea, at least – surely, he would not want me to die of dehydration – but the biscuit... Now that was quite different, and it had tasted so good too! Another time, when I found myself in a Nepali home and being served with lots of delicious little spicy dishes, I made a snap decision to defer the day of fasting for twenty-four hours so as not to upset my hostess. Again, I suspect the Lord understood. On yet another occasion, however, my response was different. I had been showing some important officials around the hospital, but just as I was escaping from that ordeal, the Brahmin doctor said, "We would like you to join us for the feast at 2pm." *What to do?* High caste Hindus are very strict with their fasting, so, feeling he might understand, I took a deep breath and said, "Thank you very much but it is a little difficult as today is a fast day for me." I am not sure who was the more surprised at that – him or me! I don't think he was offended; rather, I hope, he was challenged by the discovery that Christians also took their religious observances seriously. Eventually, I gave up my weekly fasts – on the basis that I could not continue to work efficiently without both sleep and food. Perhaps it had not been a sensible idea in the first place for a busy obstetrician?

As it eventually worked out, most of my time in GZH/WRH was concurrent with the extension work and before the new buildings were opened in 1987. However, the early months of that year were exciting ones for the INF team and INF as a mission. At our Annual General Meeting and conference, we agreed our revised constitution and were challenged to more intercession and a bolder witness to the Lord. Among the hospital team, both in emergency and in maternity and theatre, we saw evidence of God's healing in miraculous ways and exciting answers to prayers. But at the same time there was some opposition as INF was excluded from the new housekeeping department and forced to negotiate handover of the pharmacy and maintenance departments – inexplicable as we had put so much effort into promoting and developing these departments. My own involvement also came to an abrupt and unexpected halt in mid-1987. Originally, I had planned to finish clinical work at the hospital at the end of June and then spend three months prior to home leave handing over the finalisation of the hospital equipment and gathering information on INF (with the aim of possibly writing a book). It was not to be.

One Tuesday I received a letter from home saying that my mother was about to go into hospital. The following Tuesday I was at her bedside. That final week was incredible, much longer than its 7 x 24 hours. I had to pack up my house (furniture, food and personal effects) completely. I had to hand over all the paperwork and details regarding the hospital equipment, although, miraculously, the person to carry it on had already been found. I had to reconcile various accounts with the administrator in readiness for the auditor's visit. I had to tie up innumerable ends of personal, mission and hospital work. And before I could even start on all that, I had to get permission from the Civil Surgeon, Dr Sinha, to be released immediately from all clinical work. But by 10.30am on the Saturday, I had finished all the official jobs and was only half an hour late for church. I'm not sure how I did it but perhaps it was because the Lord God "daily [bore my] burdens"[95] and "kept my eyes from closing"[96].

After the service I set out on a whirlwind tour of Pokhara to say goodbye and explain the situation to many of my Nepali friends. From the airground (where I collected my plane ticket for the following day), I went south to Sonam's and shared *momos* and Coke with her. She cryptically asked, "You could back to Pokhara sure or not?" which I think meant she hoped to see me again. Returning up the bazaar, I called in for a chat (and an omelette) with the Dhewajoo family, but as only Ram Gopal was home, I had to go farther up the bazaar to her parents' house to meet Rashmi and the two children. From there I dashed over to Lamachaur to spend a short while with Mrs Mouse and then finally arrived on Shyam Malla's doorstep almost at the same moment as he arrived home from a picnic. Sadly, there were others I did not manage to see – like Prem Kumari (an ex-patient who had wept when I read her the story of the prodigal son), as she did not live locally. Back at WRH, I saw Dr Kusum (with husband Iswar and son Anuraag). She said, "Do keep in touch." Then, after the final packing and a very short night, Bhim Kumari (my helper in the house and one of the very few Christians who worked in WRH), together with her husband Rikhman, was on my doorstep to say goodbye. I sincerely hoped it would not be too long before I saw them all again.

While I was away Rashmi wrote:

> *"...in your absence, the hospital seems lonely..."*

---

[95] Psa. 68:19.

[96] Psa. 77:4.

In fact, I was away over a year, first looking after my mother during her terminal illness and then doing mission deputation for several months.

18

Nepal Janne

Going to Kathmandu

Left: Royal palace (that was). Right: Kathmandu valley.

STRANGE AS IT MAY SEEM, I never got to Kathmandu until I had been in Nepal for a whole year. When I had first entered Nepal, it was overland from India via the southern border and along the Sunauli-Pokhara Road, and not by air. I started work a week later and was not due any holiday until I had passed my first language exam – nearly a year later. In addition, as there was no road from Kathmandu to Pokhara in 1970/1, I needed time to save up for the air fare of about 80 to 90 rupees. This was equal to the amount I received in my hand (after deductions for meals on the compound) for one month's work.

On that first visit with Joyce (remember the head cook at the Himalayan Helper house party[97]), we travelled part way by plane, part

[97] See Chapter 2.

way by foot and the final few miles by peanut lorry.[98] In those days the big city was not a big city at all. It still had few vehicles and a lot of green areas – it was generally quite pleasant. I once read that when King Prithvi Narayan Shah first viewed Kathmandu from an overlooking ridge and saw the beautiful green valley, he determined to conquer it. If he were reincarnated(!) now, I am sure he would turn tail and run back to Gorkha, away from the concrete jungle and air pollution. In the 1970s Kathmandu was the end of the hippy trail. Just round the corner from the main police station, not far from Aunt Jane's café and Freak Street (where all the world travellers hung out) several shops advertised, "Hashish" – quite openly and quite legally!

My second visit was a lot shorter and a lot less happy. I was on my way home to the UK to be with my mother after my father had died.

After that I didn't bother going to the city again for many years, but when I was Equipment Consultant for GZH and later still, when I was Medical Director, I had to visit Kathmandu regularly. By then the Pokhara-Kathmandu road had been completed and so I had the option of commuting by night bus[99] – considerably cheaper but unquestionably unenjoyable. To say the road goes straight and due east from Pokhara to Kathmandu is only partly true. It does – until the last 29 km. From Naubise (meaning literally '29') it winds up the hill around a series of Z-bends to reach the top of the ridge and then descends into the Kathmandu Valley. A 7.30pm start from Pokhara and about twelve hours or 200 km later, still awake and very stiff and tired, I used to arrive in Kathmandu, ready to start work.

Actually, that's not quite true; I first had to wash off the layers of encrusted dust, dig out some suitable city clothes, find something to eat, and – if possible – catch up on sleep, before I was ready to face HMG/N. Up to the 80s and early 90s even, taxis were inexpensive and the roads not clogged with private vehicles, so travel was the easier part of the day. The harder part happened inside the offices. They were open for six (or seven) hours a day and the time passed very slowly – and if I had forgotten to take a (big) book or my Rubik's cube (which I never did manage to solve), this felt remarkably like infinity. Nothing happened

---

[98] See Chapter 19.
[99] See Chapter 14

quickly. Officials often kept us waiting – possibly on purpose, to demonstrate who was really in charge. Catching the *thulo manchhe* (office-in-charge), whose signature was vital, was usually only feasible between 10.00 and 10.30, during the first half hour of the working day. All too often I was told, "Come back tomorrow (or next week)." Mostly, our discussions were conducted in a Nepali-English amalgam. Sometimes their English was better than my Nepali; sometimes my Nepali was better than their English. While most appreciated the efforts we made to converse in Nepali, on one occasion a group of officials deliberately conversed among themselves in Newari, well aware that had they used Nepali, we would have understood. The only redeeming bit of any visit was when we were served hot, sweet, milky Nepali tea, although in later years they gave up on the milk (though whether for economic or health reasons I never discovered) and served *rato chiya*[100], which left my stomach lining much less happy. The best part of the day was after 4 or 5pm when I could escape and enjoy an ice-cream or some other junk food in one of Kathmandu's tourist eating holes.

Much later still, in 1998, I moved to live in Kathmandu. Some people thought I was crazy, but it seemed to be what God wanted me to do, so I went. Some years later, when INF had divided itself into INF/Nepal and INF/Worldwide, the international office shifted to Kathmandu, and we had long discussions about that as by then we all knew a major earthquake was long overdue. Was it safe? Of course, it wasn't totally safe (but then, neither was staying in Pokhara), but since when has following Christ been a safe option? However, I obediently bought a quake alarm, which gave me an estimated 15 seconds' advance warning to disentangle myself from the mosquito net and get to safety, away from any falling masonry. (I later discarded it because it squeaked every time a big truck went along the road.) I also seriously thought of learning how to abseil so that I would have an alternative route of exit from my top floor flat.

Living in Kathmandu in the 90s and 00s was significantly different from living in Pokhara in the 70s and 80s, although some things were the same. Household *bahinis* were more sophisticated in their dress but not necessarily in their housekeeping tasks. Buses and taxis were ubiquitous,

---

[100] Rato chiya – lit. red (i.e. black) tea.

but as time went on, the fares they charged were iniquitous. Owning my own transport was great – except when there were petrol shortages. On many occasions I had to leave my scooter in a petrol queue overnight just so that I could purchase a tankful (five litres) of fuel for the following week.

The houses we rented were bigger and posher, but that did not automatically mean the plumbing worked. And when the power cuts started with a vengeance, living in a big house dependent on electricity was arguably more frustrating than living in a village hut with kerosene lamps and a wood-fired *chulo.* In 2008 I regularly got up in the middle of the night to print out my M.A. thesis as that was the only time there was sufficient power to run the printer. When I moved to Bagdol, I finally bought an inverter, something I should have lashed out on years before. This brilliant invention used to suck electricity out of the mains when the current was on and then regurgitate it into my appliances when the current was off. By this means I could even use computer and printer together, but not the iron or the electric kettle.

While I lived in the north of the town, water was plentiful, though what emerged from the tap was often brown and smelled of iron (crudely put, it reminded me of the hand-washing water after I'd done a delivery). Once I moved to Lalitpur in the south, however, I began to suffer with everyone else in the area and depended on regular tanker supplies. There was just never enough water for the rapidly increasing population of the Valley. Every big house had an electric pump to propel the water from the pipe to the roof, and in Jawalakhel the switch was in the landlord's part of the house. This was frustrating as they never pumped a full tank. One day only the daughter-in-law was at home, and when I asked her to switch it on, she declared that she couldn't do it because she had her period. I knew that a menstruating woman could not touch a water source but this seemed to be carrying the tradition beyond any reasonable interpretation.

Kathmandu can be very cold in the winter, so when my landlord installed a solar water heater in 2006, I was very happy. Unfortunately, Kathmandu can also be quite foggy in the winter; hence no sun and no hot water. Only in my last house in Bagdol did I enjoy the luxury of gas for heating the living room and water as well as for cooking – except for one period of about three months when no gas cylinders were available.

But I shouldn't complain; I never had to cope with the much harsher privations during the earthquake and then the five-month Indian border blockade in 2015/16.

On the other hand, there were many advantages of living in the capital. One was the shopping – in supermarkets, which by the late 90s were pretty much like Western supermarkets, except that they did not sell British-style sausages. Fruit and veg were also usually plentiful and no longer just seasonal. There were bakeries that sold bread that was worth buying if my *bahini* was off sick and I was too lazy to make my own. This was a far cry from the late 70s when bread was first introduced into Pokhara. In those days it was *'pau-roti ek rupiya'* [101] sold by a man riding a tricycle with a big box on the front. If you bought from the wrong company, the bread was pretty much like cotton wool, but I had it sussed and used to go direct to the best factory and buy it hot – and then it was quite tasty. The later Kathmandu loaves may have been higher quality, but so they should have been when they cost 90 times as much.

Another joy of being in Kathmandu was eating out, although the tourist area of Thamel was quite a distance from where I lived. Nearby, I had two favourite eating haunts. One was Roadhouse – for pizzas. Usually I went with a friend but sometimes I would go on my own, buy a 12-inch bacon pizza, eat a 120-degree slice and then take the rest home for the next two days; that way it didn't feel like extravagance. The other was Sing-Ma for Malaysian food. It had been established by Jason, with whom I had studied at campus when I first moved to Kathmandu. I was one of his guinea pigs who patronised the restaurant even before it opened, when the staff were still in training. I always chose cashew chicken but discarded the chillies and followed it up with a fabulous cheesecake – delicious but pricey, so we only went there for special treats. For a simpler Nepali snack, the Bible Yatra[102] team patronised the Dragon Restaurant for *momos.* It was situated opposite the fire station, and the accompanying sauce that Jeevan always brought back for us was so hot, it could well have been cooked over the road.

Another plus of living in Kathmandu I discovered during the warmer half of 2008 was that for the princely sum of around 35p I could swim

---

[101] Pau-roti ek rupiya – bread (yeast bread) one rupee.
[102] Yatra – journey; see Chapter 24.

for half an hour each day. I lost weight, became fitter and had a clearer head, which meant that I wrote more sense in my dissertation.

The most important downside of living in 'the big smoke' was just that: the pollution. In 2002 I wrote that Kathmandu "chokes upon its love affair with the internal combustion engine".[103] Like most motorcyclists (and a lot of pedestrians) I used to go everywhere with a mask and still had continual sore eyes and sinusitis. Even wearing gloves, my hands were perpetually dirty. Three factors were to blame: one, the fumes from the vehicles (few of which would have passed an MOT); two, the dust from the potholes in the roads (and some roads had more potholes than road surface); and three, dirt from rubbish by the side of the roads (for it was rarely collected). The worst time to travel was, unsurprisingly, rush-hour, but even in the middle of the day, when people should have been in their offices, there were traffic jams. Misjudging this doubled the time needed to cross the city and more than doubled the amount of gunge I inhaled. Some years ago Kathmandu boasted several roundabouts, but it became apparent that Nepalis either didn't like roundabouts or else didn't know how to use them; most disappeared overnight and were replaced with traffic lights. But Nepalis didn't seem to like traffic lights either (or perhaps they were all colour-blind). As a result crossroads began to resemble the board in the middle of a game of Chinese Chequers – all the players hemmed in and no one able to move in any direction.

In early 2009 an earlier quip about people in Kathmandu no longer planting rice but only bricks and buildings became an unpleasant reality for me. The school next door suddenly decided to extend, and their new five-storey building shot up rapidly only inches from my bedroom window. Denied the air, the sun and the only view I had had of the mountains, I decided to move house again, but it was a good decision as the new landlady in Bagdol was as brilliant as the former one had been irritating.

Living in Kathmandu was also sometimes like living inside a political cauldron...

On 1st September 2004 (known locally as 9/1), twelve Nepalis were assassinated in Iraq. They were undocumented migrant workers but otherwise quite innocent. This triggered a very unpleasant riot as the

[103] A quote originally about Istanbul, in *Belshazzar's Daughter.*

people of Kathmandu blamed the government in general for not doing enough to get them released, and the overseas employment agencies specifically for sending them there in the first place. Inadvertently, I was caught up in the demonstrations. I had been teaching in Banepa and then spent the night in Dhulikhel. Up there, on the rim of the Kathmandu Valley, no one knew what was happening down below, so it was only when I got back to Banepa that I heard that the road was blocked. No big problem – this sort of thing happened a lot. It had even done so in a minor way only the week before, so I reckoned a small scooter would probably be allowed through. Promising to return if the road was really unpassable, I determined to get home if at all possible. I was led to believe that the block was only on the Arniko Highway[104] and so I thought that once I reached the ring road everything would be OK. I could not have been more wrong. I did get to the ring road – by ignoring the police and skirting the burning tyres – and then found that I was trapped; behind me, and in both directions along the ring road, every junction was on fire. My house was more than ten kilometres away on the opposite side of the city, but I had come too far to turn back; I just kept going. When rioters tried to push my bike over, I accelerated. At every crossroads there were angry young men burning tyres and office furniture (from the employment agencies) so I wove in and out of the fires. I did stop just once when someone threatened to throw stones. I acted the stupid expatriate until they let me go and then put my foot down again and eventually I arrived home safely, before the curfews were enforced. I have to confess, I actually rather enjoyed this adrenaline-powered ride.

For the next couple of years, things got worse rather than better. By 2005 the Maoists were effectively in control of most of the country, except Kathmandu, which was crawling with security forces. I learnt never to drive on the bumpy potholed roads close behind an army truck if I valued my life. The soldiers used to sit with their guns balanced on their knees and pointing backwards, and I believed what I had been told: that they had no safety catches. There were almost daily *bandhs*[105] and strikes and then the Maoist rebels introduced a strategy first used by King

[104] Arniko Highway – it runs from the Kathmandu Valley ring-road, via Bhaktapur (one of the three cities of the Valley) to the Chinese border.

[105] Bandh – strike or stoppage of traffic and/or closure of shops.

Prithvi Narayan Shah in the 18th century. This was the *'nakha-bandhi'* or blockade of the Valley, fairly easy to achieve as there was only one really major road into Kathmandu. Inevitably, this led to shortages, huge price increases and a (bigger-than-usual) black market. Then in February King Gyanendra seized the reins of power and suspended the Constitution. At first this seemed to promise hope for a peaceful settlement, but the longer the King clung onto his renewed role as absolute monarch, the further these hopes receded. The people of Nepal – whatever their political allegiance – ganged up on him, and after three weeks of street demonstrations in 2006, he was deposed and Nepal became a kingless kingdom. When they remembered, the newscasters told us the weather "in the country" (not kingdom) was fair. In fact, the weather was unusually cold that year while, in contrast, the political climate remained hot.

After nearly a decade the Maoists at last began to disarm, but there was still sporadic violence, street demonstrations and tyre-burning in protest (on just about any pretext). There was much talk about the peace process but little action. Political wrangling continued for a further two years until in 2008, after 239 years, the Shah dynasty came to a sticky end; the proud monarchy of Nepal was defunct. The country was officially declared a republic, but as everyone except perhaps the politicians could have foretold, that did not automatically bring peace and development. Many years of power struggles over the presidency and the prime ministership followed. Thus, during my final five years in the country, Nepal was no longer the simple, friendly, peaceful place it had been in 1970. Only after I had been back in the UK for two years did I hear that the new Constitution had at last been promulgated.

19

Chhuti

Holidays (and auspicious days)

Judy Crook and Diana Johnson with Val (2003).

ONE PRIVILEGE OF WORKING IN NEPAL has been that I got the chance to spend many holidays[106] in some pretty exotic places – like the Himalayan foothills, Chitwan National Park, and the Annapurna Sanctuary. While I never made it to Everest Base Camp, I did visit the Mountaineering Museum in Darjeeling. I braved the disputed border area of Kashmir, shopped in Delhi and Kolkata, and journeyed near the Golden Triangle. I lazed on beaches off the east and west coasts of India, and bathed in the South China Sea, but the most memorable swims were in the Persian Gulf, where the water was far hotter than any bath I ever remember. In Emirates I saw the world's tallest building and, heavily

[106] Chhuti – holiday.

disguised in a burqa, visited a famous mosque. In between these more exceptional destinations, Judy, my old school friend,[107] and I had cold holidays in the UK or hot holidays in other parts of Europe. I enjoyed Greek islands most, not least because souvlaki followed by yoghurt and honey is one of my favourite meals. These were also safe destinations as I could read the Greek script and so locate a pharmacy in case of need – although, happily, that never arose. Perhaps the one spot that I found the most attractive – apart, of course, from revisiting the Abersoch of my childhood – was the little stream outside Philippi where Lydia had been baptised somewhere around AD 50.

My first holiday in Nepal began – and ended – in style. Joyce, the one I had first met in 1967, and I flew to Gorkha and then walked, via many villages, vaguely retracing Prithvi Narayan Shah's route of conquest backward until we reached Trisuli, at the edge of the Kathmandu Valley. We got there just fifteen minutes after the last bus had left but we weren't the only latecomers and, along with the others, we hitched a lift on a peanut lorry. At every village it stopped to load more peanut sacks and at every stop we climbed farther up the pile of sacks until we were perched overlooking the driver's cab. As it gradually got darker and windier, we got more and more hungry, but the only remaining food from our trek was a tin of condensed milk. Thus, two very sticky friends alighted in Kathmandu, not sure where we were meant to be going or even where we were. The only other thing I recollect from that holiday is returning by plane with an oversized cauliflower or a large wheel of cheese (I forget which now) – a present for my stay-at-home friends in Pokhara.

I used the rest of that holiday month to go trekking in the west of Nepal. I'd been 'confined to barracks' in Pokhara for a whole year and was determined to see something of the country and needed to stretch my legs. During the first week I headed off north-west to Jomson. That was as far as I was allowed to proceed as the Nepalis and Tibetan Khambas were having a set to on the Chinese border. It was on the way back that I met the *bhut.*[108] Then, after getting back to Baglung, my *bhurria* and I turned due west and walked solidly up and down for two days. That was

[107] See Chapter 1.
[108] See Chapter 13.

not just masochistic pleasure; I was due to collect one of the Shining Hospital nurses from Musikot and bring her safely back to work after her holiday. The family could have escorted her but this way we made sure she came back and was not married off instead. Trekking back to Pokhara, Phouda, an ex-leprosy patient, carried our luggage and in retrospect I am mortified to think how heavy it was for him. We took an interesting route via Ridi and emerged somewhere near Tansen, but on the way passed an old Rana palace, no longer occupied. Being me, I climbed the wall and explored the empty mansion, only to discover that the bathroom was about twice the size of my little hut in Pokhara and even had a bath. I assume the noble Rana must have made arrangements to fill his bath but it was also clear that he had omitted to share these amenities with the surrounding villagers. They still had to trudge a long way down to the river for every bucketful of water.

In those early years, when I was working at the Shining, I usually chose to walk off into the sunset on several holidays, but always with a porter to carry my stuff. I can picture the *bhurria* now with a large case and bedding roll balanced with a strap across his forehead and walking for eight hours a day; that's like climbing up and down Snowdon one and a half times every day carrying a rucksack bigger than you are. On another trek I lost my porter (he went one way and I went the other), as I was lagging behind and had not seen him turn off the path. That experience reminded me of the little narrow path I had decided to follow in 1954. Walking in the hills is so like living the Christian life. There's a lot of ups and downs; and it's always best to keep one's eyes on the guide – be he a Nepali *bhurria* or Jesus.

The trek that I enjoyed the most, largely because of the stupendous scenery, was to the Annapurna Sanctuary. To break ourselves in gently, we had planned that on the first day we would only go as far as LAC[109], the Agricultural Centre on the hillside outside the little village of Lumle. Leaving Pokhara, with our trusty black umbrellas for support, we marched past the Hyangja Tibetan Camp and then through the dry rice fields of the Suikhet Valley. Then, sharing the path with several mule trains (and remembering to keep on the inside of the slope), we climbed

---

[109] LAC – Lumle Agricultural Centre.

the steep hill to Naudara for a *chiya*[110] stop. After that there was a stretch of lonely hillside to Kanre and then Lumle. We used 'No. 11 Jeep' as there was no motor road in the 1970s.[111] LAC was an agricultural ODA[112] project to rehabilitate retired Gurkhas; and our night there was, predictably, the most luxurious overnight stop on the trek. From there conditions went downhill while we trudged uphill – and north – to Chomrong, where we stayed at a lodge owned by an ex-Gurkha captain. The villagers made sure we knew which trail to take; the wrong one would have led us to the new (but unfinished) bridge with no struts and supports, only a nasty drop to the river below. Next stop was *not* a bivouac in Hinko Cave (really an overhanging rock) as a new tourist lodge was open for the season.

The next day we arrived at Machhapuchhare Base Camp under the shadow of the twin peaks of Fishtail Mountain, and from there it was just a few hours west across a glacier to reach the Annapurna Base Camp. In those days I was tough and walked in rubber flip-flops, but finally, near the snow line, I exchanged them for a pair of boots. Up there in the sanctuary, it was cold, and got even colder overnight as the flimsy bamboo hut gave us minimal shelter. I never warmed up as I had to climb out of my sleeping bag every couple of hours to answer a call of nature; I had discovered the downside of taking diuretics[113] to prevent altitude sickness. Although the sanctuary was a bleak and lonely place, inhabited only by a shepherd and his sheep and our one little temporary tourist 'lodge', it was stunningly beautiful. It was more than worth a night of shivering to be surrounded by 360 degrees of magnificent snow peaks.

---

[110] Chiya – tea.

[111] The road, and ribbon development, came much later and has ensured that there are no longer any lonely stretches. After Naudara, the Baglung Highway now veers off towards Paundur to reach Kusma and eventually Baglung. Not long after this road was opened, I rode my little yellow Honda, with its little yellow fuel tank, to Baglung and back, but I had to carry spare petrol with me as no petrol pumps had yet been built along the way.

[112] ODA – Overseas Development Administration. Now DfID (Department for International Development).

[113] Diuretics – more commonly known as water tablets.

In later years, when trekking became part of my work with the Leprosy Control Project, I opted for less energetic holidays. In 1989, before it became the 'big smoke', I spent a week in Kathmandu and a couple of times in the 90s I even stayed at home in Pokhara, but more usually I went to India. There were, however, two other important holidays in Nepal: one when Regina and I visited East Nepal by bus; and the other when Judy visited and we 'did Nepal', including a trek to Muktinath beyond Jomson. The most memorable bit of the holiday with Rejina was the visit to Chitwan,[114] although we also explored the Eastern *Terai,* Janakpur and a tea estate in Ilam before ending up in Darjeeling, where it was so cold and damp, we rapidly descended to Siliguri to dry out and warm up.

The 2003 holiday in Nepal with Judy, from school, and Di, who cannot sing, was incredible, and I did a lot of things I'd never done before, despite having lived in Nepal for so long. Judy, as a first-time visitor, put some of her impressions into writing:

> *"Himalayan mountain peaks – golden at dawn, rosy at dusk, often peeping through the clouds above the forested foothills. Rivers rushing down gorges – reminding me of Val's lifestyle: even on holiday Diana and I were always running to keep up with her! Terraced hillsides (just like the pictures), rice growing and then being harvested. Rapid urban development on the outskirts of Kathmandu as once-fertile fields are now 'growing' big houses. The paved city ring-road lined with rubbish. Road travel: a real experience with buses, lorries, taxis and motorcycles – mostly belching out black fumes – all fighting for spaces but miraculously avoiding cyclists, pedestrians, dogs, cows and chickens... Our route into town involved two kilometres of potholes, hardly wide enough for two vehicles and frequently narrowed by electricity poles stuck nearer the middle than the edge of the road, which is lined by shops opening directly onto the street. Dozens of Hindu temples and Buddhist stupas everywhere, happily co-*

[114] See Chapter 14.

existing. In contrast, Christian Church buildings have a low profile but those I visited were all full on Saturday mornings."

And that only gives an introduction to her experiences.

We made a long trek in the hills – to Muktinath (*mukti* = salvation), so called because it's where many pilgrims go hoping to achieve just that. All along the route there were temples and stupas, and on the way back down the hill, at Kagbeni, I chatted up one of the lamas[115] and was struck by his comment, "Christianity is so easy." Too late I realised I should have explained that while it may have been easy for me to receive salvation, it had been far from easy for Jesus to achieve it for me on the cross. Judy didn't mention the swaying bridges and tiny footpaths across slippery landslides, perhaps because she didn't like them very much; or the time when I was the only one of the three of us brave enough to go for a dip in the sulphurous water at Tatopani. She left out the tale of our night at Ghorepani Hill; that time it was the Maoists I chatted up and arranged a 50% discount on the extra fees they were charging regular tourists.

We also visited the old palace of Gorkha (from where King Prithvi Narayan Shah came before he conquered and united the rest of Nepal), and took a Land Rover trip to the Chinese border (where we put our feet across the border on the Peace Bridge). We flew within five miles of Everest, rode an elephant and went for a jungle walk in Chitwan National Park, and went up and down in Nepal's only cable car at Mankamana. We saw the sunrise – and mountains – from Poon Hill, Serangkot and Nagarkot, and did a host of other touristy things like shopping in Thamel and visiting the Darbar (palace) squares in the old cities of Patan, Bhaktapur and Kathmandu, which twelve years later suffered so much damage in the earthquake. She only alludes to it, but Judy survived a hair-raising ride on the back of my scooter through the streets of the capital. Despite being a botanist, Judy did not mention the visits I arranged to the Godavari Botanical Gardens and Balaju (which I certainly cannot forget, as my sandals fell apart). And she missed out the week in Pokhara altogether, when we pretended to be real tourists at Lakeside. We explored Phewa *Tal* by canoe, walked around Begnas *Tal*

---

[115] Lama – Buddhist holy man. Some lamas also function as witchdoctors.

(overlooking Rupa *Tal*), visited Mahendra *Gupha* (cave) and Devi's waterfall, in between meeting all my Nepali friends.

I hasten to add that not all my holidays were as long or spectacular as this one was, but I can recommend that when you do go to Nepal, you spend at least a month, starting in late September. Don't go in the monsoon (June to September) or your holiday, and photos, will be washed out; and forget the winter (December to February) as you will need excess baggage to transport all your warm clothes; while summer (May to June) is just too hot and dry.

I must have visited India at least ten times: once to Kashmir and once to Goa, twice to Sikkim and twice to Gopalpur-on-Sea; and umpteen times to West Bengal (Mirik, Darjeeling, Kalimpong or Siliguri), Shillong (Meghalaya) or Dimapur (Nagaland) to teach Bible Yatra; Bangalore to attend a medical conference; and later Delhi, Shimla, Dehradun, Mumbai and Pune to visit IMI[116] projects and a Nepali friend called Janak BC. Most times this entailed using Indian Rail,[117] which always managed to provide the unexpected. I recollect the stations being so-o-o long, although this may have been a false impression created by my train going in and out of Lucknow all night. Booking Indian Rail tickets at the last minute is dicey so when I noticed an attractive offer to book my tickets in Pokhara, I gladly snapped it up. Reaching the border, however, my glee soon turned to gloom. There were no rail ticket reservations. Instead, I had serious reservations about the motive of the hotel proprietor who wanted to offer me an evening massage. After spending an anxious night blockaded in my room, I jumped up and down until I got a refund and then adjusted my itinerary. That was the year – the very week – that Mrs Gandhi was assassinated. When I eventually got to India, people kept saying I looked like her – so perhaps it was all to the good I was delayed, or those bodyguards might have taken a second pot shot at me.

The first time I went to India, no visa was required as I had a British passport, but all too soon this changed, and since then Americans have found it a lot easier to get into India than Brits. The system was streamlined (a little) over the subsequent years, but for a long time we suffered from retribution for all the injustices (real or perceived) of the

---

[116] IMI – India Migrant Initiative; one of INF's Diaspora programmes.
[117] See Chapter 3.

British Raj. Rain, hail or sun, I had to stand in the road outside the big embassy gates until the stated hour. Then, allowed to enter but only a few yards past the gate, I had to wait fifteen minutes in the next queue to obtain a number that entitled me to stand in a third queue for forty-five minutes (or more). After a short interview, if the man liked the look of my face, he gave me a form and, having completed that, I then had to wait in a fourth queue for thirty minutes (or more) for the privilege of paying 300 rupees for a telex (later fax) to the UK to check whether I was an undesirable. A week later I had to go through the first two queues again to get inside and discover whether I was desirable enough to be given a visa or not. If my name was on the list then I could complete the form, pay the fee and, with any luck, collect my passport in the afternoon. Nowadays I have given up trying to apply for an Indian visa as it has mostly to be done online which is beyond my geriatric abilities.

One thing I especially liked about the Indian cuisine was the availability of *chapatis*[118] as an alternative for rice. *Sukkha roti*[119] and omelette (preferably without the chillies) remains one of my favourite breakfasts and beats Indian 'toast' hands down. *Chapatis* are served hot from the pan, placed into a cloth-lined basket and covered to keep in the steam and stop them going hard. Toast served like this is unspeakably awful.

The first time I ventured into India had been in the 1970s – with a nursing colleague. We went only as far as Darjeeling, an area where I could make myself known in Nepali – if English failed. I still have vivid memories of that holiday and its residuum of the British Raj: the manager of the hotel who called all his patrons 'passengers'; proper English sausages for breakfast at the dairy; afternoon cream cakes at Glenary's, a very English restaurant near the Chowrastra; a five-hour Nepali church service (which we walked out of long before it finished); and returning to the plains on the little narrow-gauge 'toy' train.

Some years later my old Bible College friend Dot and I went with Vera and family, which included their two small children, to the seaside. That brings back a very different set of memories: drying nappies out of

---

[118] Chapati – thin pancake of unleavened wholemeal bread cooked on a griddle.

[119] Sukkha roti – lit dry bread – the Nepali name for chappatis.

the train window; swimming and sandcastles; pushing Dot onto the train because she was wearing a back support; fish for breakfast, dinner and tea (or so it seemed); the lack of ice creams; suffering a painful boil; and exploring the fascinating markets in Calcutta (as it was then) on our way home.

My next foray into the remnants of the British Raj was to Kashmir in 1980. Jammu-Kashmir is a unique state that epitomises the religious and political tensions of India. Jammu, on the plains, is strongly Hindu; the Sri Nagar plateau is fiercely Muslim; and up in Ladakh there are Buddhists. We stayed on a houseboat on Dal Lake – a beautiful spot – but, unfortunately, I remember it for the most vicious attack of diarrhoea I have ever suffered. I never went back, for political – and medical – reasons: I suspected the lake was used for both water supply and sewage disposal.

I visited Gopalpur with Joyce (another Joyce – from my church in Liverpool) and later Goa with another mission family. These were nice warm and leisurely seaside holidays, but the time Di and I went to Mirik and Sikkim in 1998, the weather was quite the opposite. Mirik is a delightful little village not far from Darjeeling, which boasts an artificial boating lake. The surrounding hills beckon for lots of lovely walks – except that as Mirik and mist go together like fish and chips, it is all too easy to get lost. All year round the climate is unpredictable. How the locals ever manage to dry their washing is beyond me. If they start the washing in the sunshine, it's raining by the time they are ready to hang it out. If they start in the rain, it might just be sunny for them to hang it on the line, but by the time they've popped inside for a cuppa, it'll be raining again. Sikkim is more reliably sunny or snowy (great for viewing the mountains) but can also experience fog – as we found out. It's also cold and no one had warned us about this. I think the only time I was warm on that holiday was when I borrowed a swimsuit and went for a dip in a hot spring – and perhaps when we surreptitiously supped some *chhang*[120] in the hotel.

When working with Nepali migrants in Malaysia, it was logical (and economical) to take holidays back to back with the non-stop migrant ministry. In early 2008 I spent two-and-a-half weeks lazing by the sea

[120] Chhang – Tibetan-style millet beer supped through a bamboo straw.

and a swimming pool in Prachuap Kiri Khan; that's in the narrowest bit of Thailand not far from the Burma border. As I was on my own, all I did was alternate between swimming, eating, reading and working on my Nepali Proverbs research. The first time I had ventured as far as Thailand, however, had been nearly twenty years earlier when Gaynor, Diane and I had luxuriated on the beach in Phukhet before exploring Chiangmai. (You met these friends in Chapter 8 in connection with plum plus cheese and onion quiche.) Spicy fried chicken and sticky rice eaten sitting on the hot sands near the hotel and shopping for pretty cotton blouses in the night market are what I remember most. In 2009, after attending a conference in Pattaya (south-east of Bangkok), I stayed on for a week's break by the seaside. It was a bad mistake. Don't ever think of holidaying there; I've never seen such a dirty beach. In 2013 I was back in the civilised bliss of Prachuap, this time with Heike, a colleague who shared my passion for Diaspora ministry. We also visited Chiangmai but the night market had gone downmarket since 1990. I never found any replacement pretty cotton blouses, but it was hard to miss the red light area in the middle of all the ordinary stalls. In 2011 Heike and I had holidayed briefly in Malaysia – on Tioman island (off the south-east coast), where Heike got sunburn and I got insect bites; and Langkawi island (off the north-west coast), where there were no insects, just a swimming pool and a borrowed car. We were both happy; Heike was in the shade and I in the driving seat.

Understandably, for financial and cultural reasons, I never really holidayed in the Middle East, but in between teaching Bible Yatra and visiting migrants in Doha, I did get to swim in the Gulf and also enjoyed about three days' extreme luxury, courtesy of a Nepali staff member at the Abu Dhabi Hilton. On my one and only visit to Jordan I was taken to Mount Nebo and to see the Dead Sea and the River Jordan, both of which I discovered are very much smaller than on the maps I still use for Bible teaching.

INF Nepali staff got annual holidays but usually spent them with their families and did not travel out of the country as the expatriates liked to do. There were plenty of Hindu festivals and holidays[121] that punctuated the otherwise routine existence of ordinary Nepalis. We didn't celebrate

[121] See Chapter 4.

these ourselves but as most people had no time to be ill during festivals, we had less work to do and those times felt like extra half-holidays.

For Hindus and Christians alike, hatches, matches and despatches, especially weddings and funerals, are also important occasions, although celebrated very differently. Hindu rituals are much lengthier than Christian ones; weddings may last three days, and funeral rites go on for at least thirteen days. I've been to one or two Hindu weddings but only to the final 'social' bit and the feast, and never to a funeral, although I have watched the sad processions winding their way down to the *ghats* on many occasions. Christian Nepali weddings are far less exotic – similar to ones in the West, with a church service and vows and a feast afterwards. The groom always used to don formal Nepali dress but nowadays fashion favours a Western suit. The bride always used to wear a white sari, a custom undoubtedly imported from the West via India and, to my way of thinking, totally inappropriate – white being the colour worn at Hindu funerals. Nowadays, however, there seems to have been a contextual compromise and Christian brides mostly wear pink saris, while Hindu ones wear red, which is the colour of victory and rejoicing.

Hindus cremate their dead by the riverside; Christians, until now, have buried theirs. Many times this insistence on burying has deeply offended Hindu neighbours as they fear the ghosts that they believe roam around until a body has been burnt. Today, because of this and because of lack of suitable grounds for cemeteries, Christians are beginning to consider cremation, but are largely still bound by tradition and, as I see it, a not very well thought out theology of death and resurrection. That, however, has never been the biggest personal problem for young Christian men in Hindu families. There was, and still is, huge pressure from relatives for a son to perform the rites of *kiriya*[122] for his father, but the church regards anyone who does this as an apostate. As with the cremation-burial debate (or the red-white wedding dress conundrum), maybe it need not be quite as clear cut as that; some of the rites are undoubtedly Hindu but others are perhaps merely an expression of mourning.

One other important event I discovered was the *udghaten,* or 'opening', and it had a protocol all of its own. Dress was formal: the men

---

[122] Kiriya – Hindu funeral rites traditionally performed by the eldest son.

in *daura-suruwal*[123] and black *topis;* the ladies in saris. Nothing happened until the chief guest arrived and he (invariably a 'he') was often an hour late. Then all the important people had to be introduced and requested to sit on the platform. Next, they all had to make a speech. The result was that the *udghaten* was so formal and long-winded that it turned what should have been a joyous celebration of something new starting up into a boring half-day assembly. Only the refreshments at the end made it worth attending.

Until the monarchy was overthrown in 2008, the King used to make regular visits to each of the development regions. While the King was still regarded as an incarnation of the god Vishnu, these were very auspicious events for the local people. These royal visits also had a more practical knock-on effect in that preparation for them included getting various development matters – like bad roads – fixed. INF was not usually considered important enough for a specific visit but occasionally this happened. I remember the Queen coming to the Shining in the early 1970s and I wrote about this, and other royal visits, in *Himalayan Vision:*

> *"Rani Aiyo,*[124] *Rani Aiyo," screamed a frantic Kanchha*[125] *as he rushed down from the Shining Hospital Compound to warn the expatriates of the auspicious visit of his queen. In his excitement, his grammar fell far short of the expected level of Nepali royal honorifics, and the event also caught the mission on the hop. Gerald Turner only just had time to change out of his shorts, while Mary Thomson was destined to meet Her Majesty in the lungi and rubber flip-flops she wore for operating...*

I missed this event but was more involved in a later visit of their Majesties to GZH in 1985.[126]

> *Visits from the British Royal Family, on the other hand, were accompanied by strict protocol, which, in the quaintness of their customs, reflects the days of the British Raj. The first, in*

[123] Daura-suruwal – Nepali men's traditional dress.
[124] Rani aiyo – the queen has come.
[125] Kanchha – One of the peons; Effie's youngest son.
[126] See Chapter 16.

1961, found the entire mission being presented to Queen Elizabeth at the air ground, there being no road for her to travel up to the hospital. Exactly how our intrepid pioneers overcame the problem of not having quite enough pairs of long gloves to go around, I leave to your imagination. On a subsequent visit in 1965, there still being no motor road, Prince Philip made the trek up to the Shining, while the Queen waited at the air ground. Many years later Prince Charles also visited Pokhara, but by this time formalities were minimal. There were no formal expatriate presentations, but a few INF-ers lined up with the rest of the population to see the prince. One, who had dressed respectably in a sari for the occasion, recollects his remark that she had "gone native".

My own turn to meet the Queen came in 1996 in the UK – and no, I didn't wear a sari!

20

Jet Lag

Home assignments

Left to right: childhood home; the bungalow; maisonette.

DID YOU HEAR THE JOKE ABOUT the little boy?

Q: "What do you want to be when you grow up?"

A: "A missionary on furlough."

Quite clearly, he knew very little about missionaries or about furlough. I discovered that even most adults – including devout Christian churchgoing adults – did not know a great deal about missionaries and especially about missionaries on furlough. Furlough (or home leave, or 'home assignment' as it's now called) is hard work – and often quite lonely. It's an upside-down existence; you're free in the daytime when everyone else is working and have to work in the evenings when everyone else is relaxing.

Over the years I think the most frequently asked question I encountered was, "And when are you going back, then?" As a conversation opener, this gambit left a lot to be desired. It also used to leave me feeling somewhat unwelcome and at times tempted to respond, "As soon as possible." The other most frequently asked question, often following close on the heels of the first, was invariably, "And are you having a nice holiday, then?" That also used to annoy me, not because I'm mad at my 'friends', but because of the connotations of 'furlough'. This is an antiquated term, which, according to the dictionary, means rest and recreation, holiday, unpaid leave, unemployment or even something akin to parole. While for me it did certainly contain odd bits of some of those, it was definitely not unemployment. My home leave in 1977/8, consisted of 7,000 furlough hours spent in covering 26,000 miles, in 8 different countries, visiting more than 80 cities, towns and villages, for purposes of locum, statistics, holiday and rest plus an average of half a deputation meeting every day for 5 months, and all of this entailed sleeping in 40 different beds and 4 aeroplanes. After that the thought of returning to 'work' in the East became increasingly more attractive. This was typical. No, furlough was not (just) holiday! Delivering babies (in Nepal) is one thing, delivering stirring messages to church audiences (in the UK) is quite another, but both are hard work. Happily, over the years furlough morphed into home assignment – a far more accurate description of what we are really expected to do.

To be fair, in the far-off days when furlough was the acceptable term to use, missionaries got their 'holiday' while travelling home by boat. I was one of the last few 'boat people' to arrive in Nepal; but after that I always travelled by air, whisked across several time zones, my circadian rhythms all out of synch, and always arriving with jet lag and sometimes with other weird accoutrements too. With infrequent (five-yearly) leaves and no real-time Internet information, I would always turn up in the UK wearing something not quite right for the fashion or the season, although I did manage to avoid arriving in the cold in white sandals – one of Dot's more notable achievements.

The first time I returned to the UK, I thought I was about to be put straight onto the next flight back to Nepal. The man in front of me in the immigration queue was asked how much a bottle of milk cost. I had no idea and don't think I'd even known before I went to Nepal. I assume my mother had always paid for her milk; I just drank it – or that from a hospital residency. But it turned out they didn't ask people like me, who looked as though they lived here! I was allowed back into the land of my birth, but it was not too long before I began to wonder whether that had been such a good idea.

I had arrived, and that in itself was a minor miracle. To date I have not been hijacked (for which I am genuinely thankful to God) but most other air travel catastrophes have happened to me at some time or another. Once, when I was *en route* to Ethiopia, ticket in hand, I walked confidently up to the check-in counter at Tribhuvan Airport in Kathmandu, to be greeted by an airport official who looked me directly in the eye and declared, "But Madam, you went on Tuesday." As by then it was Thursday, he was forced to admit that I hadn't and was also forced to find me a seat on the next flight to Delhi.

Even getting to the airport was sometimes the biggest achievement of the whole journey. In the early years, when Kathmandu had no traffic jams, it was travelling from Pokhara to Kathmandu that could be difficult, not getting the last few miles across the city to the airport. But by the noughties, traffic had become horrendous and strikes ubiquitous. Just my luck, then, to have a flight on a *bandh* day. Happily, I was already living in Kathmandu, but as walking the five or so miles was not a reasonable option with a suitcase and a box of books, I was forced to use some authorised transport from a nearby hotel. Two rather wobbly trips on my scooter delivered these heavy bags to the hotel the day before the flight. Then a short morning walk to the hotel the next morning reunited me with my luggage and I was then ready for the hair-raising taxi drive through the backstreets of the capital (avoiding the demonstrators) to reach the airport.

In 1986, on my way home for a holiday, at about three o'clock in the sleepy darkness of the tourist class cabin, as I was dozing uncomfortably suspended somewhere over Eastern Europe, there came a request over the loudspeaker, "Is there a doctor on board?" In my youthful enthusiasm to be helpful, I forgot all the possible legal tangles if the case turned out badly and confessed to my medical qualifications. A very relieved stewardess led me through the dividing veil and into the inner sanctum of the first class cabin to meet my patient. She turned out to be a very large and a very important personage, travelling to London for medical treatment for some obscure complaint for which she was already taking several lots of medication. My confidence pulled the rip cord on its parachute and left me, but as there were no other medics queuing up to help, I grasped the borrowed stethoscope and attempted to examine her. It was not so much the dim light in the cabin which made this difficult (I was used to examining by candlelight) but rather the vast size of the patient. Eventually, I arrived at a diagnosis of sorts and then, with much courage, administered an injection. Finally, after assuring the aircrew that it was safe for the patient to continue to the UK, I returned to my seat praying hard that we would reach Heathrow safely before the lady's pain returned. Air India were so grateful that I had saved them the hassle and expense of an emergency landing in somewhere not too friendly like Albania, they later sent me a present.

In the early years we always travelled via Delhi and before the new airport was completed, we had to share the terminal building with migratory mosquitoes who also broke their journeys there. When my father died suddenly in December 1973, I had to return home urgently. Kathmandu to Delhi was painless, but then, after spending a long time negotiating a last-minute booking on a London flight, I went to a hotel (the same one all those with stopover had gone to). It was a bad choice and an expensive one. After just two hours of sleep, we were due back at the airport at 4am. It was a bad night – and it got worse. I was sharing a taxi with a UMN family who also used to work in Pokhara, but halfway to the airport the taxi ran out of petrol. While Larry and I ran up and down the deserted dual carriageway, waving our arms to attract an empty taxi, Phil was looking after two very small and very sleepy children. To add final insult to injury, the check-in clerk then booked Larry and me into the same seat.

Some years later, on my way back to Nepal but when the new transit lounge was functioning, I found myself once again in Delhi. I managed to avoid being hustled with the crowd through immigration (a fate only slightly better than death and much more expensive than a funeral, with all the visa and airport taxes that become involved) and getting separated from my luggage, but then I discovered I was sentenced to well over eight hours locked in the transit lounge. The luxury of air conditioning, a choice of many toilets and no friendly mosquitoes as in the old days did little to offset the inconvenience of a very long fast – all because I had no US dollars. Now that there is no longer a British Raj in India, the airport no longer accepts sterling pounds. Only just before I expired from dehydration did a kind-hearted Air India official issue me with a voucher for one small cup of coffee. Since then, guess what – I always carry a pocketful of dollars.

By the 1980s the favoured airline had become Bangladesh Biman, but only because it was the cheapest. Travelling west, the flights seemed to link up with no trouble at all; returning eastwards, there was always a delay, and an unscheduled overnight stopover in Dhaka. This was so regular we planned for it by packing overnight essentials in our hand luggage. But once I faced a different problem in Dhaka and it was all because I had lashed out and decided to fly direct from Birmingham – a doubly galling mistake. First, I found out that Birmingham International Airport charges far more excess baggage than London Heathrow, such that I almost had to resort to a whip around to pay for it. My resulting discomposure probably explains why I watched unquestioning as an official labelled my precious cases 'Dhaka' (not Kathmandu). In Dhaka, as usual, I heard they were sending us to a hotel for the night. That was no big problem but my luggage was. When I enquired they assured me that it would go straight to Kathmandu, although I deemed this extremely unlikely as it was labelled 'Dhaka' and told them so. No matter how many times I said this, no one believed me – until, probably just to be rid of me, one man agreed to take me around the back and prove, once and for all, that my cases were safely stacked ready for Kathmandu. Predictably, what he proved was what I had feared; he found two lonely little cases located somewhere in limbo behind the rubber flap of the carousel, where I assume they might well have stayed for eternity. He was apologetic and hastened to relabel them while I smiled happily and courteously refrained from saying, "I told you so."

Later still, our choice of route shifted to stopovers in the Middle East in Qatar or Emirates – supposedly bigger and more efficient airports, but sadly not always so. Returning from a visit to the UK in 2005, I had a short stopover in Doha and on arrival in Kathmandu found that my luggage had not caught the connection. At first I was not too worried as it seemed everyone's luggage was delayed. But then a couple of days later, when everyone else's cases had turned up, mine stayed missing – and never reappeared. I was disappointed not to have my treat of some English pork sausages and still wonder what the Qatari Muslims who found them thought; perhaps that's exactly why they never put them on the next flight for me?

Jet lag is reputedly worse on west-east travel but perversely I found it worse in the opposite direction. It was always harder arriving back home in the UK than in Nepal, and going back to Nepal one time I virtually stepped off the plane and into the operating theatre in Pokhara. Strange but true, reverse culture shock was also more of a jolt to the system than the original. In Asia people made allowance for the fact that I looked and sounded different – they accepted I was peculiar – but back home in the UK, where I looked normal, people still thought I was peculiar. OK, so maybe I *am* peculiar and it's nothing to do with culture shock...? The first time back in the UK, I went around in a complete daze for several weeks, overwhelmed by the extraordinary amount of choice of even simple items in the shops and unable to travel very far because buses no longer had friendly conductors to advise me how much I needed to pay. If I did venture onto public transport, I never had the right change and never knew from which secret slot my ticket might choose to emerge.

Re-entry into Nepal (i.e. getting through customs) was another hazard to be faced at the end of 'furlough' before life could finally return to normal in Pokhara. Despite the cost of excess baggage, I always yielded to the temptation to take some goodies back and in time I became quite an accomplished smuggler. I travelled once with three tape recorders, only one of them mine – but then at Kathmandu Airport my helpfulness was nearly my undoing. Waiting for the baggage check in customs, I overheard a conversation with an unfortunate tourist. The customs officer kept asking him, "Wakky-Takky Chha?" What on earth was he on about? But then I suddenly realised that he meant a tape recorder (walkie-talkie) and obliged with a translation. The tourist's machine was then examined and duly registered in his passport (so he would be obliged to take it home with him). I expect *he* intended to do that anyway, but *I* didn't; all three of my machines were to be left in Nepal. This could have been a problem, but wasn't: happy with my translation assistance, the officer whisked me through without any further ado. And as he didn't ask, I didn't tell him I had them.

He was a nice customs officer but many are not. They are trained to home straight in to the single most embarrassing article in your case and then hold it up for everyone around to see and laugh at. If you are thick-skinned enough to cope with that, having an embarrassing item (like the baby's dirty nappy) on the top of your luggage can be very useful, or so

I was told, but for me – no marriage, no children, no nappies. I have, however, effected entry with a six-foot kite for my language teacher's children; and for the hospital, a box of leprosy medicines (which no one dared to touch), an LSD[127] type of drug (for my anaesthetic colleagues), a bag of old spectacle lenses, and enough reusable plastic syringes for all the hippies in Kathmandu to remain high for at least the next decade. The rules stated that importing "decayed beef" was not allowed. This was reasonable in a Hindu country where the cows are sacred, but as even the most dedicated cow-eater would not touch decayed meat, I felt I had a clear conscience to take back OXO gravy granules. I regularly smuggled them in, in unlabelled plastic bags, intending, if asked, to say they looked like coffee granules. This, of course, was strictly true, though perhaps not the whole truth. Another rule displayed on the board in Tribhuvan Airport declared that bringing in more than half a pound of 'sweat' per person was illegal. In the hot season there can have been very few innocent travellers.

While my mother was alive, I used to stay with her during my visits to the UK. As she lived in Sutton Coldfield, this provided me with a very convenient base in the Midlands from which almost anywhere else I went was equidistant. It was so convenient that I used to return home to see Mum in between each trip and felt virtuous about doing so. I was therefore more than a little put out when she complained that I only came home to wash my hair and my sweaters.

Over around ten visits to the UK, I have begged, borrowed, hired or bought a selection of old bangers, and some of the hassles I had with them were equal to those concerning transportation back in Nepal.[128] One Christmas Eve was more than usually exciting. On return from a late-night service at church, I saw flames starting to spurt from one of the headlights. Remembering just in time that water is not a good idea to put out electrical fires, I grabbed handfuls of earth and threw them onto the lamp. Although that seemed to have done the trick, I could not be absolutely sure, so I moved the car as far from any other vehicles as possible – just in case – and in doing so, must have awoken the whole estate, as metal garage doors make a heck of a row in the middle of the

[127] LSD – Lysergic Acid Diethylamide – a hallucinogenic drug.
[128] See Chapters 14 and 15.

night. Then I went to bed and prayed hard... and my prayers were answered: I awoke on Christmas morning to discover that I still had a car.

The next near tragedy was even more hairy. With a new (to me) car with brakes duly adjusted, I drove to South Wales and then noticed that one hub cap was missing and all the wheels were wet. Being in Britain in the summer, I just assumed this was due to rain – until a couple of days later it dawned on me that we were in the middle of the hottest and driest summer for decades. The wet must therefore be brake fluid, but as nothing unforeseen had happened on the way down the motorway, I reckoned it was OK to drive up the Rhondda. Not a good decision and no doubt unpopular with my guardian angel, who was probably hoping to take the weekend off. By the time I reached Brecon, wheels and tyres were covered with fluid and even I began to worry a little. At last I decided to seek advice. By then everyone (except my guardian angel) had gone off for the Bank Holiday, but eventually I found one garage mechanic. He said he couldn't fix it and told me not to go anywhere. As I needed to get home that night, I calmly informed him that I planned to drive back to Birmingham up the motorway, but the look he gave me was one usually reserved for ghosts (presumably because he thought I would soon be one). He responded, not particularly reverently, "God help you, then," and I said (slightly more reverently and sincerely) that that was exactly what I was expecting to happen (at which I suspect my guardian angel groaned). I set off armed with a couple of cans of brake fluid and lived to tell this tale, which indicates one of two things: either the whole situation was not nearly as serious as he had indicated, or guardian angels work a great deal harder than we usually give them credit for. As the garage put it right free of charge, I suspect it was the latter. You may feel that it also indicates that I am a prize idiot where car maintenance is concerned – and you could be right.

Before the days of satnavs (of which, more later), navigation when driving alone could be hazardous. Reading a map and driving at the same time is difficult if not dangerous, and hand-drawn maps are often dodgy. I was following the instructions in one of these to the letter. The final directive said to take a dead-end road into the dale. I did, but it turned out to be the wrong dead-end into the wrong dale to the wrong farm. Then, because I couldn't get the gate to the deserted farmhouse to stay open long enough to drive in and turn the car around, I had to turn in a narrow, muddy lane with an even muddier verge and ditch. I too was muddy by the time I arrived an hour later.

Years later I acquired a satnav, but – as everyone who has one knows – this just created a different set of problems. One time the machine also sent me down a dead-end – not into mud, but onto MoD[129] land. The thought of becoming shot at put my previous ditch escapade into perspective.

Never trust a satnav in London. Mine directed me unerringly towards the congestion charge area until I forced it to 'recalculate', but even then it didn't give up; it tried to send me on the Woolwich Ferry instead of through the Blackwall Tunnel. On the way home, too, it remained fixated on the ferry and congestion charge route. Since then I've learnt some tactics and I think I may now be winning the battle of the satnav.

So why didn't I use public transport? Because it's impossible to carry a case of respectable clothes, a projector, slides and a selection of books by bus and train. Occasionally, when I didn't have luggage, I did leave the car at home, but that didn't automatically ensure stress-free travel. Late one evening, when I had missed the previous bus by about five minutes and faced a half-hour wait in the cold, dark and dismal cavern that passed for the Birmingham bus station, a young man came and joined me in the queue. He soon began to tell me, embellishing the tale with all the gory details, that he had just had a circumcision operation. I started to pray for a miracle, that for once the bus would come early. Finally, the fellow offered to show me the results of his operation, so I smiled and said, "Thank you, but I'm a doctor; I've seen a lot of similar operations. I'm not really very interested." Never had I been so glad I was a medic. Then... my miracle arrived – not the bus (that was too much to expect), but the young man just walked away.

In Nepal I sometimes had to make do with a tree, but in Britain there was always a bathroom. I had always naïvely imagined that all bathrooms were situated upstairs in some approximate proximity to the bedrooms, but I was wrong; some of my friends kept their facilities downstairs. Fortunately, I am an early riser and so was never caught wandering through the kitchen in my pyjamas while my hostess was

---

[129] Ministry of Defence.

cooking the breakfast. But there was one home where the family watchdog was bedded down in the kitchen, and that bothered me: how to avoid a doggy lick instead of my normal morning ablutions? The ultimate ignominy, however, was where the one and only bathroom led off my hosts' bedroom. Having to make use of a commode in the guestroom meant I never stayed there more than one night and was heartily relieved(!) when Hilary and Roger moved house.

There was a very different bathroom anomaly in another friend's house: a strange odour, but definitely not soap, talc and bath salts, nor even of lavatory cleaner. It emanated from the mice in the bathroom cupboard, kept ready to feed the snake that lived in the living room – in a box, I hasten to add. Judy once invited me to fondle Ben, saying he was not poisonous; he was a squeezer but too small (he didn't look at all small to me) to do any real damage. I refused to put this to the test, even though she added that even if he did wind himself around my neck, there would be plenty of time to grab his tail before my breath was taken away. As the very idea had already left me gasping, I was far from reassured.

Many families keep a little library in their loos, and on one home leave I conducted a simple survey of the different varieties available. I discovered three grades of reading material. As most of the homes I visited were Christian, the provision of a scripture calendar in the loo was hardly unexpected. Personally, I did not find it too moving! In others the religious devotion was either deeper or the owners chronically constipated. How long would you need to spend 'enthroned' to get through a thick volume like *My Utmost for His Highest?* My favourites, however, were the Readers' Digest, other magazines or joke books.

Some bathrooms in the UK may be a bit unusual but they do all have many modern advantages. It was so relaxing to sit on, rather than squat over, the loo, although I found it hard to adjust to cleaning my teeth under the running water from the tap without the slightest danger of contracting amoebic dysentery.

But bathrooms (or snakes) were not my only problem. Gardens, too, had their pitfalls. Di had gone to work and I was to leave her parents' house at a more civilised time when the South Circular would not automatically be a sentence of three hours in a traffic jam. I knew that the family kept bees (and had enjoyed the honey), but I didn't realise they had other unusual 'pets'. In blissful ignorance I ventured into the garden to say goodbye and thank you to her mother, only to be attacked by a couple of ferocious geese. I beat them off with my handbag and then beat a hasty retreat – never to return.

One of the professional hazards of being a missionary on furlough was being overfed. Most people assumed (correctly) that a diet of *daal-bhat* in Nepal was monotonous and enjoyed feeding us up on the fat of the land while we were home in the UK. That tended to result in my becoming one of the fat of the land. Just occasionally, however, the system broke down. A couple of days before I was due to visit an old friend from Liverpool, her husband phoned to enquire what time I would arrive. I assumed that he wished to synchronise the evening meal with the time of my arrival, and so I clearly said that I would be coming direct from work, leaving at 5pm and arriving at about 7pm. On arrival I was offered a cup of coffee, but not wishing to spoil my meal, I declined it. Several hours of chatting later, I was offered a hot chocolate and a biscuit before bed and this time I accepted with alacrity. On other visits to this family I was, as everywhere else, overfed, and so I can only assume it was all a genuine misunderstanding and not a deliberate attempt to keep my weight down – much as that was needed.

A lot of my time on leave was spent speaking about my work in Nepal at various meetings. To survive I discovered I needed three things: patience, tact and a sense of humour. In the early years I bent over backwards to avoid saying anything political but often had to emphasise that Nepal is Nepal, it is not part of North India (and never has been). It is not Naples, nor is it Natal in southern Africa.

Many of the meetings I spoke at were attended by the older generation of supporters. These were stalwart prayer warriors but, sadly, many were caught in a time warp. While by my second and third home leaves, the towns of Nepal had mostly dragged themselves into the 20th century, these ladies (and they were invariably ladies) hadn't, and still thought we missionaries lived in mud huts and were surrounded by 'lepers' (ugh!) and uneducated (savage) children. One day I was so pleased; I had got over the fact that there were now hospitals in Nepal, and had explained how I worked in one of them delivering babies. But then one dear lady asked if there were any schools in which these babies could subsequently be educated. I fear I blotted my copybook by telling her a bit too bluntly that there were at least 15,000. She remained silent for the rest of the meeting, but I do hope she continued praying for Nepal and for me – even if I didn't deserve it.

Back in the 1970s, 80s and early 90s we had to rely on slides – and projectors. One meeting I remember all too well as it was so bizarre. Everything was set up. The screen was perched delicately on the piano and the projector balanced on an ancient table, but no sooner had the first slide appeared on the screen than one gentleman jumped up and declared that no one could see properly. What he meant was that *he* could not see properly. Realising immediately that suggesting he move to the front row was not going to work, I switched off the projector while he searched for something suitable to raise its height. I balanced the slides carefully on a chair by my side, waiting for him to return with the obligatory pile of hymn books – the normal church solution to this common problem. But this guy was clearly not into normal solutions; he soon came back but with his arms full of saucers! I rejected them and again he rushed off, but whether in embarrassment or enthusiasm I never discovered for I was far too busy picking up my slides from the floor where he had scattered them with his coat tail.

A meeting that proceeded without some hitch was rare. Projector bulbs popped at the crucial moment, plugs were the wrong size, and when leads were too short, no one knew where an extension could be found. Even slides used to turn themselves upside down. I thought I had learnt from every conceivable experience and began to carry around with me a bag of spare bulb, adaptor and extension lead. Then one day I plugged in and nothing happened. I tried the next socket and again nothing happened. This church was clearly in need of a rewire. At last I found a socket that seemed to work, but as I released the extension lead, the projector went off yet again. I picked up the lead and back the light came. I repeated this manoeuvre until it dawned on me that it wasn't the church but my extension lead that was playing up. As there was no handyman in this ladies' meeting to help me out or find another lead for me, I had to recruit a friend to stand and hold the lead in just the right position throughout my slide show. It worked.

Although I later progressed to using PowerPoint presentations, this did not eradicate all the potential pitfalls; it just upgraded them. I was still dependent on a functional socket, plug, extension lead, screen and projector – and also a computer, which had to talk nicely to the projector.

It was usually that last bit of communication that broke down, and solving that problem was generally harder than picking up slides or holding extension leads. How to change rhomboidal into square images and retrieve important text titles cut off at sides or top and bottom is way beyond my capabilities.

During my first couple of furloughs, I'm pretty sure I bored everyone to tears with my exceedingly traditional missionary talks, using a style barely different from the lantern slides of my esteemed predecessors decades earlier. Things slowly improved, paradoxically as churches hosted fewer missionary meetings and I was able to spend more quality time with my personal supporters. I tried inventing creative ways of getting over what I had seen God doing in Nepal – combining a set series of slides (later a PP) with a carefully prepared commentary to make a more professional presentation. That, incidentally, removed the need for me to prepare a new talk for every meeting. I dreamed up an interactive programme, describing a problem scenario that led on to group discussions about how the missionaries should have tackled it. That proved popular and the idea was even taken up by the mission. I showed a video of the Nepali church and invited discussion about it afterwards. I even invented a couple of games to illustrate what it meant to be 'called' to Nepal, or to work in a village community health project. On one home leave I raised awareness of, and funds for, Bible Yatra by jogging – my target being to jog a circuit the same number of times as there were chapters in the Bible. In case you are wondering, there are 1,189 chapters (and just for the record, there are 31,173 verses and 807,361 words) but you could have googled that – like I did. Nowadays my hips remind me that this was not the brightest of my bright ideas.

Children's talks were also not my forte but what I lacked in talent I made up for with effort. I designed games and quizzes and 'spot the difference' pairs of pictures of life in Nepal, and created a whole programme of information, games, language and even food-tasting. I invented a quiz called 'Who wants to be a missionary?' It was rather like the TV show *Who Wants to Be a Millionaire?* except for the money! My final invention was a 'Let's be a migrant!' activity.

21

What – Me?

Medical Director, OBE and new things

(Late 1980s to late 1990s)

Left: INF headquarters in Pokhara.
Right: Val and Rajani in Medical Director's office.

AFTER MY MOTHER DIED IN DECEMBER 1987, I stayed on in the UK for about another nine months. That time was like a normal (hectic) home leave[130] but with three significant differences. First, I had to sort out the flat and contents I'd inherited from my mother and decide what I would do with it all when I returned to Nepal. From then until I returned permanently to the UK in early 2014, I decided to rent out the flat (not always a happy experience) and so home leaves always started with getting my personal effects out of the loft and ended with putting them back again. Second, in 1988 I attended a Walk Thru the Bible (WTB) seminar at a friend's church and this so excited me that I asked

[130] See Chapter 20.

permission to use this teaching in Nepal.[131] And third, another friend, when discussing my future with me, indicated that she believed I would soon be doing something very different. I think I had assumed that I would try to return to WRH but what she said made me consider other options. Perhaps not a prophecy but it was still fulfilled: when I did return, my role in INF had changed dramatically.

If I was not to return to clinical work at WRH, then the job that I wanted was Health Projects Director (HPD) in INF. The only trouble was that in 1988 Pat (the Pat we met in Chapter 12) was still filling that role, so I was asked to be Acting Personnel Secretary until Mida (the permanent incumbent) returned from her home leave in the Philippines and took her job back. This was a bigger change than I had envisaged but, bizarrely, I believed it was the right thing to do – that it was where God wanted me for that year at least.

I was given a little office in our Pokhara headquarters. It had a big crack in one wall, one outsize desk, two large filing cabinets, an enormous noticeboard, an overflowing wastepaper basket and, of course, my new Amstrad word processor; but I was able to escape from it at times to see people in their homes, or visit some of our outstations. My work involved writing letters (literally, *ad inf)* and memos *(ad nauseam);* drafting, re-drafting and amending personnel-related policies; compiling agendas for the Personnel Committee and later doing (mostly) what the PC had told me to do. I had my fingers in pretty much every pie, or, put another way, a whole lot of new hats to wear, including Acting Director for a brief three weeks in 1989. In Personnel I also had responsibility for some aspects of our children's education, housing (including guesthouses) and language and orientation, as well as needing to relate to all the Home Ends, keeping the personnel records and statistics, dealing with some applications, designations and assessments, and home leave arrangements. I had some new-fangled electronic gadgetry to help me, but when the electricity went off (as it frequently did), then I had time to talk with people! More reliable help came from the supporting team in the department.

I think I coped with the personnel job adequately but probably not brilliantly – mainly because I am very much a paper person rather than a

---

[131] See Chapter 24.

people person. Thus, the one specific contribution – perhaps predictable – that I made to the department was to sort out the Personnel files. I trust that that was of some help to Mida and her successors.

Then the next year the HPD post became vacant and I was appointed to start on 1st January 1990. With fifteen years' medical experience in various programmes of INF in Nepal, I was undoubtedly better qualified for this job, which I then held for about seven years. This time round the coordination included all the medical projects that INF was involved in: initially TB, Leprosy, Community Health and Training; and subsequently, the Hospitals' Assistance and its associated Technical and Laboratory Services Programmes, Medical Supplies, Drug Education and Community Based Rehabilitation. Along the way I once again acquired several extra hats to wear. I produced the *Health Projects Digest* (an internal news bulletin for our medical projects), juggled the applications for medical student electives and was re-elected to the mission leadership committee. Within the first eight months in my new job, I had nearly finished sorting and colour-coding the office, made at least three working visits to Kathmandu, begun to update our Technical Resources Library, chaired a Health Education Strategy Seminar and started to make contacts with other non-governmental organisations. I had also visited Ghorahi and Surkhet (in the Mid-West) by road, Baglung and Burtibang (in the West) by foot, and Jumla (in the remote north-west) by air. Another time I visited health posts and hospitals – and church groups – in Nawal Parasi, to see if this might be the next new project area. It was not to be but still encouraged Lok Bahadur, the 'bishop' of Nawal Parasi. He wasn't really a bishop; that's just my nickname for him, as he was the senior pastor who had started almost all the churches in the district (and a couple of other districts too).

1990 was also the year of Revolution and then political 'freedom' in Nepal. One of the things that struck me most in the middle of this was the willingness of the intellectual and professional groups – doctors, lawyers, lecturers – to publish articles on human rights, knowing that they were putting their careers, and in some cases their freedom and even their lives, in jeopardy. Under similar circumstances, would I have been as willing to stand up for my beliefs and support freedom for others? Apart from the time of the spring demonstrations, all this had hardly affected our project work, but what did disrupt my plans was having to attend innumerable NGO meetings to debate any and all issues "in the changed political context". Optimistically, we anticipated that as Christian expatriates we would have more open opportunities for supporting the churches in the future, and this made me think how I might ultimately respond to this challenge. As a result, in 1995 I enrolled in a distance learning degree in Theology. True to form, I used to do some of my New Testament Greek homework sitting in the back of a Land Rover during my various out-of-Pokhara visits. I even started thinking about an M.A. with a view to perhaps being able to teach in a Bible College afterwards.

1996 was another auspicious year. It was then that I moved house (yet again) and INF moved into its new international headquarters in Pokhara and my title was changed from HPD to MD (Medical Director), not that it made any difference to my work or workload. By then I was also serving as the director of our Health Services Partnership (HSP) – also renamed but formerly the Hospitals Assistance Project, or the 'HAPpy Project', as we liked to call it. Most of our input was into WRH but we also worked with district hospitals in Beni and later Surkhet, with some clinical but mainly technical (equipment) support. We forged links with the Medical Doctorate in General Practice training programme of Tribhuvan University and for a couple of years I edited (and largely wrote) *Frontline,* a small journal for this group. There was progress everywhere we looked, but re-reading my newsletter from Mar/Apr that year I can't help laughing when I see what I wrote.

> *We are also approaching new horizons of communication: no longer does e-mail mean e for envelopes. Just think of the possibilities of prayer requests via the Internet!*

Also in 1996 I heard (incorrectly, as it transpired) that 'Mrs Mouse' had died and (correctly) that Shyam Malla had received a long service medal for his work in the bank. Amidst all this change, 1996 was also the year when I started very seriously thinking of a new future for myself. Then by the end of 1997, I had handed over the MD job and the HSP work and "moved out from the security of an INF visa". My colleagues in INF threw a farewell party for me and presented me with a farewell book. One person wrote, "...you will be missed in INF," although I was not leaving INF altogether but only an INF visa post. Another person wrote, perhaps more accurately or prophetically, "Now the training's over, time for the real thing..."

When I reflected on my own tortuous medical career, I realised that over the years INF's work had also changed quite significantly – a microcosm of evolving medical mission around the globe. During my time in Nepal, I witnessed some of the most significant changes. For the first twenty to twenty-five years, like the earliest medical mission pioneers, we had delivered curative services. Until INF arrived in 1952, there had been no modern medical care in the whole of the west of Nepal. *Baidyas* and *jankris* treated patients – the former reasonably well within the limits of their herbal practice; the latter often very badly and expensively. Fractures were left to heal on their own – with deformities and disabilities resulting. Patients with conditions requiring operations just died, and untold numbers of mothers also expired in childbirth. TB patients coughed and spluttered their way to an early demise, infecting whole families *en route;* 'lepers' were totally ostracised from society but often lived long years in the jungle, lonely and disabled. It was therefore not surprising that the Christian love and care given at the Shining Hospital and Green Pastures made us popular with the people, but paradoxically, it also made our future work harder – when we had to move with the times. The village clinics (Baglung, Sikha and Beni) in the 1960s and the Pokhara town clinics (Tirsapatti, Baidam, Dungasaon and Kunahar) in the 70s and early 80s were also primarily curative, although the emphasis in the MCH clinics gradually shifted towards community care and involvement.

By the late 1970s, however, the tide of medical mission had definitely turned towards community development, prophylaxis and health education. INF jumped on the bandwagon. We became deeply involved, alongside HMG/N, in leprosy – and later TB – control. In the 1980s and early 90s, we started two community development programmes – first in Burtibang in the remote north-west of Baglung District; and later, in West Myagdi, centred on the scenic hill village of Takum. Disease control and health education were rightly seen as vital to improving the health of the people. Providing rural communities with water, sanitation, literacy, agricultural and health advice was regarded as the way ahead. Curative clinics were outdated. The Shining had closed and our role in curative medicine – apart from caring for long-term leprosy patients in Green

Pastures and seconding a few people to work in WRH – was minimal. The trouble was that the pendulum had swung too far over and hit the floor with a bang, destroying the delicate balance – of life, death and health in Nepal. Sometimes it seemed that we were trying to persuade communities that it was better to immunise their children than treat them. In a way – at least in the long term – that was true, but it should never be at the expense of treating those who are already sick. I had always argued for such a balance between curative and community services, and this was perhaps partly why I had returned to hospital work for several years in the 80s. I argued but the matter was not in my hands.

Looking back, I think the real problem, ironically, was the development of the Nepal Government Health Services. They made excellent five-year plans but sadly these were rarely fully carried out. The concept of a network of local health posts, small district hospitals, larger zonal hospitals and major regional hospitals was brilliant, but it soon broke down. While some facilities were not constructed, many of the buildings were erected although the staff, equipment and supplies never appeared. We knew and understood why: the budgets were limited. Doctors and nurses who themselves had escaped from remote villages and received training did not want to take their families back into such 'primitive' conditions. Those from rich city backgrounds simply refused rural postings. HMG/N was supposed to provide the curative framework and NGOs, like INF, were meant to fit around this with community and other activities. Theoretically, a non-government organisation is flexible and able to carry out activities or meet needs that are outside the scope or budget of the government. In our case, however, we were restricted by our agreements to working alongside the government – a role I dubbed 'para-government' – and so we had limited room to adapt or innovate in our programmes.

In the very beginning (from 1952), NEB (later INF) worked according to the terms of a simple letter of permission given by the Ministry of Health, but from the mid-1970s onwards we were dependent on the signing of five-year agreements with the government both for the projects we were able to run and for our expatriate visas. Working with any government has its problems and in the run-up to each set of new agreements, we found it increasingly hard to second-guess the government of Nepal. One rather trivial, albeit frustrating, problem was the terminology. At first HMG/N called what they did 'projects' and so we ran (smaller) programmes for the government projects. Some years later they reversed these terms, so we ran (smaller) projects for the (bigger) government programmes. Happily, the acronyms looked the same and the work we did was much the same! We had a similar problem with the reporting systems: sometimes they wanted disease-based reports, and at other times location-based reports. It all caused a lot of hassle and extra paperwork but, happily, did not significantly affect the real work.

Over the years our community development itself developed. We started off by telling a community what they needed and then providing it for them. As they did not always see eye to eye with us bossy westerners, uptake was understandably not always what we had hoped for. This was the implementation approach – and happily, we learnt from it and moved to a facilitation strategy. This involved helping a community to see their own needs and then advising them how they could themselves change things, meet their own needs and access the necessary services to achieve development. This was the essential difference in approach between Burtibang and Myagdi.

Well before I became Medical Director, another new emphasis had entered the agenda of medical missions: training. Right from the beginning we had given training to our Shining Hospital nurses, lab and X-ray technicians and later to the TB and leprosy paramedics; and also retrained our nurses to run MCH clinics. Most of these ventures resulted only in in-service trained staff whose qualifications were not recognised by the government, but later we encouraged (and then released) those who had the ability and education to enrol in formal government training schemes. When two Midwifery Sister Tutors ventured into the domain of nurse training at the Pokhara campus, this aspect of our work became even more formalised. The surgeons taught their junior colleagues, but no sooner had a doctor been trained than s/he was transferred to another hospital. Of course, their expertise benefitted the whole country and patients in other regions, but it was frustrating for our INF secondees in WRH to have to keep starting again.

The inability of the government to extend its services through all the districts and provide comprehensive care in the remote areas left many communities without medical help. For a while INF secondees helped to develop district hospitals in Beni and Surkhet; and still today in those centres where INF has other programmes, some assistance is given at district level. But even this left vast numbers of people in isolated communities without access to secondary or tertiary care. This need, together with Ellen and Mike's deep Christian concern for such people, inspired them to start a Camps programme in 1993, and over the following years more than 100 surgical, gynaecological, dental or ear camps have been conducted, treating over 4,000 patients in many remote locations each year.

During the years I was based in our mission office in Pokhara, some weird things happened not only in our medical projects but also in our mission community...

In 1988 at our annual conference, we washed each other's feet. There's a biblical precedent for that although Jesus' words were probably never intended as a literal command. As a symbolic act, however, it was powerful. At the time I wrote:

> *The exercise was completed. The dirty water was thrown away. And we could forget the whole embarrassing incident – or could we? The symbolism had been enacted, a commitment made and the relationships altered for ever.*

In 1993 a rumour began to circulate that a wealthy Indian foundation (the Manipal Pai Group) planned to establish a medical college and hospital in Pokhara. In view of what the government had told INF in the mid-70s, this was strange – but turned out to be true. Subsequently, several other private hospitals and nursing homes were established in the town – all of them needed to cope with the burgeoning population.

In that same year the INF TB and leprosy projects began discussing a merger, which came to pass in 1995. I described it as an arranged marriage but not in the usual (Nepali) sense. Both partners already knew each other well. They had even been living together! Since 1973 INF had been involved in both TB and leprosy control in the Mid-Western Region and over the years the clinics in Ghorahi and Jumla, and later the Training Unit, had worked together quite closely. But now it became a formal union, arranged by the respective 'parent' projects.

One day back in 1994, in the centre of Pokhara town, when I was buying the sort of provisions that marked me as a non-tourist, I had an unexpected conversation. The shopkeeper asked me, "What organisation are you with?"

"INF," I replied, but by the puzzled look on his face, it clearly meant nothing to him. I tried again – "Shining Hospital" – and then suddenly he remembered.

He smiled and said, "I was born there." And soon we were friends, but it made me think. Times had changed – a lot.

Even after I had left the Medical Director role, INF programmes and activities continued to change – and still do. As a result of the hard work of the expatriate and Nepali project staff, both the prevalence and the incidence of TB began to fall. The work was therefore eventually handed over to GON, although TB remains as a potential threat in Nepal – and more so as HIV numbers increase. As leprosy was eliminated (as a community health risk), it became harder to get donors to give towards its final eradication or to support disabled people living with the ravages of leprosy in their bodies. On the other hand, other resources in the leprosy project – including staff skilled in dealing with patients with neurological damage – have more recently been deployed in caring for those with spinal cord injuries and amputees. This put the mission in a unique position to help many disabled as a result of the 2015 earthquake.

In 2002 I was invited to give the Rendle Short Lecture at the annual Christian Medical Fellowship Conference in the UK. From my experience of thirty years in Nepal I suggested that medical mission was changing and speculated that the new challenges of the emerging paradigm might be largely prophetic ones, addressing issues of injustice, inequality, corruption, immorality and idolatry at both personal and society levels. INF was already moving in the direction of patient advocacy, and even well before I left Nepal, INF (as it originally had been) had voted itself out of existence and begun again as INF/Worldwide, handing over most of its medical and development work to a national Christian NGO – INF/Nepal.

In the next fourteen years INF further extended its concern to pastoral and palliative care, more community help for people living with disability, and – in the wake of the earthquake – disaster aftercare and preparedness programmes. Green Pastures and the new ear hospital are being developed as centres of excellence. The Camps programme has been renamed Outreach, and Integral Mission is a high priority. New ideas are being mooted to achieve local financial stability. Young Nepali professionals have been inspired to live out their 'faith@work', strategic partnerships (mostly in training) have been encouraged and smaller local NGOs supported, while the Diaspora programmes (now concluded) helped to promote safe migration and advocacy for vulnerable migrants. As well as these mission changes, there were also two other major developments obvious even before I left Nepal: a progressive handover to national medical professional colleagues; and an increasing responsibility taken by Nepali churches for various aspects of medical work alongside their ongoing prayer ministry. Today the majority of the work of INF in Nepal is led by experienced Nepali Christians who see their work as service for God, in the same way as we expatriates did over the preceding years.

INF has always been essentially a medical mission, despite different emphases over the years. This was the role that God gave us right from the beginning when any overt church involvement was prohibited by law. It is humbling and significant that many Nepalis have become Christians, in part because of our help during their illnesses or accidents. Sometimes it was through the love and skill of the medics, sometimes it was through prayer by (Nepali) Christians, and perhaps most often through a combination of the two. One early patient in the Shining Hospital later became an evangelist with a ministry stretching all across Nepal and into diaspora countries. Hundreds (perhaps thousands) of leprosy patients found a new hope and a control for their dreadful disease; some even, complete cure. Churches have sprung up in almost all the communities reached through the INF programmes, usually as a result of the witness of Christian staff members – although sometimes many years later.

By the end of 1995, I had been in Nepal for twenty-five years, but this was far from being a record among my colleagues. Once again I was starting to wonder if the future might hold another change for me, and then came that memorable day in November...

I was *'oo bhayo'* or, for those not familiar with Nepali symptomatology, I was feeling like death warmed up. I had the flu but had struggled into the office under what was undoubtedly a misapprehension that the place would collapse if I had a day off. The phone rang. I picked it up and a voice on the other end enquired whether I would take a call from the British ambassador. Even with the flu clouding my judgement, I knew better than to say no. When the ambassador came on the line, he told me that I had been nominated for an OBE[132] in the upcoming New Year's Honours list. "What, me!" was the best response I could muster under the circumstances. Apparently, the Queen wanted to know if I was willing to accept it, but as it seemed churlish to even think of saying, "No, Your Majesty, I don't want a gong," I said, "Yes, thank you," and then had to keep it a secret until 1st January 1996.

I remember that New Year well. As a sort of reward to myself, I took a few days off and went to Narayanghat where Di and I celebrated in style in a posh hotel near the Chitwan National Park. I think Di was initially puzzled as to why I suddenly wanted a break – quite out of character; and I felt strange until I was eventually able to explain the real reason to her. But when I returned to Pokhara, the secret was out and everyone knew. After that there was another long wait until the investiture on 17th July 1996.

A chance to meet the Queen was definitely not to be missed, so I booked a flight to the UK in the summer of 1996. The plan was to combine the visit to Buckingham Palace with a holiday with Judy. It proved to be an expensive but exciting trip. Eventually, I found a suitable blue suit and a hat (not easy as my head was still small even if my ego had grown bigger), bag and shoes to go with it – and borrowed a pair of matching gloves, which in the event I never wore. The day of the investiture was even more harrowing. I couldn't remember whether we had been instructed to say 'mam' or 'marm' so I dared not say either. In fact, I said very little; I was struck dumb, an occurrence I deeply regret. I wish I had been able to have expressed some gratitude to all my colleagues in Nepal. After all, I was very conscious that this award reflected as much the contribution of INF as a whole to the development in Nepal as it did to my own efforts. As some of my friends reminded me, OBE really stands for Other Blokes' Efforts. I remembered, however, to curtsy and walk backwards and then it was all over, bar a relaxing meal on the way home with Terry and Mollie (my mother's cousin and his wife) and Alison (from INF) – and then the holiday. Once back in Nepal, I was brought back to earth with a bang when I heard the local children

[132] OBE – Officer of the Order of the British Empire.

calling out their rather rude greeting, *"Hello; guhu-ko dolo,"* which, literally translated, means, "Hello, lump of excreta." However, it did shed new light on St Paul's words in Phil. 3:7-8: "But whatever were gains to me, I now consider loss for the sake of Christ. Indeed, I consider everything a loss compared to the surpassing worth of knowing Christ Jesus my Lord, for whose sake I have lost all things. I consider them garbage [KJV – 'dung'], that I may gain Christ..."

I had begun my career in the early 70s as a humble (well, perhaps not particularly humble) medical officer in the Shining Hospital and then gained some training and experience in TB and leprosy as well as MCH clinic work. Along the way I had also developed some understanding of community health work in the villages. In the 80s I had been 'promoted' to specialist obstetrician in GZH/WRH and also acquired knowledge of hospital administration and supplies through my equipment work. Then I had been 'promoted' again to Health Projects/Medical Director during which time I set up a small medical library and coordinated all the INF medical projects. I had also been British Warden, liaising with the Embassy concerning safety and other issues. By the mid-90s, therefore, there was no other senior medical clinical or managerial role for me to be 'promoted' into. I had my gong, given for "services to the British community and health care in Nepal". I had reached my limit but was not convinced that it was therefore time for me to leave Nepal. So, in 1997 I began seriously to think about another very significant change of career.

As far as real trail-blazing in Nepal was concerned, however, I got into the act almost twenty years too late – fortunate, as I am not made of the same sterling stuff that pioneers are made of. Only very infrequently (once) did I have to deal with a snake in my bedroom and I only lived in a mud hut for five years, and even then it was not one I built myself. Nor have I ever dug a pit latrine. There have been, however, places I visited that sensibly no one else from our mission had ever been to. One was the remote village where the only crop they grew was hashish, but even then an American anthropologist had got there before me. And the other was the place where I sustained 500 flea bites. Sadly, this record never got into the Guinness Book of Records as official authentication would have required irritating, itchy and insufferable repetition. I have been bitten by a dog but as the brute had already bitten the rest of the village first, you couldn't call my experience original. Hardly ground-breaking but innovative in its own way is the fact that I'm the only one who ever completed part of my language exam on a bus.

In the early days just about the only Western foods you could buy in Pokhara bazaar were peanut butter, coffee and honey, which was lucky as a wimp like me would never have survived on tea and home-made marmalade. Sixty plus years ago, when the real pioneers first walked in to Pokhara, there were virtually no roads in the whole country. By the time I arrived, roads were also arriving and soon came night buses too, but those who used them were not pioneers, they were martyrs.

I thought (mistakenly, as it turned out) that I was cut out for village medicine. I could walk fast but was not nearly adaptable enough to last. As far as I am aware, I also became the first and only member of our mission to be assaulted while walking the trail to Baglung. I'd left my senior colleague safe in the overnight 'hotel' and generously accompanied a local man to see and advise on the diagnosis and treatment of an elderly relative. All went well until on the way back we reached the barren bit of path across an old landslide. Suddenly, the guy grabbed me and his intentions were all too clear and appalling. I struggled, and a combination of superior nutrition and better protection as I cried out, "Help! Jesus, help me," won the day. I chucked the man's *chappals* down the hillside and ran as fast as I could back to my colleague.

Sometime later, in Ghorahi, I had another chance to prove my character in a village. Again, I failed miserably; however hard I tried to help with the cooking, I was unable to keep the wood fire alight by judicious blowing through a bit of hollow bamboo. I gave up and let Betty N do the cooking while I gained a reputation instead for immaculate colour-coded leprosy records.

Many years later, however, I became an expert in neo-pioneer-ism. The first time was when I brought an Amstrad PCW into Nepal. Without a regular electricity supply, that was surely a cutting-edge act of faith equal to those of the bygone pioneers.

In 1987 my mother was diagnosed with terminal cancer of the oesophagus and I spent an extended period of time in the UK looking after her. When she died I completed my normal home leave, during which I attended a Walk Thru the Bible seminar in a nearby church. This light-hearted and yet accurate and interactive teaching so impressed me that I obtained permission to translate the material into Nepali. It seemed absolutely ideal for a semi-literate church membership – and for their leaders. And so I became a 'pioneer' once again. I called it Bible Yatra[133]. Teaching opportunities gradually expanded and I was keen to see the programme pass into Nepali hands. If it was something that was blessing people then it needed to have a secure indigenous future. And if this was God's plan too, he would surely fix it for me.

By 1997 I had been INF Medical Director for some years, but felt convinced the mission needed a fresh approach I was unable to give. After much prayer and consultation, I resigned and explored the option of staying on in Nepal with a campus visa to study Nepali. This was unconventional pioneering that no one in the mission had ever attempted before. And I did it because there was a challenge running around in my head: *move outside the security of a mission visa.* There was also a strange passage of scripture that seemed to back it up. Numbers 32 and Joshua 22 tell of the two-and-a-half Israelite tribes who chose to settle on the east of the Jordan. I had always felt that these people had missed God's best for them by not crossing the Jordan. However, this time a new thought struck me: that they were actually pioneers in a kingdom that would later expand way beyond where they settled; by the time of David, their tribal lands were well within the borders of Israel.

At the time, with my medical qualifications and experience in Nepal, an INF visa was pretty well assured; a campus one was dicey – especially as I already spoke fluent Nepali! I moved; I got the visa. I started studying and I began to develop Bible Yatra – and then INF visas became insecure. Already in 1998 HMG/N unaccountably clamped down on 'extra-curricular' activities, with huge delays in granting INF visa extensions, and in 1999 some INF expatriates were expelled. Then in 2003 all my former colleagues who had been in Nepal for more than ten years were required to leave – but with my new visa under a different ministry, incredibly, I could stay. That proved the challenge must have been from God. It also proved that obedience (like honesty) is the best policy. For thirteen years I survived on study, research and business visas until I had

---

[133] See footnote 101 in Chapter 18. See also Chapter 24.

fully handed over Bible Yatra and it was officially registered as a Nepali NGO, BaYaN[134]. God fixed it!

As I approached 65 I didn't retire but had one last bash at becoming a pioneer – two really. Before my brain gave up completely, I was studying for my second degree, some forty years after the first, and had been visiting the UK for a summer course. On the way back to Nepal, Qatar Airlines lost my luggage (fortunately only clothes and sausages, not my notes and books) and then, in place of any reasonable compensation, offered me an extra baggage allowance when I next booked with them – as if I would ever book with them again. But I did, because they were the cheapest and I had another course the following year. I didn't need excess baggage but was definitely going to claim it – but what for? Out of the blue, inspiration struck, surely of divine origin. I could take Bible Yatra books to Doha. I could arrange a seminar in Doha. Brilliant. And so began a ministry of visiting Nepalis in the diaspora, mainly in the Middle East and Malaysia.[135] No one had done that before either.

---

[134] BaYaN – Bible Yatra Nepal (also written BYN); see Chapter 24.
[135] See Chapter 25.

22

The BBC

Bishwa Bhasha Campus and other studies

(Late 1990s and early 2000s)

Bishwa Bhasha Campus – building and student group.

YOU PROBABLY THINK YOU KNOW what the BBC is, so this may surprise you. While working in Nepal I discovered that the acronym BBC means three things. The first is, of course, the British Broadcasting Corporation. The BBC world service radio programmes (no television when I went to Nepal) are a lifeline to world news for many expatriates. The second was a small radio/electrical shop in Pokhara bazaar called BBC Radio. When I first discovered it, the name really puzzled me – until I found out that the proprietor was a man called BB Chhetri. And the third was Bishwa Bhasha Campus (aka Campus of International Languages) where I studied Nepali and Sanskrit and later researched Nepali Proverbs, between 1998 and 2008.

When I left Nepal for home leave at the end of 1997, I planned to return in mid-1998 and enrol in BBC in Kathmandu, thereby improving my Nepali at the same time as obtaining a student visa. In my spare time

I intended to continue my theological studies and teach Bible Yatra, gradually building up relationships with more Bible Schools in Kathmandu.[136] However...

It was with a significant degree of fear and trepidation that in 1998 I obeyed what I believed God was saying to me about moving outside the security of an INF visa. My friend Di was already studying at BBC, with the vision of challenging the Nepali church to undertake outreach to deaf Nepalis through befriending them, and by learning and using sign language. Happily, she did not need to sing to achieve this and her deaf friends wouldn't have minded if she did! She was the one who also challenged me to try to get a student visa. I decided to apply for the Nepali course and study for as many years as I could while using my spare time to establish Bible Yatra and maybe develop other teaching ministries too, although I was also genuinely interested in refining my own Nepali speaking and writing. I had, of course, an extensive medical vocabulary and a pretty good biblical one, and my grammar was reasonable, but there was plenty of room for improvement and for learning and understanding more Nepali literature, history and culture.

Enrolling at campus was rather like registering a motorbike[137] as it entailed numerous trips to the bank and campus offices. You couldn't enrol without paying the fees but on the other hand, you couldn't pay the fees without a bank account. You couldn't open a bank account without a visa but to get a visa you needed to be enrolled in campus. In the end I achieved the impossible and turned up for class on the first day of the semester, which for a while I thought would also be my last. I was forced to admit that I did already know some Nepali, but then, so did several other students. We were all accepted anyway, probably because the campus depended on our fees, which were around ten times the level that Nepali students were required to contribute!

Moving to Kathmandu was challenging in other ways too. Living in 'the big smoke' meant exchanging one house in the middle of a quagmire for another at the end of muddy lane. It was also significantly more expensive than living in Pokhara and on top of that, I had to pay my campus and student visa fees myself, whereas visas in INF had been

---

[136] See Chapter 24.
[137] See Chapter 15.

gratis, which reminds me... Did you ever hear the story of an elderly lady who faithfully supported a missionary (in some tropical county, not Nepal) from her pension? After receiving a letter describing how they ate fresh pineapple (in her eyes a real luxury), she promptly stopped her support! I'm not sure whether this story is true or apocryphal, but just so you understand, fresh mangoes and pineapples were a couple of the culturally affordable blessings of doing God's work in Nepal. As God had told me to move, he was the one who provided in a variety of different ways, including gifts, over the next few years.

The first year of Nepali study was easy – I could do the work standing on my head. Two hours daily in class and five minutes for the homework and the rest of the day was mine to teach and develop Bible Yatra. Second year was still not hard – it did begin to stretch my brain cells a little, but I still had plenty of time to work on Bible Yatra. The only slight problem was that because we were required to attend 80% of classes, it meant (if I wanted to continue getting a visa) that I could not travel outside Kathmandu during term time. Some students stopped attending once they had a visa but campus authorities soon got wise to this and reacted by giving us visas for only six months at a time – even just three months one year. In contrast I determined to study with integrity as well as get on with the Bible Yatra work, and as a result I became great friends with my professor, Dr Balaram Aryal. This led to my helping him with corrections to the English (and even occasionally the Nepali!) of the Nepali language coursebooks he was writing. Third year really stretched my aging grey matter but was very informative as we studied Nepali poets and other authors. I even managed to write a few short poems myself. One was about modern Kathmandu – its tourists, poor people and political struggles with the Maoists – written in the same style as the ancient 'Kantipur' (or Kathmandu) penned by the famous Bhanubhakta Acharya. More usually I just wrote up my notes in Nepali – to practise writing fluent prose (very useful while I was writing the Bible Yatra book), but sometimes I also created short stories. The most memorable was a

Dr Aryal.

seasonable one about Four Wise Men. It proved to be an oblique, but acceptable, way to share my faith and the real meaning of Christmas. We also studied Nepali History, which explains why I know far more about that than British history. At the time I could reel off all the Shah kings in chronological order, and probably – with a little judicious revision – still could as there haven't been many new ones since! Later Dr Aryal and I co-authored a small book on the history of Nepal in maps. I took the information from his lecture notes and then did most of the computer work – typing, layout and graphics. In case you're wondering, it was in English – but sadly is now out of date and out of print, as political events have overtaken us. The other main subject at campus was Nepali Culture, covering all the main ethnic groups and their different customs. I acquired a deeper understanding of Hindu culture and philosophy. I learnt a lot and discovered many customs I had never heard of before. I also discovered with horror that I had probably made many more cultural bloomers than I had ever realised. Every year I topped the campus exam lists but that was only because the competition was not great: some students didn't bother; others had not had the same thirty-year start on the language that I had had!

After three years and three proficiency certificates in Nepali, I was still a long way from handing over Bible Yatra, so I enrolled in Basic Sanskrit for a year. There were only two of us in the class and one of them dropped out before the end of the year; it was not me. Again I came top! Sanskrit is a very interesting, and complicated, language. It has 3 genders, 3 numbers, 8 cases and umpteen tenses – and everything has to agree with everything else. And, as if that were not enough, classical Sanskrit stringsallitswordstogether without any spaces. The only bit that was relatively easy was the vocabulary: as Nepali is derived from it, I could guess the meaning of a large percentage of the words. All through this time I had been working on the Bible Yatra Handbook – a written form of the seminars. I completed it at the end of that academic year along with Sanskrit and heaved two very big sighs of relief.

I had already been studying other subjects by extension. In 1994 I completed a short correspondence course on 'Starting to Write' with the Open College of the Arts. I was given a Grade 'C', and if you have struggled to read this far, you may be feeling that that was overly generous.

In the mid-1990s I had also enrolled in the Open Theological College (OTC) and took all my first year courses from St John's, Nottingham as a corresponding student. Contrary to advice and the expectation of the college, I skipped Old Testament and New Testament Introduction and chose instead OT Prophecy and NT Greek (something I had always wanted to study). I really enjoyed all the topics (especially Creeds and Ethics) and although the assignments were relatively easy, it took me several years to complete all six modules as I was coincidentally holding down two INF posts. In fact, it took three years for the first three modules (while I was in Nepal) but just three months for the final three (when I was on home leave in the UK). I completed 'first year' in 1998 and returned to Nepal to study Nepali and continue my theological studies with OTC second year.

I found that there was a huge jump in standard between the first and second year theology courses. The files were about five times bigger than those in first year and the assignments invariably took me at least twice as long as the recommended times – and no one has ever called me slow! But I persevered and finished second year in 2002 with a Diploma of Higher Education in Theology. By that time I had decided that studying 'Westernised' theology to degree level was not relevant to my ministry in Nepal. The last thing the Nepali church needed was a mediocre expatriate theologian – but just maybe a missiologist could be useful?

By 2003 the Bible Yatra handbook was completed and I had trained and mentored one Nepali teacher but there was still a way to go before Bible Yatra would be able to stand on its own two Nepali feet. I was also receiving more invitations to teach in Bible Colleges. My time in Nepal was clearly not yet over, but I had absolutely no desire to return to BBC and study tonal Tibetan, or Newari, and second year Sanskrit was not even an option to be considered! The answer was to engage in some research. I chose Nepali Proverbs, probably under a misapprehension that it would not be too demanding. I was – after some not particularly difficult negotiation – granted a three-year research visa under BBC as that was the simplest way to do it, even though I knew it would not lead to any official academic recognition. That hardly matters as most people seem to think I got a Ph.D. for it anyway – even if I didn't. For the amount of labour I put in, I certainly deserved one.

By early 2005 I had read 30 books and accumulated 4,500 proverbs which I had entered into a grid on the computer. That made me feel good, as though I was nearly 'home and dry', but in fact it was only about half the estimated total I would ultimately collect. I plodded on – between BYN seminars and M.A. assignments – and when 2007 arrived I thought the thesis might be nearing completion, but again I had miscalculated badly. One big problem was that so many proverbs were duplicated. The same proverbs appeared but with their clauses in reverse order. Synonyms were ubiquitous. Spellings were atrocious – either wrong or just old-fashioned. Sorting all this out took months – years, in fact. In early 2008, while I was on my own in Malaysia and Thailand, I was able to get a lot of it done, but I was still at it when in Pattaya a year later. In between, back in Kathmandu, and until I ran out of petrol (during a shortage), I was commuting each evening up the hill to the little town of Kirtipur where KB Basnet, one of my former M.Div. students, spent hours helping me understand some of the more colloquial proverbs and so preventing me writing something very stupid. Finally the write-up was completed, although I still had to check the spelling, vocabulary and meanings prior to extracting examples to illustrate the thesis, and work out how to insert spreadsheet pages of examples into the basic word-processed document (probably the most difficult part of it all for an oldie like me). Then I had to print out several copies, each of 700 pages – mostly in the middle of the night when there was some *bijuli.* Don't ask me how I did it, but I did, and then in mid-2009 it was finished and submitted.

Then in March 2010, to my great surprise, as part of the Great [Nepali] Poet [Laxmi Prasad] Devkota Centenary Celebration, I was given an award for my "continuous dedication to promoting Nepali literature and ... tireless efforts in taking Nepali language to the international arena". I'm not sure I would describe my proverbs research as either continuous or tireless, but it was a great honour and another chance to wear my best sari.

As one is supposed to do, I gleaned quite a bit of wisdom from those Nepali proverbs. "Easy to say, difficult to do," sums up my whole five-year project, but, "The mouth that really wants to eat will not be stopped by the moustache," explains why I persevered. Sometimes I felt I was going nowhere fast – rather like the Israelites when they first left Egypt and were trapped between the Egyptian army and the Red Sea; the Nepali equivalent being "a stream in front and a landslide behind". Perhaps I should have given it all more careful thought before I started, on the grounds that it is always good to "prepare yourself for a tiger hunt when you go after a jackal". However, progress did come – slowly – and "drop by drop the pot [was] filled; letter by letter some knowledge [was] acquired". One proverb declares that "an idler's lips are full of proverbs", but idleness was the last adjective you would have used about me during those years!

Many proverbs are internationally or interculturally understandable, but I learnt (the hard way) never to depend on this; it could lead to catastrophic mistakes. "What takes a year for a man to do, takes a woman just a moment," was, for a while, my favourite proverb until I discovered that in the Nepali context it had a distinctly unsavoury sexual connotation. "One spit dries up; one hundred make a river," would be a good slogan for an anti-TB campaign, although, "The wealth of the poor are their children," would not work quite the same in a family-planning programme. "One ear, two ears and the wide field" could refer to constructive health education or destructive gossip. "It's easier to swallow chewed food," is not the most aesthetic description of the way we simplified the Bible story in BYN, but a fairly accurate one. I had long discovered that "one hand cannot clap" and that I needed Nepali colleagues in Bible Yatra, but it was also not so long before I also discovered that "the penknife is sharper than the *khukuri*[138]" as the team were teaching more effectively than I ever had.

Nepali religious proverbs almost all refer to Hindu deities, festivals, places and beliefs, but a few contain wisdom that is equally applicable to Christians: "If God is on the right hand, then who can do anything against me?" seems to say much the same as Rom. 8:31[139], and, "Contentment is great happiness," is similar to 1 Tim. 6:6[140]. "If God gives, then oil will come when you grind sand," sounds a bit like Mark 10:27b, "...all things are possible with God", but I think it's usually interpreted far more cynically. "He who worships God, belongs to God,"

[138] Khukuri – Nepali fighting knife or sword.
[139] Rom. 8:31b – "If God is for us, who can be against us?"
[140] 1 Tim. 6:6 – "But godliness with contentment is great gain."

sounds good but is it really the right way round? I think in my case I worship God because he has loved me and made me his own. "You reap what you sow," is identical to the English biblical proverb from Gal. 6:7 and "not seeing the buffalo walking on his own back but seeing the lice walking on another's back" is an even more graphic version of the speck and the plank from Luke 6:41.

There are dozens – hundreds, if not thousands – of Nepali proverbs that are philosophical and moralistic and many echo the sentiments of English proverbs and even Biblical teaching. A lot of them use the symbolism of wildlife – both flora and fauna – and their meanings are easily guessed: "It's not the tiger in the forest but the one in the mind that eats up a man;" "When the bulls fight, the calves get trampled on" (think child abuse); and, "The elephant got through but its tail got stuck," which sounds suspiciously like the camel that got stuck trying to go through the eye of the needle, although it's not quite the same and is more often used as a riddle about a needle and thread. I love the picture of humility portrayed in, "When the bamboo grows, it bends down," as much as I love the parabolic beauty of wild bamboo clumps, and then, "When rice grows, it bends; when millet grows, it stands upright," expands that idea to mock the negative arrogance of others. Such uppityness is also amusingly captured in, "If you're a queen and I'm a queen, who will fetch the water from the spring?" "The fragrance of a flower spreads in the neighbourhood; the essence of a man reaches beyond the hills," reminds me of 2 Cor. 2:14-16[141]. Others are more literal and some have English equivalents: "As long as there's life, there's hope;" "Without suffering, wisdom does not come;" "Righteousness remains; sin shouts from the housetop;" "Putting salt and vinegar on a cut wound;" "Gold is tested by fire;" "Good work; good wages;" and, "What is bitter at first but sweet later is good." Others are metaphorical: "An empty vessel makes the most noise," and, "Give him a finger and he will swallow your fist."

All those are fairly self-explanatory, but without some knowledge of Hinduism you may remain puzzled about the meaning of others. "To go

[141] 2 Cor. 2:14-16 – "But thanks be to God, who ... uses us to spread the aroma of the knowledge of him everywhere. For we are to God the pleasing aroma of Christ..."

to Pashupati (a big Hindu shrine in Kathmandu) and sell dried fishes" means you can take advantage of a pilgrimage to do some business at the same time, or as in English, "kill two birds with one stone". The man referred to in, "All night he read the Ramayana; in the morning, he asked whose wife is Seeta," is clearly an extreme example of, "The sorrow felt at a funeral and the wisdom of a sermon do not last long," for the Ramayana is a popular and (usually) well-known Hindu epic about Seeta and her husband Ram. You can guess the meaning of, "Rubbing the donkey and washing it with the water of the Ganges will not make a donkey into a cow," and, "The tiger will not stop killing the cow because it heard the [Bhagavad] Gita (one of the Hindu scriptures)," but both make even more sense once you are aware that the cow is a sacred animal in Hinduism. So, too, "The heavenly cow, although she is Laxmi (one of the Hindu goddesses), is just the wife of the bull," which seems to sum up the traditional patriarchy and derogatory attitude to women. Quite a few proverbs, like, "Let it be late but let it be a son," I found had this same sort of gender bias towards men. A lot of the older ones were downright vulgar and I cannot resist the temptation to include just one example for your edification – "The shit is bigger than the baby." – as it rather aptly describes some of the infants I used to treat with D & V.

Once you grasp the importance and hierarchy of caste (although it is now officially outlawed) in Nepali culture you may begin to understand that "to give up caste for a bowl of cheap *gundruk* (dried sour vegetables)" is rather like "selling your birthright for a mess of pottage (lentil stew)" as Esau reputedly did in Genesis 25. "A Chhetri (warrior caste) is spoiled by luxurious living; a Newar (business caste) is spoiled by feasting," reflects the quirks or characteristics of some of the different caste groups. So, too, "A naïve (i.e. simple and trusting) Magar (one of the hill tribes), what he says, that he does," and, "A Sarki's (a low-caste leather-worker) god is not worshipped; it (the cow) is shooed away." Traditional high caste wisdom is that "there is no caste above the Brahmin (priestly caste); no body above the *tupi* (tuft of hair on a Hindu man's head)," but I also discovered, "Every living being is a Sarki (tanner) because everyone has a skin; when the skin has gone, in the end all are one," which shows a far greater depth of understanding of the equality of human nature.

Likewise, if you know your history and are aware that King Ram Shah (17th century Gorkha king and predecessor of Prithvi Narayan) was renowned for his righteousness and justice, and that Banares was famous for its Hindu scholarship, "If justice is lost, go to Gorkha; if learning is lost, go to Banares," makes complete sense. Sadly, the more recent history of Nepal has been far less commendable: "Like king, like subjects" reminds us that Nepal's problems were not all on the side of the (now ex) Royal family; "yesterday a king, today a man among men" describes exactly the fate meted out to ex-King Gyanendra between 2006 and 2008; and "ruined king, ruined court" aptly depicts the state of politics following the fall of the monarchy. Since the mid-90s and even before, ordinary people have complained, saying, "Leaving the nose, it goes to the ear; leaving the ear, it goes to the nose" (if it's not one thing [wrong], then it's another). Everyone in Nepal knows that "you cannot get *ghiu* out with a straight finger", meaning that you can only get things done through bribery or corruption. They also know that all too often "the headman of the village shits on the path" (sorry, that's another vulgar one but does rather nicely describe the not-so-nice behaviour of rather too many officials). Other politicians or leaders have been caught out "saying Ram, Ram (one of the Hindu gods) in the mouth, a dagger in the pocket", but I don't need to explain what that means.

If you had spent as many years in Pokhara as I did, you will know that "to speak of Phewa Lake in front of a Pokhara person" is the local equivalent of "taking coals to Newcastle" or "teaching your grandmother to suck eggs". "No Mahabharat (Hindu epic story) without Arjun (hero of the epic)" means the same to Nepalis as, "There is no smoke without fire," does to us. "What's the use of an education when one must plough to earn one's rice?" must have been exclaimed by many in the past, but these days there are many Nepali migrants from remote hill villages for whom "to tell about Kuwait, to understand about the *Dhiki* (village husking and grinding machine)" has literally come true as they now understand both local (national) and international issues as never before.

As many as there are varieties of family relationships, so there are huge numbers of family proverbs. One of my favourites is, "A one-eyed uncle is better than no uncle." "Parents always think about their children; children only think about stones and logs," may sound out of date but substitute 'getting stoned' and 'logging on' for the original words and you could be describing some family problems today. The traditional Nepali family had three generations living together, often with more than one wife per husband, and a unique – and generally not very harmonious – relationship between mother-in-law and daughter(s)-in-law. If you bear that in mind, "One wife is ace, two are trouble, three cause vomiting," makes perfect sense. So, too, "Sometimes it is the turn of the mother-in-law; sometimes that of the daughter-in-law," and, "Everyone thinks his own children and someone else's wife are pretty." Big families the world over have squabbles, so sometimes literally, "When brothers quarrel, the villagers rob them." Nepal has also struck the generation gap: "Although the old man has 12 sons and 13 grandsons, yet his sack is on his own shoulder."

Some proverbs uncannily reminded me of my personal experiences on trek or with some of Nepal's wildlife; for example, "All the day – no rupees, all the night – only fleas," and, "A gnat can make an elephant cry" (I assume in much the same way that mosquitoes drive me mad). From bitter (or should I say *biter*) experience, it is simply not always true that "a barking dog does not bite", but certainly, "The dog's tail does not become straight even if kept in a pipe for twelve years" (and I'll leave you to guess what that means). When walking in the hills, "pulling a creeper may [well] precipitate a landslide", and sometimes "the stream is crossed, the stick is forgotten", but except in those rare instances in Exodus and Joshua, "a flowing river does not turn back".

Proverbs (sad to say) are starting to disappear because as "the old man dies, the language changes" but there are some new ones emerging. The traditional, "Warm yourself by a log fire; listen to the words of an old man," has morphed into, "Warm yourself by a heater; listen to the words of a minister;" while, "Consider your throat before you swallow a bone," has become, "Consider your neck before you buy a high-neck [jumper]."

Finally, "The one who cannot dance says the stage is crooked," and, "The one who cannot write says the pen is crooked," while I just blame my computer for all the errors in this book. Nevertheless, "What happens in early days makes a story for later years," so I hope you are enjoying this one.

Fully convinced that "rest is rust", while in the UK on home assignment in 2004 I looked into the possibility of studying for an M.A. in Mission. At that time most colleges were only offering a course over a full academic year, which would have meant being out of Nepal for at least a year. That was just not possible for three reasons: Bible Yatra was not yet ready for me to leave them on their own for that long; I didn't wish to ask INF for leave of absence; and I had no desire to alter the happy relationship I had with the British tax office. Then I discovered that Redcliffe was starting a new blended course: two three-week summer schools over two years and all the rest of the work done by email/extension. This seemed to provide the best of both worlds: meeting with faculty and fellow students at the summer schools and the chance to study but stay in Nepal, developing BYN, and not paying any taxes to the British government. I applied for the first year of this new course and was accepted for the summer of 2005. The clinching pull towards Redcliffe was one of their module options – The Use of Metaphor and Narrative in Christian Mission – which seemed a perfect fit with my interest in the genre of proverbs.

In May that year I discovered that I needed to read two huge books on post-colonialism and globalisation before attending the first summer school. Acquiring them in Nepal was the first challenge; reading them the second. They almost (but not quite) put me off. I don't think I knew much more about globalisation after wading through them than before I started, and so I arrived in Gloucester not sure that I was really prepared. I need not have worried; my three fellow students were equally bemused. In retrospect, however, of all the modules I studied, this was probably the most useful as it gave a solid academic background and understanding to my developing Diaspora ministry and writing.

Two summers and four modules later, when I got back from my prolonged visit to Malaysia in early 2008, I heard that Brent had almost finished his dissertation. That galvanized me into action as I was not about to be outdone by him. I had already scribbled over seventeen thousand words in my draft write-up, but then immediately I set in motion the email survey (which I'd kept putting off) and shortly received more than a hundred responses, mostly from friends and contacts in Asia, Europe and Africa. How was I then – short of a minor miracle – to record the findings of the survey in the remaining thousand words? Somehow I did it; computers are so helpful when it comes to deleting, cutting, pasting and rearranging paragraphs! I had proved that traditional proverbs can be a very useful method of Christian communication for pre-evangelism, preaching and teaching, and also for counselling.

In 2008 I graduated from the University of Gloucestershire gaining an M.A. with Distinction in Global Issues in Contemporary Mission. To my surprise I found that younger people apparently now consider it cool not to bother going to a graduation ceremony, but I couldn't resist the temptation to visit the UK and receive a second degree approximately forty years after my first – an extravagant but fun decision. This bit of paper then automatically qualified me to do some teaching at a higher level than most of the BYN seminars so I began to discuss other possibilities, including mentoring some Nepali students doing a semi-extension Master's course in Leadership. I also toyed with the idea of myself doing a Ph.D. – investigating the use of Nepali proverbs in Christian communication by linking up my secular proverbs study and my M.A. work in order to leave something of value for the Nepali church. To date this has not happened because I was soon too busy with Nepali diaspora activities – or maybe because I was just too lazy to fit it in.

Perhaps I was also too ambitious (or conscientious) or perhaps it was just because I spent rather a lot of time with Bible Yatra that the Nepali proverbs research had been far from complete at the end of the initial three years. Bible Yatra was a lot nearer to handover but that too required more time. When my Nepali tutor pointedly remarked that my three years' research time had expired, I began to get worried as it seemed unlikely I would receive a research visa extension. What to do? Then, in a strange 'coincidence', a friend offered me the chance of investment in his business just at the time when I did not know how to proceed. Within a couple of weeks, I had a business visa for a year and it cost a lot less than the research one – and no campus fees to cough up either! I was later able to renew it once, and so I was provided in a miraculous way with the extra couple of years I needed to finish both projects.

In 2009 I finally handed in my proverbs thesis to Tribhuvan University in Kathmandu and set about revamping it into a book – which was eventually published in 2010 as *Sitting in my House; Dreaming of Nepal.* Even before that not-very-successful writing course in 1994, I had cherished an ambition to become a published author. I first succeeded in

2003 by self-publishing *Bible Yatra, Maps of Nepal* (with Dr. Aryal) and *Daughters of the Millennium,* the latter being a piece of 'faction' produced as a gift for my prayer supporters. The autobiographical bits were fact and the rest – about life for Nepali ladies – fiction, but based on fact. In 2005 I started to think about writing up some of the thrilling testimonies of Nepali believers – especially the ladies'. I'm sorry to say that never got done; in this case I'm sure it was laziness – and perhaps also disobedience.

The English version of the BYN handbook, *Bible Journey,* came out in 2012, and that same year, having by then experience of teaching in several colleges, I published five books in simple English for Nepali Bible College students. The first was *Introduction to Study Skills & Research Methods,* which was the result of trying – with difficulty – to teach this subject to students with minimal relevant background understanding and little clue about research, using libraries or academic writing. The other four were a set of *Introduction to the Bible – Vol. 1 Bible Survey, Vol. 2 Bible Structure, Vol. 3 Bible Formation and Vol. 4 Bible History, Geography, Customs & Culture.* Volume 1 was the basic material from *Bible Journey,* while most of the additions from the original were included in the other three volumes along with a lot of new material, which I had tried to simplify and summarise for students overwhelmed by English theological texts. Between ten and twenty colleges, I discovered, were insisting that their students learnt in English, although in my not particularly humble opinion, this was making them bite off more than many of them could chew, especially in their first year. For a while I had help with the promotion and distribution of these texts, but in the end I didn't stay long enough in Nepal to discover how useful they were proving.

Originally, I had hoped to write further books in the series; it never happened, but in 2011 while I was attending the HIMGlo Summit in Hong Kong, Mr RC Timothy of EKTA Books suggested that I might write about Nepali migrants. *The Nepali Diaspora: Migrants, Ministry and Mission* took longer than anticipated but was eventually published in 2014 by EKTA, already out of date when it rolled off the printing press – such was the speed of development in the Nepali diaspora.

Today I am still writing, but a post on Facebook by Heike, my Diaspora colleague, in 2015 confirmed that I had achieved my aim to become a published author. She walked into the EKTA bookshop and asked, "Where can I find Val Inchley's book?" to which the assistant answered, without even batting an eyelid, "Which one?" In the Bible, in Ecclesiastes 12:12, it says, "Of making many books there is no end, and much study wearies the body," a text that could legitimately summarise this chapter!

23

Jai Masih

The Nepali church

Ramghat Church, Pokhara (in the 1970s).

IN 1970 WHEN I ARRIVED, almost twenty years after the first church had been founded, there were perhaps 1,000 Christians in Nepal. No one knows for sure as no records were kept. In 1983 I quoted figures of 150 churches and 15,000 believers; in 1992, more than 70,000 baptised Christians attending more than 500 churches; and by 2002, maybe 400,000. Today there are almost certainly over a million, although some claim only around 2% of a total population of around 29 million. Again, no one knows for sure as not all churches keep records and the official census figures could be biased. This expansion (initially of about 40% per year) indicates one of the fastest growing churches in the world and is a modern mission miracle.

Some would date the Christian history of Nepal only from the middle of the 20th century, but this discounts the early efforts of Capuchin monks, ignores the outreach to Nepalis living in India and – most importantly – overlooks the volume of longstanding prayer for Nepal from even farther afield. God's purposes were much wider reaching. In fact, the first Roman Catholic missionaries entered the country at the very beginning of the 18th century. They were allowed to teach, preach, heal and establish a small church. Sadly, some sixty years later, when King Prithvi Narayan Shah became ruler of an expanding Nepali nation, all these believers were exiled to Bettiah in India and never allowed to return. For the next two centuries, there were no known Christians living in Nepal, although once or twice some tried to enter the country and were repelled. Among them were Sadhu Sundar Singh (who may have been martyred in Nepal) and the family of Dr Rajendra Rongong, who himself later settled in Nepal where he became an academic and church leader.

The founder of INF, Dr Lily (Pat) O'Hanlon, had received a very special Bible verse from God – it could hardly have been more specific:

> *...But the land wither ye go to possess is a land of hills and valleys, and drinketh water of the rain of heaven: A land which the LORD thy God careth for: The eyes of the LORD thy God are always upon it, from the beginning of the year to the end of the year.*[142]

For around seventeen years Pat and a growing number of colleagues had worked in Nautanwa, on the Indian side of the western part of the southern border of Nepal (and in Assam), but they were not the only ones in the Nepal Border Fellowship waiting – and praying – for the country to open up. There were others, both expatriates and ethnic Nepalis; in the east, in Darjeeling, Kalimpong and Sikkim; in the south; and in the west; all of them longing to enter Nepal and share the Good News of Jesus. At last, after the 1950/51 Revolution, God's promise was fulfilled as small groups, mostly of medics, were allowed to start work in Pokhara, Kathmandu, Tansen and later Amp Pipal, Okhaldunga and Dandeldhura. With Nepal only just beginning to emerge from feudalism,

---

142 Deut. 11:11-12 (KJV) – emphasis mine.

this was a special kind of pioneering mission. It was unique in another way too. All those who participated in the two major mission advances, having experienced some of its problems in India, determined not to introduce denominationalism. Even the strict no-proselytizing rule imposed on foreigners was something of a blessing in disguise as it meant that the Nepali church was independent and self-propagating right from the very beginning. That was a tremendous strength, although the flip side, that many of the early leaders were quite uneducated, meant that Bible and theological knowledge developed more slowly than they might otherwise have done.

To date, the Nepali church has been rather like the New Testament Church – in several ways. The early Christian believers were passionate and many experienced persecution. So, too, the first Nepali Christians. By the end of the New Testament, the oldest church – in Jerusalem – was only 60 years old; the first modern Nepali church turned 60 only in 2012. The way God has used political events to allow church development in Nepal also reminds me of the way he used various powers – like the Assyrians, Babylonians, Persians, Greeks and Romans – to further his plans in the Old Testament and Inter-Testamental periods.

The first Revolution (1950/1) allowed Christians to enter Nepal, but there were penalties for those who evangelised or converted. One year's imprisonment was the penalty for converting to Christianity – usually interpreted as being baptised. A six-year sentence was decreed for those who "caused someone else to convert". To my knowledge only one pastor actually spent as much as four-and-a-half years in prison, although over the years many were jailed for shorter periods. It was costly to convert; the early Nepali Christians were courageous and strong in their faith. Churches were few and small, and 'sort of' underground, but their members deeply committed. The expatriate missionaries were prohibited from proselytising which restricted our practical input – but not our prayers. The church grew.

In 1960 the Nepal Christian Fellowship (NCF) had been formed – to provide links between churches scattered across the country. At that time all churches were essentially independent, but NCF organised conferences and trainings, and kept leaders in touch with each other. Now known as the National Churches Fellowship of Nepal, it has remained the largest grouping of churches, although there are now several others. In 1996 another organisation, the Nepal Christian Society (NCS), was formed. This linked together most of the main Christian groups (they prefer not to be called 'denominations') in order to be able to present a united voice on Christian matters before the government. It has continued to do this over the subsequent years.

1990 was the year of the second Revolution in Nepal. In a Christmas 1989 internal prayer bulletin, one of our Nepali secretaries had prophetically(?) but incorrectly typed "a light for revolution to the Gentiles..." Suddenly the country changed from being a repressive one-party Panchayat system to a multi-party democracy with political freedom and increasing freedom of speech/press, although initially nothing official was said about freedom of religion. Nepali Christians and mission expatriates were all hoping that this would be incorporated in the new Constitution. If so it would have been far-reaching for the church and of great significance to us in INF. In the event, the document turned out to be disappointingly vague on the subject. The new situation did ensure some degree of freedom that enabled the church to emerge from its semi-ghetto and led to the establishment of many training organisations and Christian NGOs.[143] An historic meeting of the NCF was held in the Royal Nepal Academy, at which at least five well-known Christian leaders spoke. Pastor Robert expounded Rom. 13 on why Christians are loyal to the authorities, while Resham Raj explained why Christians pray. The assembly was attended by a few prominent politicians and human rights leaders. However, because the law of the land was never altered, there remained a legal loophole for continuing persecution. Although Christianity seemed to have been legalised, proselytism was still prohibited. Nepal remained very much a Hindu country.

As early as 1991 the combined Pokhara Youth Fellowship was able to present a Christian drama, *The Supreme Sacrifice,* at the Pokhara town hall (next door to the police station!) to about 600 people. At *Desai,* when we heard that 200 Christians from village churches in Nawal Parasi had not been able to hold a big meeting as they had no large cooking pots to do the catering, we provided the pots, and two weeks later they had their belated conference at *Tihar* time. And at Christmas that year, for the very first time, the government wished the Christian community a

---

[143] See Chapters 24 and 25.

"Happy Christmas". Christian employees were authorised to take the day as a holiday and in Pokhara (and other places) churches celebrated by taking out a procession through the town, distributing thousands of tracts telling the story of Christ's birth.

In 1992 INF celebrated its 40th anniversary – using the city hall in Pokhara – and I was able to conclude my official speech with the words, "Not one of all the LORD's good promises failed; every one was fulfilled."[144] To be able to include a Bible verse in a formal speech before government officials was amazing! At that time several people reminded us that 'life begins at forty', and in the midst of the rising political tensions, rapid church growth and radical changes in health policy and programmes, INF also realised that we needed new life and a new vision (from the Lord) for the next forty years...

In that same year 700 had attended the Western Regional *Desai* Christian conference in Pokhara, 300 went to a regional youth conference, over 200 to a ladies' conference and more than 100 were present at a local church day. According to the National Planning Commission, Nepal's population was growing at the rate of about 1 a minute or nearly 500,000 every year. The church too was now growing exponentially, and in 1993 a local newspaper reported that during the previous three years, more than 125 new churches had opened in the Kathmandu Valley alone. The correspondent indicated that the conversions must have occurred through allurement, threats or force as he could not believe that Nepali people would convert themselves to Christianity and visit churches regularly of their own free will! Little did he know! Patently, true religious freedom had not yet arrived in Nepal.

Then, in October 1994, 1,100 church leaders, representing almost all the main church groupings and parachurch organisations, gathered in Kathmandu for the Nepal AD 2000 Congress on Evangelism. It was an historic event for the Nepali church. The theme was 'Partnership in the Gospel', and despite the presence (for the first time, officially) of denominations, delegates demonstrated a genuine desire to unite and mobilise for evangelism and church planting. Of course, it has not worked out as smoothly as planned; opposition continued as harassment, and strained relationships (because we are all still human) continue to be

[144] Josh. 21:45.

an issue at times. I attended the regional follow-up of this in Pokhara the next year, and one of the things we did was look at the distribution of churches and outreach by plotting it on district maps. I remember at least one pastor disparaged this approach as "unspiritual", and yet years later I was so thrilled to see a group of leaders in one of those same districts actually doing their 'spiritual' planning kneeling on the floor around a map!

In the pre-1990 era nearly half of the believers experienced some form of persecution, and this increased significantly in the late 80s. In 1989 Radio Nepal had even announced that citizens should inform on neighbours whom they thought were Communists or on any who did not wear a *tika* (i.e. were Christians). Then from the mid-90s onwards came suffering for Christians (as well as others) at the hands of the Maoists. By 2002, however, a new generation of Christians was emerging who had never faced such difficulties. For some there was still family opposition, but internal divisions and the infiltration of sects and cults were the new problems for the new age.

In 2008, after the dissolution of the monarchy, Nepal was provisionally declared a secular republic, with presumed religious freedom; and for the next seven years the church made the most of all the increased opportunities this gave. However, when the new Constitution was finally promulgated in September 2015, it ambiguously declared Nepal a secular republic but at the same time denied true freedom of religion by adding a clause to the effect that attempts to convert from one religion to another should be punishable by law. This was followed in early 2016 by the debate in parliament of an extraordinary bill aimed at criminalising conversion for any reason. The idea had been mooted several years earlier but I think most people believed it had been dropped as turning the clock back more than two hundred years. It clearly hadn't. This draft bill made even sharing of beliefs punishable by a significant fine and up to five years' imprisonment (plus deportation in the case of foreigners). At the time of writing, we now know that the constitution states, "...any act to convert another person from one religion to another, or any act or behaviour to undermine or jeopardise the religion of another will be punishable by law."[145] This is clearly undemocratic and

[145] Nepal Constitution 2015, Article 31 (3).

totally in conflict with the Universal Declaration of Human Rights to which Nepal has signed up, and it could have substantial effects on the Nepali church and on mission work. However, the Nepali church of today is far bigger and stronger – and more vocal than it was in the past. And, more importantly, Christ, who is the head of the church, has promised that nothing can ultimately overcome it.[146]

When I had first arrived in Pokhara, there was only one church in the valley, but in the 1970s two new congregations started up – one in Lamachaur (near the boarding school) and the other in Bagh Bazaar (within spitting distance of the Shining). By the time I left Nepal 43 years later, there were at least 43 accredited churches linked into the Pokhara Christian Community, plus some other small fellowship groups. Over the years I was a member of three churches in Pokhara and one in Kathmandu, and visited many more in various towns and villages.

Ramghat Church has the distinction of being the very first church established in Nepal when the country opened up in the early 1950s. It was a good hour's walk from the Shining Hospital so in the early days I could only attend when not on duty. Ramghat began with the pioneers (Nepali and expatriate) meeting in a simple bamboo structure, and the building has been extended six times over the last sixty-five years. Like many churches, at least in the towns, it is now a large modern building with carpeted floor, glass windows, electric guitars, microphones and loudspeakers. Most people, however, still sit on the floor – men on one side and ladies on the other. I remember, though, when the windows were just shutters, which, when left open in the summer, allowed sheep (and goats!) and dogs to drop into the services too. As the congregation grew, the amount of floor space decreased to little over two square feet per person! This was literally 'close fellowship'.

So that I could attend even when on call, I later began going to Bagh Bazaar, although Pastor Hari was a controversial figure at the time. In fact, the church remained a bit controversial for a long time and there was at least one major split. The ladies, however, whom I had the privilege of teaching for many years, were passionate about their faith. Many were illiterate but then they did not need to read in order to pray

[146] Matt. 16:18.

– and pray they did. Some also went out on the preaching teams and returned with thrilling testimonies of how the Lord had spoken through them. Like me, many were not very good at singing, so when Dot or Vera were not around, we just made a "joyful noise unto the Lord"[147].

Ps. Hari Thapa.

When I went to work in GZH in the 80s, I moved back to Ramghat Church, and I described some members of that fellowship in a magazine article of around that time:

> *Worship was just starting as Maya*[148] *came shuffling in and squeezed into a non-existent space against the wall. Crooked, stumpy toes protruding below her sari revealed the ravages of leprosy but the smile on her wrinkled old face told a happier tale. Pastor Jiwan was leading the service: he is a first generation Christian, young and enthusiastic. Not long ago he and his wife lost their first baby, a tragedy shared by all too many Nepali families. From the front, Deependra, one of the three elders, unfolded his unusually long legs and stood to read the notices. Better educated than anyone else in the congregation, that cannot always be easy for him. In front of me was the motherly figure of Maili, mature in her faith and a leader amongst the women, while out of the corner of my eye, I caught a glimpse of Som Kumari scooping up the youngest of her six children to breastfeed him discreetly under her* kasthto, *before his cries disturbed the worship. She is a simple, illiterate village believer but straightforward when it comes to obeying the Lord. Across the aisle from us, Chandra started to pray – and pray. He got so caught up in his conversation with the Lord, the rest of us sang a song. Then, from the back of the church, I recognised Daud's voice and turned around for*

[147] e.g. Ps. 98:4 (KJV).

[148] A few of the names have been changed as I cannot remember them all!

the encouragement of seeing his radiant face; one hand raised in worship, the other, paralysed since youth, hanging limply by his side. Next to him Resham prayed aloud. From a high caste background, he has a real gift for sharing Christ which is undeterred by once spending a year in prison for this very reason. Finally, David got up and went to the lectern. Thirty-seven years ago he became the first pastor of the first church in Nepal. Now he is a frail eighty-seven-year-old – until he begins to preach.

David and Premi Gurung.

Half of these people are now worshipping in heaven, but the new generation is not really so different.

In 1989, when I had settled into my new office role in INF and was based in Bagh Bazaar, I returned to that congregation. With no hospital duties I had more time to get involved in the church, and over the next two to three years I taught a systematic series of studies going all through the Bible with the ladies' fellowship. Many years later I again met Goma and Chandra Rana, who had been emerging leaders in those days. I was thrilled to hear how they had been encouraged by the teaching both of the Bible and on how to lead meetings. We reminisced about how shy they had all been in the beginning and about the way-out type of meetings I had led. Those included a pilgrim walk to the river and up the nearby hill; an Easter celebration including a Passover meal; and a demonstration, by walking round and round the church, of how the Israelites could approach God in the Temple. But there was one thing that really bothered me at the time, and that was the overall low level of literacy. A small informal survey had revealed that 50% of the women were effectively illiterate. Although that was just the figure for the church I attended, I had little reason to doubt that it was much the same in most churches – probably much worse in village areas. We began to pray that an adult literacy scheme would soon take off – and, with a little outside motivation, it did in 1990. That same year saw new freedom for churches in the wake of the political changes, and the annual report recorded 85 baptisms, 48,000 Gospel portions distributed, visits made to at least 30 scattered groups and daughter churches established in two places (Burtibang, and Baglung where INF had worked for many years); that was not considered extraordinary. No wonder the church needed to rebuild.

Until the buildings were later extended, there was just thin lino over the cement floor, and a tin roof. We therefore used to take our own cushions to survive the two-hour-plus services. I also have earlier vivid memories of Bagh Bazaar in the monsoon – ones which explain why I wore my wellies to church. Although it only took about five minutes to get there, I had to squelch through the forest of wet grass on the compound, splash through the puddle immediately outside the gate, skate over the slippery mud of the old parade ground, slosh through the potholes along the bit of tarmac road and finally sink into the quagmire in the alleyway leading to the church. I wonder if Isaiah would have written, "How beautiful on the mountains are the feet..."[149] had he ever sat cross-legged with us, his feet caked with copious smelly mud? And, if it rained during the ladies' fellowship, we just stopped and prayed, as the only person who could hear anything above the din of rain pounding on the tin roof was God.

Almost all Nepali churches have daughter churches – often several – and Bagh Bazaar was no exception. Many of the leaders spent a lot of time out on preaching tours as the Nepali church has always been very strong on outreach and evangelism (although sadly, I discovered, somewhat less so on follow up and deeper discipleship). For this reason I was really excited about the opportunity to get involved with the small

---

[149] Isa. 52:7.

one-month training for the house group and daughter church leaders. These were mostly village people who did not have the required academic qualifications to get into a Bible College (not that in 1993 there were many seats available anyway). There was also no time to waste; village churches needed their pastors then and not several years down the line after they finished a long college course.

By this time there were at least six churches in the Pokhara Valley and all were growing, although some had come into being by division rather than multiplication of the original fellowships. Before 1990 there had been no denominations (except for Assemblies of God in the south-west) and no cults, but freedom brought both into the country, although more so in Kathmandu than Pokhara. However, it was not so much false teaching that the churches struggled with but the relationships between their leaders. In this situation INF was privileged to act as a mediator. For some years Graham, our INF Executive Director, had tried to bring the leaders together, to little avail, but then a new initiative, inspired mainly by Richard (who had married Joyce), and later, John (a later Executive Director), set in motion some seminars for younger leaders. These were held on INF premises (neutral ground) and the tea breaks – when they really got to know each other better – were probably more effective than the teaching sessions. After several years this led on to the formation of the Pokhara Christian Community, which still stands today as a powerful example of churches and their leaders praying and working closely together. After some years a series of ladies' seminars was also held. Later still a social wing called Asal Chhimeki Nepal (ACN), meaning 'Good Neighbours', developed out of the PCC.

By 1995 I had moved to one of the offshoots of Bagh Bazaar. Kunahar was on the eastern edge of the bazaar and by the industrial estate. A lot of members were Gurungs; others were *sukum-basis*[150], which indicated that the church was poor and many members were uneducated. The pastor then was Rikhman (and husband of Bhim Kumari – of custard powder fame). Before long I was regularly teaching the ladies and even served as a deacon. Later I literally helped design their new building. I had persuaded them that putting windows on both sides would stop the congregation falling into a stupor during the services in the summer and

[150] Sukum-basis – squatters on free government land.

that the extra expense for that could be offset by not having a window immediately behind the preacher's head. That window also would have sent people to sleep, as they closed their eyes to avoid squinting at the preacher's silhouette. I felt I had made a really useful, if not particularly spiritual, contribution. The new church building was eventually opened in 1997, but I left to go to Kathmandu the following year. However, I kept in touch and visited regularly, and in 2001, as one of my study projects, I worked with the youth to initiate some community outreach.

Ps. Rikhman and Bhim Kumari Ranabhat (Kunahar, Pokhara).

When I moved to Kathmandu in 1998, I began attending Ashish Church, pastored by a younger relative of Pastor Hari. While that church was being rebuilt, the monsoon rain used to seep in around the edges of the temporary structure – especially on the ladies' side. There was one memorable day when Raju (the assistant pastor) told the ladies off for fidgeting and standing up during the sermon – but then, he wasn't sitting in two inches of water. The new building was eventually opened in 2002 and as the main church hall was two storeys up, we were well out of the way of any floods. Pastor Sundar and his wife Sarita became friends of mine.

Ashish was in Samakhushi in north Kathmandu and near where I lived in Gongabu – so near I could walk to church. Later when I moved across the city, commuting became less easy – but there was only one day when a *bandh* stopped me using my scooter and I had to attend a more local fellowship. There was, however, one other day when I was nearly trapped in Samakhushi as a sudden all-out strike blocked all the roads around the church. Happily, someone lifted my scooter over the barricade so that I could then weave my way back home along an 'interesting' and unusual route, following the stream and avoiding all the main roads. Over the sixteen years I was a member of Ashish, I was deeply involved with the ladies' fellowship and again led them systematically through the Old Testament books and many other series of Bible studies. In 2007, when Sarita started an early Saturday morning (pre-service) Bible study, she asked me to teach Bible Yatra as a precursor to the later studies. It took us several weeks and the ladies were far more regular attenders than the men! At the end I set them an exam so they could get certificates. Results were hardly spectacular in academic terms, but then, I didn't expect them to be as most of the ladies had never had any formal education. In other ways, however, they clearly appreciated and benefitted from the course.

Sundar and Sarita Thapa
(Ashish, Kathmandu).

Ashish is also where I met both Ramesh and Shyam. Shyam became the first Bible Yatra teacher[151] and in 2002 Ramesh adopted me as his 'mother'. At the time he had been thrown out by his strict Hindu family and was studying at Bible College. Ramesh (aka Harka Bahadur) is a

[151] See Chapter 24.

dynamic go-getter. Over the years he acquired a B.Th., an M.Div. (from India, with some help from me) and later an M.Th. (from America) plus a wife (from Nepal). They have two children (Beulah and Baradan) and Ramesh pastors his own church, various daughter churches, runs training courses, does translation and is involved with other Christian organisations and NGOs – and he may even still be doing some studying. (That's typical of many pastors.) Both of these men lived with me for a while – Ramesh, while on holiday from seminary and while preparing to get married; and Shyam, when he was working with Bible Yatra. Shyam once exploded my pressure cooker while I was away in the UK, but that was Shyam all over – far too heavenly-minded to think of earthly practicalities!

Ramesh Khadka and family.

One of the other churches I visited many times was the first church established by 'the bishop' of Nawal Parasi, Lok Bahadur.[152] He had founded almost every church in the district (and a couple of other districts too). Back in the 80s, I think it was, when there were just thirty families who had believed, the government officials suddenly realised what was happening. Not having read the Bible, they tried to put a stop to Christian activity by resettling all the families (except their pastor) in three widely separated areas. But once again, "those who had been scattered preached the word wherever they went".[153] To the government Lok Bahadur was

[152] See Chapter 21.
[153] Acts 8:4.

notorious, but I don't think he was ever personally arrested during the Panchayat years; he always seemed to have just left the village before officials came looking for him. He was the most amazing man: a village farmer with minimal education and a praying wife. He used to pastor the church in his house and regularly visit all the daughter churches for teaching and encouragement. At the same time he promoted the development of his own village and surrounding area and fought for the rights of the villagers whether they were Christians or not. Over the years I taught Bible Yatra in his church and spoke at a couple of ladies' seminars, but I always felt he and his faithful church members had far more to teach me than I them.

Ps. Lok Bahadur Tamang (Nawal Parasi).

In the beginning church congregations met on a Sunday, as in the West, as this had been one of the provisions agreed in the original letter of permission given to Dr O'Hanlon. In the 50s hardly any children went to school and as everyone had to milk their buffalo every day of the week, all days were much the same. By the late 70s, however, schools and colleges were growing fast and an increasing number of Christians were starting to work in government offices; Saturday had become the national day off. So, after a lot of discussion and heart-searching, churches agreed to change their meeting time.

Today most Nepali churches have just one service – on a Saturday morning – but that one service usually lasts as long as (or longer than) two British services put together, although admittedly many members do not manage to arrive within the first half hour. This is quite understandable in the villages where many will have walked perhaps two hours to get there; not quite so excusable in the towns. Every week there are new people who attend for the first time: family members or friends invited by new Christians; others just curious. Mothers feed their babies (under their *khastos*) during the service and small children commute between their mum and dad – from one side of the church to the other. Some of the oldies can't last and have to pop out in the middle; others fall asleep. But I have come to the conclusion that sitting listening and learning is not the only benefit of the service. Illiterate old grannies feel comfortable, safe and relaxed and just enjoy being in the presence of God and other Christians.

Praise and prayer have a special place in Nepali services and most include a time of 'mass prayer' i.e. everyone praying out loud together. I confess that while sometimes this can be very moving, at other times I found it less inspiring. Sometimes the cacophony got to my ears as I could no longer hear myself think how to pray, let alone actually pray. At those times I just gave up and prayed quietly in tongues, and assumed that God could sort it all out even if I couldn't. Many times I have been put to shame by the passion of Nepalis praying and literally expecting the answer to pop up almost immediately. But just sometimes I felt that God might perhaps expect us to answer our own prayers in a very natural way without a miracle from him. After one fellowship meeting a lady asked me to pray for her small son as he had an itchy rash on his hands and especially between the fingers. I hardly needed to look at the child to know this was Scabies. I'm quite sure I did pray but also suggested that a liberal application of soap and water and Benzyl Benzoate might help God out a bit.

Nepalis are also very conscientious about regular fasting, which is probably one good thing that has been carried over from their former Hindu heritage. Many come 'fasting' to the Saturday services, but this usually means simply that they haven't eaten rice; by that token I could say I always fasted before going to church! However, missing a rice meal is a far greater sacrifice for Nepalis than for me! Missing a chance to pray is different; they just don't do it. The first time when opening a teaching session that I said (as one does), "Let us pray..." I was taken aback when everyone did just that and all started praying out loud together.

In the beginning, and even up to 1990, it was very costly for a Nepali to become a Christian. Before they openly witnessed to their new faith in baptism (usually in the local river) they had to be ready to go to jail or be disinherited by their family. This gave the early Nepali church an amazing strength and spiritual depth. Today things have changed. New Christians are often baptised within the safety of a church building.

While some are still disowned by their families or communities, there is generally a lot more tolerance. After 1990 outright persecution and imprisonment largely turned into harassment. Sometimes I wonder if this has been diluting the passion of the church, but then, who am I to talk; the Western church has been wishy-washy for decades.

In the 70s several church leaders in Pokhara were arrested and at least one spent time in jail. Our mission leader had also been apprehended, but as all the Nepalis bravely declared that their decision to follow Christ was theirs alone and that there had been no coercion or allurement, the charges against him did not stick and he was released. Apart from that, and a stricter need to adhere to the non-proselytising clause in our agreement, the expatriates in the mission were barely affected. I was, however, at a Nepali house fellowship when a mob turned up and burnt all the hymn books; and another time, when we were celebrating with the young people down near the river, some Hindu youths arrived and started throwing stones. But it was the Nepali Christians who bore the brunt of the opposition – and for many years. After the Referendum of 1980 but before the Revolution of 1990, it seemed that there was a new burst of anti-Christian activity and several of the local fellowships experienced both harassment and actual persecution. This mood was fed by an International Hindu Conference early in 1988. Then came 1990 and in the aftermath of the political demonstrations and victory for freedom and multiparty democracy, all the Christians in prison were released. Since then, until now (2018), only a few have been imprisoned – and usually on trumped up charges, not always religious. But things may now be about to change again.

In the early days our hospital only took one day off a year – Christmas Day. It started the night before, with the young people from the church congregating at Green Pastures (in the south of the Pokhara Valley) for a nativity play and then carol singing their way from Christian home to Christian home all the way up to the north end of the bazaar. They usually reached the Shining Hospital and the compound, where I lived for my first few years, just in time to wake me up at about 4am. In the early 1970s, when there was only one church in the Valley and no public transport, come 9 o'clock we all walked for an hour to reach the church and there celebrated Christ's birth together with a service followed by a feast of chicken curry and rice. In later years, as the church multiplied, there were more carol singing groups and after the freedom of 1990 this became an opportunity to sing and witness to our neighbours. After 1991 Christian employees were allowed to take the day as a holiday and subsequently Christmas was even declared a national holiday – although I understand this was rescinded for a while. As the number of Christians increased even more, churches got together to organise Christmas rallies and other joint celebrations. *Bada Din* (or the 'Great Day'), as Christmas was known, was always a time when it was reasonably acceptable to talk about the baby of Bethlehem.

As the years passed and Pokhara became more of a tourist destination, and Christmas began to be celebrated in the form of cards, trees and food, INF responded by organising a multinational carol service and singing (English) carols inside, and later outside, some of the main hotels at Lakeside. While those who could sing in tune did this, I was amongst a few others who handed out Christmas tracts and tried to explain to the locals what we were doing.

Earlier in the tourist season one year, Richard and I bought some Christian books and gave them to a few of the bookshops around the lake. When we checked up some months later, many of them had moved from one shop to another and we assumed this meant they had been bought in one place and then sold before the tourists returned home. Who knows how many had a good read this way?

Because originally Sundays were our weekly holiday, we also got Easter Sunday off, but not Good Friday. Every year I wondered why we did not take this chance to share the meaning of Jesus' death, and I don't think this was just because I wanted an extra day off. Then in the 90s Christians were granted the right to celebrate their own important festivals and this has usually been done in traditional style by having a street procession and a mass meeting in a park or even a public building.

The first Nepali Bible was a translation done by William Carey at the very beginning of the 19th century, but, as far as I am aware, it was never widely used, perhaps largely because Nepal had just been firmly closed to the gospel. The second translation was completed in Darjeeling by Padre Ganga Prasad Pradhan about a century later. This was the Bible that was used by the Nepali Christians in India praying for Nepal to open up. However, by the time the first groups of Christians went into Nepal in the early 1950s, the language in the country had changed again and new believers found this version old-fashioned. Very soon the Bible Society was established and work begun on a new translation, although when I arrived in 1970, there was no complete Old Testament, just a New Testament and Psalms in one volume and a second volume we called the Hexateuch (the Pentateuch plus Joshua, which was as far as the translators had got). The first modern full Bible was published in 1977. Since then the Nepali Bible has been fully revised more than twice, a Simple Nepali Version has been produced, and today it is also available in digital format for computers and phones.

I had not been long in Nepal and struggling to read through my Nepali bible when I realised some of the problems the translators had faced. For example, the word used for 'sin' is the word used also by Hindus, but their understanding of sin is more ritual than moral or spiritual. The word used for the 'ascension' of Jesus literally means 'he went to heaven' – fine, except that this same word is also a posh way of saying someone important has died. As Nepalis are more concerned about their daily rice than their daily bread, the Lord's Prayer is sensibly translated as, "Give us this day our daily food." 'Baptism' has ended up as 'baptism' after a debate as to whether it would be better rendered as 'ritual washing', which is not quite the right sense. Names too were debated; should they be Nepalised (e.g. Matti for Matthew) or follow the Greek (e.g. Mattheus)? The former system won. Even the titles of the New and Old Testaments have changed from the original *Niyam* (rule or law) to *Karar* (agreement, contract or promise), which is generally agreed to be more appropriate.

As a Bible student and teacher, this is all really good news, but sadly there are all too many Nepali Christians who are still effectively illiterate, although that is rapidly changing with the younger generations. Laxmi, an older member of Ashish Church in Kathmandu, told me a mind-blowing story. When she became a Christian late in life, she really wanted to read the Scriptures, but like so many of her age group, she had never had the opportunity to go to school. As she described it to me, she opened her bible and prayed, and gradually the Lord showed her how to read. She's not the only one; years before, I had met the *buhari* of one of the very early believers. She told me Tulki's story. One night an angel appeared to her in a dream. He sang the Nepali alphabet to her and showed her the corresponding symbols. From then on she began to read and even taught her daughter-in-law. And that seems a good way to summarise the spirit of the Nepali church and so conclude this chapter.

24

Bible Yatra (Journey)

BaYaN and other Bible teaching

(1988 to date)

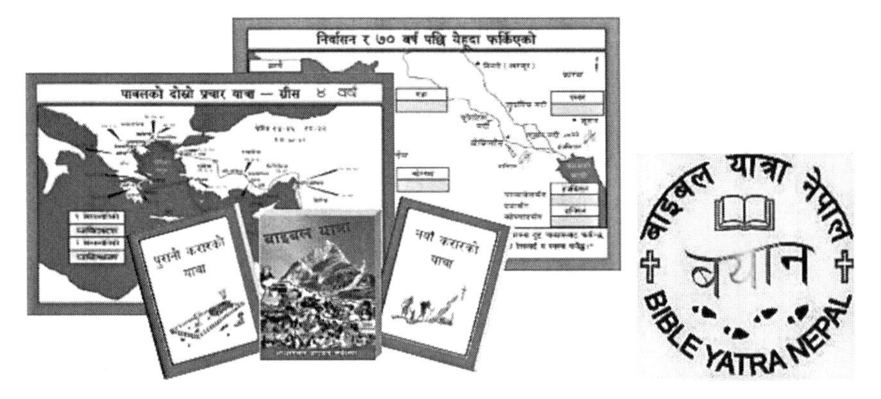

Bible Yatra Nepal – resources (posters, workbooks and big book) and BaYaN logo.

AFTER PARTICIPATING IN A NEW TESTAMENT Walk Thru the Bible (WTB) seminar in the UK in 1988, I had returned to Nepal full of enthusiasm to teach the Bible in this novel way in Nepali – but first I had to translate the material. That was not too difficult as most of it was one-word headings or Bible book titles, so I managed that easily enough and checked a few words with Goma, my Nepali nurse friend. I was ready – almost. I still had to prepare my own notes. That first time I was so nervous that I wrote down every single question I needed to ask (and their answers) so I would forget nothing. Then I had to solve the problem of presentation. Like the prize idiot that I was, I thought I needed to use the same technology as I had seen employed in the UK: overhead projection. I soon discovered that in 1991 in Pokhara it was not such a good idea. Making the overhead projector sheets was child's play compared with overcoming the electricity problem. I could pretty well guarantee it would go off in the middle (and stay off for a couple of hours), which would have brought the seminar to an abrupt halt. So, what to do? I improvised a backup system using my personal big computer backup battery; fortunately, I only lived just around the corner from the church! Then I really was ready.

The seminar had been billed as a special *Tihar* programme for the ladies. It was scheduled to start at 10am (the usual time for most Nepali meetings to start), but by 10.30am only a couple of ladies (the tea-makers) had arrived. I began to wonder if, after all, no one wanted to learn the Bible this way – and that this was their indirect way of telling me. However, by 11am we were up to about thirty and I started the first session. By 11.30am we were over forty, including a few men who had also turned up – perhaps to ensure that I didn't teach anything heretical? By the end of the day it was acclaimed as a great success.

After starting small with my own church ladies' fellowship, I began to develop Bible Yatra. Over the next decade I taught the New Testament seminar – and subsequently the Old Testament seminar – in a few churches and Bible training centres, mostly in Pokhara or Kathmandu. In those early days my computing power was limited to a simple word processor which couldn't write in Devanagri script, so I had to hand-produce all the posters (the low-tech successors to the OHPs) and workbooks – but it was worth it. Everywhere I taught, my students expressed their gratitude, saying they had been blessed as well as instructed. As a result I realized that the Lord had given me a gift in teaching (at least in this unusual way) and in the INF farewell book (of 1997) a couple of entries seemed to reinforce this: *"Orderly-brained Bible Exegetist"* (a play on my OBE as much as commendation of my Bible teaching, perhaps) and *"... one of your deeply inspired sermons..."* From Nepali Bible students too there were encouraging comments: *"You have been a big blessing to our school"* (Youth with a Mission); *"Thank you so much for your teaching"* (Ministry to Tibetan Buddhists); and *"I really thank you very much for your ministry"* (Kathmandu Theological Seminary). But then, if God was really using this method of teaching, it needed to be developed – and Nepalised – so that was what I had planned to do when I moved from an INF visa to a student visa; and from Pokhara to Kathmandu.

In my early years in Nepal, because of the political restrictions on Christians, there had been no Bible training available inside the country, so even if I had had the skill, I wouldn't have been able or allowed to teach. The only options for Nepalis to study had been occasional short-term courses run just over the border in India, or the Darjeeling Hills Bible School, the very first Nepali-medium Bible School, opened in the 1950s, in Mirik in West Bengal. But after the changes of 1990, Bible Colleges, Bible Schools and smaller training centres sprouted all over the place. All through the 90s I ran Bible Yatra seminars on my own, but then things changed...

The first two Nepalis I taught were Ramesh Khadka and SB (Shyam) Lama. That was in 2000 in my house in Gongabu in north Kathmandu. Both were keen, both were good and I had high hopes that both would join me to establish and build up Bible Yatra as a Nepali organisation. Then Ramesh returned to seminary in India with much higher aspirations than following in my footsteps; but Shyam has been presenting the seminars faithfully ever since. He has an amazing testimony. Originally a very macho trekking and white-water rafting tour guide from a hill village in Kabre, he met people from Ashish Church in Kathmandu and became a Christian. Sometime later he went to India to study for a B.Th. but contracted TB and was sent home. When he recovered he resumed his studies, but when the disease relapsed he was again sent back to Nepal, but this time with drug-resistant TB.

The doctor said that there was no point in treating him as the medicines wouldn't work. "You probably only have months to live," he told him.

But Shyam replied, "I'm a Christian and I believe God can heal me. Please give me the medicines, even if you think they won't work – and I'll pray."

That was in the late 1990s! Clearly, God answered his prayers.

Another glimpse of Shyam's character I discovered some time later. I had just written one of my regular newsletters to friends: "Hi folks, just a short note to give you an update of what is happening here. ... Love from Val." It was a full page but probably only took me a few minutes, and the same again to wing dozens of impersonal copies on their way through the ether. Then I sat chewing my fingers and counting the minutes as Shyam laboriously hammered out a one-paragraph email on my computer (and it must have taken him a good hour), something like, "Dear brother and sister in Christ, Praise the Lord! ... I am praying every day for your ministry. ... Your brother in the Lord." It made me think, was there perhaps more to letter-writing than I had so far grasped?

In 2001 Shyam officially began teaching New Testament seminars. He was good but (like me) tried to fit too many activities (Bible Yatra, church and studying for an M.Div.) into his timetable. He soon added the Old Testament to his repertoire, and then, with two of us teaching regularly, we began to introduce the seminars into more training centres and encourage colleges to include it in their curricula. In between our hectic travels criss-crossing the Kathmandu Valley, we revised the poster sets so that they looked the same as the workbooks, something I should have thought of originally but hadn't. This made it much easier for students to understand and complete the class exercises.

By this time I had already begun work on the Bible Yatra book – a written form of the seminars. I had discovered something else I should probably have realised right from the beginning: that although most students understood what we taught during the seminars, they had a tendency to forget it sooner or later (usually sooner)! The big picture of the Bible was proving just a little *too* big for those who had not been Christians for very long. Some kind of reminder was needed. From 2001 to 2003, despite my computer not always cooperating, I laboured on the book in every spare minute. I had decided to write the original text myself, to ensure that it would be simple Nepali, not the fancy variety that would have been produced by a highly-educated Brahmin doing it for me – as I wanted the end result to be easily read and understood by village pastors. Shyam's contribution was to refine my often unpolished sentences while leaving them still simple, a task he accomplished with great skill and patience. I think we only fell out once, and it was over a theological issue: whether I could say that an editor had added at least part of 1 Samuel 25. It seemed to me fairly obvious that while Samuel probably wrote the rest of the book, he could hardly have inserted his own obituary. Then Ramesh and Joseph (a pastor friend from north-east India) checked it for us. One of the hardest jobs was compiling the index (no automatic way of setting that up with Nepali script) and it turned out to be a complete waste of time anyway as most Nepali students did not understand it and never used it. We scrapped it in the second edition! Over the summer of 2003, finalising the layout and poring over the proofs, I spent long hours at the press and made friends with the printer while learning a great deal of really useful information about publishing. By September it was all finished, we triumphantly collected 5,000 copies and within a month had distributed 2,000 of them (to individuals, churches and Bible Schools). Initial comments were very positive – "they were selling like hot cakes" – but I soon realised that the real work of promotion throughout Nepal and India still remained to be done.

It also didn't take me long to realise that Shyam and I were hopelessly overworked. There were far more opportunities than the two of us could handle, especially as by 2004/5 Shyam was spending more and more time developing his church (a branch of Ashish) and only working part-time with me. He was obviously torn between the two, although later he did say, "I love teaching Bible Yatra ... we are teaching and equipping others, so that they can serve the people of God for generations to come." We started looking for colleagues and the first person we found was Mitra, another member of Ashish Church. He started well but soon got sidetracked by his upcoming wedding and overseas study options, so we had to think again – and the next candidate was Jit. Like Shyam, he was a Tamang and full of enthusiasm for teaching in this new interactive way. The son of a lama, he had been converted to Christ and subsequently completed a B.Th. at Nepal Bible College, being one of their top students. He joined Bible Yatra Nepal in 2005 and stayed with us, making a huge contribution while also completing his M.Div. and pastoring a church, until in 2013 he left to go to the USA. In 2006 Krishna, a slightly older man who had already got an M.Div. and who was studying for an M.A. in Rural Development, came on board. He too was a great teacher, but sadly, he left in 2009 to join another organisation and later establish his own church, although he has continued to teach occasional seminars for BYN. It was this team of three Nepalis, plus Jeevan, yet another dynamic young teacher and pastor who joined at the end of 2006, who really grew Bible Yatra Nepal into a Nepali organisation over the next year. Like the others, Jeevan had a B.Th. (from India) and was also studying for his M.Div. in Kathmandu. Although it complicated the seminar timetable planning, it was important that all the teachers got this extra postgraduate qualification if they were to teach Bachelor's and M.Div. level students. It certainly kept them out of mischief and also kept me in business, teaching classes when they were studying.

Current BaYaN teaching staff.
Left: Shyam Lama. Middle: Jeevan Shrestha. Right: Ruben Rai.

Fomer BaYaN teaching staff.
Left: Jit Lama. Middle: Krishna Bhandari. Right: Tejendra Buddha.

On my own I had managed only about twenty seminars each year, fitted in first around my INF responsibilities and later my campus classes, but once the Nepali team got going, numbers increased by a factor of five. 2007 was therefore a significant year for Bible Yatra. From then on the seminars were mostly conducted by the Nepali teachers in Kathmandu or Pokhara plus a few farther afield in Nepal. I had by then also taught the first Diaspora seminars in the UK, Malaysia and Qatar.

We had run eight ToTs[154] and trained around fifty teachers, although few of them summoned enough courage or confidence to go out and lead seminars themselves. I guess the benefit was more that they understood their bibles better and had more scriptural scaffolding for their sermons. We had less than a thousand copies of the big book left and needed to think about reprinting it. The original had had amazingly few errors, but what should have been a simple revision turned out to be a major undertaking as students had requested a slightly smaller size – to fit into their pockets. It took the whole team many months to retype and check the complete text in a newer Nepali font and then reformat the book in A5 layout. 2007 was also the year when we decided to appoint an advisory board and when I took the challenging step of initiating the guys into the mysteries of the accounts. I had by then also been able to set up some funding via a trust in Northern Ireland, although the income fell far short of what was needed for our budgets. In 2008 we opened a BYN bank account and then in 2009 we appointed Tejendra to replace Krishna, and Ruben joined soon after. He was a recent graduate of Nepal Bible College and since then has also got a wife and an M.Div. The handover was progressing well and I assumed I would soon be able to retire. It didn't quite work out like that. I should have known; things always take longer than you think in Nepal.

Bible Yatra, like its parent, WTB, is a very interactive teaching method, utilising rote memorisation, drama, maps and workbooks. The room is the map and we walk around this as though we were travelling around the country. We tell the Bible story and add in the actions and Bible verses to aid the students' memory. That makes it sound a bit like a Sunday school programme, and in the beginning some students did complain that I was treating them like children – until I explained that using all our senses to learn means we do much better. I have a feeling that no one had ever told them before that learning was meant to be fun. I often asked my students if they had actually read the whole Bible through and many (probably most) said no; some had not even read all of Genesis and Acts. No wonder they could not see how God's long-term plan all fitted together. Over the years many have said something like, "I

[154] ToT – Training of Trainers.

spent three years at Bible College, but only by doing this seminar have I really understood the big picture of the Bible." Wow – that was success!

We always encouraged the participants to ask questions, but this, I discovered the hard way, was something that Nepali students were not very good at because in Nepali culture no one wants to 'lose face' by asking something silly. In contrast, many years later when I taught the seminar in English in the UK, the questions came thick and fast, but they were not the same ones that I had faced in Nepal. Nepalis don't have problems with creation or miracles, but one day a student asked me, "Why did Jesus have to die four times?" Suddenly, it dawned on me that someone not long out of a Hindu background (with a belief in reincarnation) might get this idea from reading straight through the four Gospels. The life – and death – of Jesus four times over! And there was I, thinking I had clearly explained that the Gospels were like four word 'photographs' taken from four different angles or perspectives on Jesus' life.

We had lots of fun teaching, but especially in the Teacher Training sessions. Over the last 15 years, BYN has run about 25 ToTs to train young Nepali church leaders to present New Testament or Old Testament seminars. Our records show that around 300 attended but that figure includes some who came to two trainings. About 80% were young men. At first our training and marking were a bit hit-and-miss, but over the years we got more professional. We formalised the training and got stricter in our marking, making our would-be teachers pass about fifteen exams (memory, acting, storytelling, maps, posters, workbooks, use of the Bible etc.) at a high level, and over 80% made the grade, some brilliantly. We made these ToT students work from dawn 'til dusk every day for a week, and after that they still had to stay up half the night doing their homework assignments. Those who attended summer trainings had by far the better deal as we had more hours of daylight and less need for them to study shivering in the cold by candlelight during the frequent power cuts.

In 2010 Bible Yatra Nepal metamorphosed into BaYaN Nepal. It came about like this. We were increasingly aware that the government was expecting all local organisations to register, although they made this as difficult as they could for Christian groups. But should we become an NGO or a company? There were pros and cons on both sides and we debated the issue long and hard. If we registered as an NGO, the staff could not be on the board; if we registered as a company, there were more complicated financial hoops to jump through. In the end we opted for being a non-profit training company with most of the staff as executive board members, and trusted that we could cope with the accounting and tax issues. But first we had to settle the name and the logo. Actually, we already had a perfectly good and appropriate name, but the problem came when we tried to use it. Although there was no legal reason why an organisation name could not contain the word 'Bible', the local office refused to let us do so. After a hiccup of misunderstanding with our lawyer, we resubmitted the application under the name BaYaN Nepal and it was accepted, despite explaining that it was derived from 'Ba' for Bible, 'Ya' for *Yatra* and 'N' for Nepal! It was a good result even though we had to revise the logo to fit. Our stated aim even before that was to "declare or project the big picture of the Bible into the hearts of Nepali Bible students", and *bayan* is a Nepali word which means 'declare'.

During 2011 to 2014 I tried to help the BaYaN team sort out various important issues before I deserted them. We needed to increase the numbers of seminars through promotion and try to raise more funds locally – not easy, as Bible Colleges and churches rarely have sufficient funds to pay full fees. At the end of the first fiscal year after registration, we were surprised to be charged a hefty amount of tax. It was because the Nepali authorities do not distinguish a non-profit company from any other type of company, but no-one had warned us about this. Although most of the money was actually for the following year's activities, we had ended the year with a big balance – which they then taxed. The auditor commented that because we were a "transparent company", he could do nothing about this problem, which, reading between the lines, meant that there might otherwise have been some slightly dodgy way around it. This may have been a good Christian witness but it was an expensive one. After that we learnt to end the tax year with a zero balance – not always easy to achieve if the team were to receive their final month salaries on time.

The graph of the BYN statistics shows a rapid increase from 20 seminars a year in 2001 to 127 in 2007, after which the number has remained constant at around 100 per annum. This means that altogether in the last 15 years, the Bible Yatra team has taught about 1,000 seminars to more than 20,000 students. 65% of these were in Kathmandu, 30% in places elsewhere in Nepal, like Pokhara, and just 5% in the Nepali diaspora – India, Malaysia, the Middle East and the UK. Our initial priority was to teach in Bible training institutions rather than churches, but over the years the team has conducted an increasing number of seminars for churches, youth and ladies' groups, church leaders, migrant workers and even one seminar in a Kathmandu jail! Up to 2011, 74% of seminars were conducted in something like 60 different Bible training centres or schools and 8.5% in maybe 10 to 15 different Bible Colleges. Then some colleges began to insist that we should teach in English medium and against my better judgement we agreed. Funnily enough, the Nepali team were better at this than I was, probably because my English was so good. Actually, I think it was my accent that the students found hard to understand! After that various people began to suggest that I should produce the Bible Yatra book in English, as this would be useful for the Nepali students studying in English; and, if I could also make it available for other groups around the world where English was the world language and/or for those who might want to translate it into their local languages, it would be very well worth the time and effort I would need to invest into it. Over the next few years, I did make a back-translation of it in simple English, together with a glossary of difficult terms or words, and I am grateful for the help of the Wycliffe Associates in this venture. Since then I have personally taught a few seminars in English to small English-speaking groups in Kathmandu, Malaysia and the UK.

At one time someone suggested that the book should be translated into Tibetan, but then, sadly, the idea was dropped. Much later I discovered by chance that a group involved in tribal translation work was using the book as a reference for background information; that was so encouraging. For a while Jeevan, particularly, was keen for us to adapt the seminars for children; we discussed the idea *ad nauseam* and even did some research, but it turned out that that was not part of God's plan for BYN.

In contrast, when the suggestion of making a video came up, we all embraced it with enthusiasm, and in early 2013 the whole team became film stars for a month. Jeevan proved to be a natural 'hero' but the others did amazingly well too, despite a lack of previous experience and little chance to practise. We had to shift locations in the middle, but the real problem was the airport. In both sites we seemed to be directly under the flight path of Tribhuvan International Airport, and I never realised how many planes took off and landed each day until we had to stop for them all. Bob, a Christian film-maker from Canada, filmed almost twenty-four hours, including the whole of both seminars, and so, unsurprisingly, it has taken more than three years to complete the very complex editing and bring the project to completion. How he managed to edit without knowing Nepali remains a mystery to me, but there were amazingly few real errors. Just once, in the middle of the Old Testament, he joined up two lookalike shots of the presenter reading from the Bible and missed out all the intervening story, but happily, I noticed in time and restored Ruth to her rightful place between the Judges and David.

Since I first took Bible Yatra to Mirik in the late 90s, BaYaN has been back there many times, and to other places in India like Delhi. It was easier for the Nepali team than for me as they did not have to jump all the visa hurdles to cross the border. Conversely, it's been easier for me to get to places like Malaysia and the Middle East as I could always obtain a visa on arrival. Nevertheless, in 2009 we planned for Jeevan to go to Qatar (so that he could teach the one group that I as a woman had not been able to meet), and also the UAE[155]. Our plans – as so often happens – did not work out as expected. The hassles started with the money he needed to guarantee and then continued at the airport in Kathmandu where he was told that his visa was not valid – but only because no one had explained that he should have visited the website and printed out the document with an official logo on it. Someone helped him to rectify that and he did get to Doha, but never made it to Emirates as his visa was never granted – perhaps all to the good, as it would have been horrifically expensive. Even after I left Nepal, I have taught a few seminars in the UK, the Netherlands and Portugal, and the Bible Yatra team have maintained the annual level of seminars, mostly in Nepal, although in 2015/16 they took time out to help distribute aid to earthquake victims and later were hampered in their travel by the Indian border blockade.

During the initial eighteen years of my time in Nepal, I first had to master Nepali and then was far too busy with medical work to do much

[155] UAE – United Arab Emirates.

Bible teaching – or anything else for that matter. By the time my vocabulary had increased, so had the oppression from the pro-Hindu political regime, such that until 1990 expatriates needed to keep a very low profile in church matters. In contrast, during my last twenty-five years I was almost overwhelmed by all the opportunities God gave me to teach, although Bible Yatra always remained my first love. By 2010 BaYaN had become a registered Nepali training company and I was just its advisor, and although I was already informally involved in Nepali migrant ministry and visits, I had more time to accept invitations to teach for other groups or organisations.

Perhaps predictably, ladies' meetings never seemed to trigger any official radar; no one imagined that a bunch of often semi-literate women could be much of a threat to anyone, but then, officialdom calculated without the power of those ladies' prayers. But as these gatherings were never high profile, expatriates like myself were, from the beginning, able to participate – and teach. I was therefore deeply involved with the ladies' fellowships in all the churches I went to in both Pokhara and Kathmandu – with the one exception of Ramghat, because reliably attending meetings simply did not mix with my on call rota in the hospital. I taught umpteen series over the years – Bible Books, Proverbs, How to Lead Meetings etc. – and from time to time organised specials including at least one Nativity drama. I thought I was doing quite well passing on all this spiritual wisdom... until I was asked to speak on the menopause, and that was the session from which I received the most positive feedback!

Regular involvement with the ladies in my own church(es) led to invitations to lead special (joint) seminars – at first in Pokhara but then farther afield. In the middle of a seminar on the topic of Water, I used a (toy rubber) snake in a trunk as a visual aid, and nearly lost the whole congregation as they all jumped up in fright. In Kathmandu I taught a long and somewhat more sedate series on Prayer in the Gospels for the Ladies' Prayer Fellowship. Twice I accepted Lok Bahadur's invitations to Nawal Parasi. The first time was for a Christian celebration at *Teej* (the traditional ladies' festival time) in 1995. 150 ladies gathered in the original rustic church in Bartadi to learn about six Bible ladies who had trusted the Lord despite difficult circumstances – circumstances similar to those they themselves were experiencing in villages in Nepal. The second time the meetings were in Butwal. I travelled on my scooter via

Pokhara and the hill road I had first encountered on Christmas Day, 1970. It proved an unwise choice of route as the road was being resurfaced. It was a very bumpy ride and so, like the Wise Men, I returned home by a different way. My topic that time had been Burdens and my visual aids a rucksack, a day-bag and a whole pile of stones.

Those were the big meetings but there were lots of smaller ones too. Autumn 1998 was one of the many occasions when my friends declared me crazy as I drove my scooter to India (roads very much smoother across the *Terai*). On the way back, partly to relieve the saddle sores, I stopped off near Janakpur and spoke at the ladies' fellowship at Lal Gadh hospital. Some years later I had the privilege to speak at a couple of UMN meetings.

After 2006 I was regularly involved with Nepalis in the diaspora, and this included many 'interesting' visits to girls in their hostels in Malaysia. These hostels were either huge, almost bare and rather unfriendly-feeling dormitories with rows of bunk beds lining the walls, or tiny rooms where the bunks were squashed in with hardly room to undress between them. The girls living in the latter were expected to share the beds; the day shift had the bed at night and the night shift had the bed during the day! Despite the lack of facilities, the girls never lost their traditional Nepali hospitality and always managed to serve me with tea or squash and sometimes eats as well. The Christians, many of whom found it hard to get to regular meetings because of shift work, loved to have a time of fellowship – a short Bible reading, a bit of explanation and time for prayer – but even their Hindu friends were usually happy for us to pray about their problems or for their families back in Nepal. In time the numbers of girls in the diaspora increased and I was thrilled to have a small part in encouraging them. I remember three bigger meetings. The first (and it really was a first for ladies working there) was in Qatar when we received permission to invite about a dozen ladies to the home of the expatriate I was staying with. The second (which was also a first) was a Christmas party for housemaids in Oman. And the third was the first ever ladies' seminar in UAE, held in Dubai in 2014, but that was the last for me as by then I was on my way home to the UK – although Immanuel Nepali Church in Folkestone subsequently invited me to lead a ladies' seminar.

With on-call commitments in the 70s, I hardly got to any of the big joint church conferences – except for a couple of NCF gatherings that were held in Pokhara. One of these was the annual *Desai* do. Originally there was just one gathering for the whole country but soon numbers increased so much that there was one arranged in each development region, and as they continued to increase, far more than that. By the noughties, when I was in Kathmandu, I attended an NCS conference, where I was even given the opportunity to share something about Bible Yatra. My final *Desai* in Nepal was in 2013. Two conferences were planned that year in Pokhara – one for the northern group of churches and one for those in the south of the city. I was amazed to be asked to speak at the joint meetings in Ramghat Church, but also humbled and felt very privileged by this invitation. What a difference from the early days when no woman was ever allowed near the platform or the pulpit!

It was exciting – and challenging – to be in at the beginning of the seminars that INF arranged for church leaders and then to see how these grew to become the Pokhara Christian Community. In North India most, but not all, of the seminars I took were Bible Yatra; but then one year I visited Shillong, a small hill town in Meghalaya (formerly Assam), one of the early centres of the Nepal Evangelistic Band. That time it was for a missionary conference at which many young people committed themselves to go out and share the good news, not only to fellow Nepalis, but to other people groups in the north-east. Several years later I spoke at camps and seminars in other parts of the diaspora – Malaysia and the Middle East.[156]

Through Bible Yatra I had built up contacts with many Bible Schools and Colleges, and so even before I had gained my postgraduate degree, I began to be asked to teach other subjects. The first topics I dared to present were the Biblical Basis of Mission and Cross-Cultural Communication, both initially at Darjeeling Hills Bible School in Mirik, and later as background subjects for Nepalis planning to work with Tibetans. Some years later I stretched the BYN overview of the Bible into a full-semester series, covering one whole college module: Introduction to the Bible – Its Structure, Formation, History, Geography and Culture. I taught this at two or three colleges in Kathmandu, and during parts of

---

[156] See Chapter 25.

2012 I was busy every day commuting north of the ring road to one college and south of it to another. Both were off-road, the one so much so that in the monsoon I was forced to leave my scooter at the top of the hill and walk down the track to the school. I had discovered the hard way that it was almost impossible to get the scooter back up the waterfall that had originally been the path. I'm sure it was partly because of all these bumpy roads that that year I suffered an acute attack of sciatica!

In the English medium colleges, the B.Th. students were expected to produce a short research dissertation, despite the fact that most had no idea what research really was and even less idea how to write a dissertation. Statistics and graphs were pretty much like magic to them, but I already knew that from my experience with Ramesh. He had had the bizarre idea of adding all his figures together (i.e. apples plus oranges plus bananas – as it were) rather than comparing them, and wasted several hours doing that before I rescued him. I began teaching an introductory course on Study (they weren't too hot on that either!) and Research Methods. I'm not sure how much the students learnt but I certainly discovered how difficult it was for them to produce a piece of academic writing in their second (or third) language. English grammar was a challenge and especially the use of the definite article ('the') as there is no such thing in Nepali. The subtle difference between 'I am going to Jordan' (the country) and 'I am going to the Jordan' (the river) is totally lost on a Nepali audience. But perhaps the biggest hurdle was to get over to them that plagiarism was the unforgiveable sin; their assignments were full of quotations (without quotation marks) and references to important sources (without acknowledgements). I subsequently used this same material on M.Div. and M.A. level courses (the latter for DAI[157]) and also for the first batch of Elijah Counselling and Training Centre Pastoral Diploma students, and again found there was a lot that no one had previously thought to tell them about studying and academic writing.

In my last couple of years, I became involved with the faculties of two training institutions and I recollect one eye-opening discussion we had about what the exam pass-mark should be. Many of us expressed the opinion that if the future pastors did not know at least 50% of their theology, this could be a future problem, although we did concede that

[157] Development Associates International.

in other subjects perhaps the standard need not be so stringent! I enjoyed lecturing but once again I found that my students understood Indian/Nepali English better than English English! So, mentoring them one-to-one while they were planning, conducting and writing up their research assignments I found a whole lot more fun. It was probably a whole lot more profitable for them too.

Nowadays there are probably around a hundred Christian training institutes in the Kathmandu Valley alone. Some are connected with one local church and have just a handful of students; others are called colleges and award a B.Th. (although not all these 'degrees' are internationally recognised!) or even an M.Div. From the better colleges, affiliated with the Asian Theological Association, students emerge with a formal qualification and are thus able to gain entrance to overseas postgraduate seminaries. They are the future Bible scholars of Nepal. About twenty colleges teach in English, a practice that has both pros and cons. In their first year, however, almost all students struggle and I have often wondered how many important theological facts they get muddled because of linguistic misunderstandings. Reading theological tomes in one's mother tongue is hard enough, let alone in a second language. I soon discovered that using double negatives was a dangerous practice. Even if I understood what I had said (which I often didn't), many of my students certainly didn't and this was potentially a route to false teaching that I didn't want to travel.

25

After Qatar Airlines Lost My Luggage

Diaspora Nepalis and NeMUN

(2005 to date)

Diaspora book cover and NeMUN logo.

BIBLE YATRA HAD PROVIDED ME with the big picture of the Bible. Then in 2005 I had begun my M.A. studies on Global Issues in Contemporary Mission and this gave me the big picture of the world. I even wrote a short essay assignment on globalisation, which ended with the paragraph:

> *...I live in Kathmandu, in the house of an ex-British Gurkha; use a Chinese radio to hear the news of Iraq and a Japanese laptop to contact friends in Africa; I ride a Japanese-Indian scooter, wearing an Italian helmet, English underclothes, a Swiss watch and an Indian* kurta-suruwal *(top and trousers); I phone my Korean friend on a Finnish mobile to arrange a meal at the Singaporean-Malaysian restaurant, although more usually I consume organic Nepali food and bottled water (not American Coke) while dreaming of Colombian coffee and my holiday in Malta. Before that there's a mission teleconference linkup with UK, NZ and Oz before I board Qatar airlines heading for the... UK.*

After that two rather quirky things happened that changed the direction of my final few years working with INF. The first was when Qatar Airlines lost my luggage and the second was when I gatecrashed a meeting with some Malaysian visitors at NIM[158] Dhobighat Church. The first made me think about the many Nepalis I had heard about who were working in Doha; perhaps they too would benefit from Bible Yatra. The second found me offering to teach the seminar to migrants in Malaysia. These two – seemingly unrelated events – subsequently led to eight years of Diaspora ministry with regular visits to South East Asia (especially Malaysia) and the Middle East (mainly Qatar and Emirates) and much more.

Malaysia only officially started accepting Nepali workers in 2001, but by 2006, when I first visited, there were around 165,000 legal Nepali workers (plus goodness knows how many illegals) and about 45 Nepali fellowships. All the migrants were men but after that year girls too began to be accepted, and by the time of my last visit in 2013, there were at least 700,000 (legal) workers, including many ladies, and almost 100 Nepali fellowships. Most (but not all) of the groups were less than 100 strong and closely linked with local Chinese or Indian Malaysian churches, who encouraged and helped the migrants a lot. Apart from about a dozen trained pastors, who received visas courtesy of Christian

[158] NIM – Nepali Isai Mandali (one group of indigenous Nepali churches).

businessmen and local churches, most of the leaders were 'tentmakers' – themselves doing '3D' (dirty, difficult and dangerous) day jobs.

It was a similar picture in the Middle East, or 'Arab' as the Nepalis called it, although the migration to this area had started significantly earlier than that to Malaysia (in Bahrain – from the 80s). By 2013 there were around 1.5 million Nepalis in the Middle East and the majority were bound by the 'kafala' system. This was (if I understand it correctly) a sponsorship system based on ancient Arab hospitality which had degenerated into 'ownership' of workers – a form of modern slavery. Most men work on outside construction sites in temperatures of around fifty degrees. Some (perhaps many) women are promised good employment but find on arrival that they are to be sold rather like cattle in a market and are destined to become maids in large, demanding Muslim families, where they frequently suffer all kinds of abuse. The Nepali Christian groups in Qatar had links with an international fellowship but their Nepali leadership was more independent than in Malaysia. The situation was similar in UAE. Rules and restrictions on Christian meetings in the Gulf, however, meant that there were far fewer, but larger, fellowships than in Malaysia. There are probably around five thousand Nepali Christians in 'Arab', a figure at least equal to the number in the whole of south-east Asia. All the leaders had to be 'tentmakers', though a few had done some pastoral training before travelling overseas. The working hours and environment in both the Middle East and south-east Asia meant that migrant workers had little time or opportunity for leisure activities or distractions, but God – as he so often does – used this inconvenience. Christians befriended lonely new arrivals and invited them to the Christian meetings – and so the numbers grew exponentially.

I had already been teaching Bible Yatra seminars in Mirik and Siliguri, a part of north-east India where some of the Indian Gurkha regiments were based and Nepalis had worked in the tea estates for several generations. I had also taught in Shillong in Meghalaya (one of the early NEB/INF centres) and Dimapur (Nagaland) but then I also discovered how many Nepalis were actually living in India – not just in the north-east but also in the north-west (in Kumaon-Gadhwal, which in 1806-14 was briefly part of Nepal) and in at least seventeen of the major cities. Many were squatting in slums and working as (seasonal) labourers;

others were women and girls trafficked into the brothels of cities like Kolkata and Mumbai. INF/Nepal community projects were already at work in the Karnali region from where many of these migrants came; and Alois, an INF colleague, was living in Delhi and planning holistic partnerships with local Indian churches to reach these migrants. The diaspora just got bigger every time I thought about it – and then I thought about the students and professionals in the West and it got even bigger. In fact, I discovered that a 'third half' of the population of Nepal was living outside the country!

My first visit to Malaysia was a brief one over Chinese New Year in 2006, when I taught the New Testament Bible Yatra survey to ninety migrants at a camp in the Genting Highlands. On the last evening the participants were given an opportunity to share about anything special they had enjoyed or learnt at the camp. One young lad stood up and said something like, "When we saw this old lady [me!] arrive, we wondered what on earth she could have to teach us, but then we found we were so challenged by her enthusiastic teaching." That camp was a special time for me too. There I met a secondary school teacher who had been imprisoned by the Maoists. On the very day on which he had expected to be executed, he was released. I also met an ex-Maoist commander who had been captured by the Nepal army but instead of 'disappearing' him, they had given him a ticket to travel overseas. These two amazing miracles had resulted in both men ending up in Malaysia, where they were befriended by Christians and became believers themselves. By the time I met them, they were friends and brothers in Christ. Another man I met had believed largely due to the love and care he received from the Christians when he lost half his hand in an industrial accident. Later I heard of another Nepali migrant worker, who had been paralysed and bedridden in hospital in Malaysia for eleven months. Doctors had given him no hope but the Christians kept on praying for him and at last he started to recover – fast! And there were dozens of stories like that.

Not long after I returned to Nepal, my phone rang and it was Khima, a Christian Nepali migrant worker, calling from Malaysia. He was another I had met at the camp. Despite the bad line, I got the message: "My wife is now in Kathmandu. Please contact her and lead her to the Lord." I jotted down the phone number, ascertained that she knew he had become a Christian and that she had already heard a little about

Christ. Then we were cut off. By the following evening I'd arranged for us to go to church together on the Saturday. After the service we went, with other newcomers, to meet one of the church leaders. He explained to her the way of salvation, and there and then Seeta accepted Jesus as her Lord and Saviour. For a while this family seemed to be doing well, but then her husband was influenced by a false sect in Malaysia and I lost touch with them.

Six months after my initial foray into Malaysia, I used my free excess baggage allowance and stopped off in Doha (Qatar) on my way home to teach the New Testament survey to a hundred and five male migrant workers. Wonderful worship. Good organisation. Excited students. Successful seminar – despite most participants arriving after a long day's work out in the sun. But no girls! Quite a few were working as cleaners and I heard that among them were six Christians, most of whom were not allowed to attend any fellowship meeting. Then, on my way back to Nepal, I got permission to meet these girls briefly in their lodgings – a sort of ramshackle prefab with a single small fan that did little to mitigate the stifling heat. For several years after this, I visited them and the Qatar Nepali Christian Fellowship and by my last visit in 2008/9, there were over thirty ladies attending the fellowship and some had even managed to get to a seminar.

That same year, 2006, I taught in Reading in the UK, and in 2007, in Doncaster. These groups faced rather different obstacles: many members were students (or spouses) working all hours of the day and night to earn their keep, plus (I suspect) some were distracted by Western affluence and materialism. The groups were therefore a lot smaller.

Then, from 2007 until I left Nepal, I visited Malaysia and/or the Middle East every year, becoming more and more involved with Nepali diaspora activities, but it was only in 2011 that I was officially appointed as the first ever INF Diaspora Coordinator.

When visiting the UK to attend my summer course at Redcliffe College in 2007, I again stopped off twice in Qatar. On the way home I taught the Old Testament seminar, and – great excitement – I presented a short seminar for fifteen ladies. The other thrill was witnessing a baptism in the waters of the Gulf – something I will never forget, but not just for the reason you might think. A group of Nepalis at the baptism (aka church picnic) got washed out to sea in a small dinghy and the church leaders had to call the coastguard to rescue them. What with 7/7 just before I had to pass through Heathrow on my way back to Nepal, it was quite a memorable year.

In 2008 I went to Malaysia for five weeks – first teaching the Old Testament seminar at the Chinese New Year camp in Kuala Lumpur and then a hectic month criss-crossing the country to visit Johor Bahru, Ipoh and Cameron Highlands as well as the Klang Valley. I learnt a couple of important lessons about life in Malaysia. One: Malaysians only eat once a day, by which I mean that they start eating as soon as they get up and only finish just before they go to bed. And two: outside Malaysian long-distance (and even local) buses I could sweat gallons, but once inside the bus and without a sweater, I could freeze to death because of their powerful air conditioning systems. On the other hand, I received a very warm welcome from the Nepali fellowships, top-class hospitality from many Malaysian church members and a lot of practical help and advice from my INF colleague, Heike, who by then was living and studying in Kuala Lumpur while also befriending Nepali migrants. One highlight of this time was meeting the newly appointed Nepali ambassador, Dr Rishi Adhikari, who really understood the problems the migrants faced. My trip ended in Thailand where I met Anil and Gift, Nepalis leading a small fellowship in Bangkok. My plan had been to teach the Bible Yatra seminar in their church, but it didn't quite work out like that. Instead, I discovered that as most of the Nepalis in Thailand came originally from Burma/Myanmar, many were technically illegal, and so sometimes they needed to hide from the authorities. The majority could no longer read the Nepali Devanagri script, and they even found my (pure!) Nepali hard to understand.

Back in Kathmandu something new was happening – the establishment of the RDC[159]. This was originally the vision of a small group of Malaysian Christians from Klang who were involved in migrant ministry among Nepalis in their own country. Most had also visited Nepal and understood the problems facing returnees. They had seen how difficult it was even for those on a short holiday to visit their families in remote hill villages. Young men travelling in areas under Maoist control were at risk for their lives. So, the Malaysians provided the funds for us to rent a flat

[159] RDC – Returnees Drop-in Centre.

as a safe haven for them in Kathmandu. It was a brilliant and compassionate idea but between us we messed it up. The flat was great, but we didn't give enough thought to its management. It was run by a committee (!) and none of us had had the sense to see that it needed a kindly live-in host. It therefore proved less than successful and as the Maoist crisis drew to an end, the Malaysians withdrew the funding and we (the committee) were forced to take more responsibility and to pray about its future – undoubtedly a good thing.

At the very end of 2008, I returned to the UK briefly for my M.A. graduation, stopping off in the Middle East on the way there and back. I spent Christmas with a Swiss family in Salalah, in southern Oman, where there were many Nepali housemaids. Many enjoyed the lovely party we arranged, but others were prevented by their mistresses from attending. Legally, those who were Christians on arrival in the country should have been allowed to attend, but of course this rule was not necessarily followed. Those who were Hindus on arrival had no such right to attend a Christian gathering and depended totally on the goodwill of their employers.

Over the New Year I touched down briefly in Doha *en route* to an exploratory visit to the Emirates. I had been invited by an Indian pastor working with the Nepali migrants but what I did not know before I left Muscat was that he had been detained in India because of visa problems. Thus, I arrived in Abu Dhabi with just a couple of phone numbers and a rather dodgy SIM card in my phone. Things were not looking good, but then my phone allowed me to contact one of the Nepali leaders – Janak Raj Sharma. Janak had never heard of me and didn't know what to make of me, but with typical Nepali generosity he arranged for me to visit Nepalis in Abu Dhabi and Dubai and found me good places to stay. This was yet another miracle and the start of a great friendship and ministry in UAE.

Early 2009 found me back for another prolonged visit to the Malaysian peninsula – a really resourceful way of avoiding the cold Kathmandu winter. I began in Singapore where most of the Nepalis are linked with the Gurkhas and so rather different from the economic migrants in Malaysia. At the Chinese New Year camp, this time held in a rural location in Johor Bahru, were a hundred and eighty migrants, including a handful of girls and a lot of newcomers. In the first session I taught Journey Thru the Gospels in a way that made it especially clear why Jesus came, what he did for us and how we can respond to him. After that a visiting Nepali pastor filled in the gaps I had left while I taught the more mature Christians the rest of the New Testament Journey. As a result eleven people became Christians during the camp; it was a really special time. Then I headed north to Penang Island where I knew there were several Nepali fellowships, most pioneered by Kailee, a Chinese Malaysian who had worked with YWAM in Nepal. She had twisted my arm to run a BYN ToT for the leaders of her group. I did it, although her enthusiasm was not quite matched by the time available or the ability of her students. This trip also ended in Thailand – at the Himalayan Global Summit in Pattaya, where a vision for further Nepali and cross-cultural outreach, especially in the Asian diaspora, was articulated.

Home once again in Kathmandu, I assisted in the metamorphosis of the RDC into Mitra Niwas (Friends' Home). This time we made sure that all guests would be warmly welcomed by having a resident host/hostess. Our vision fitted with that of Devendra and Ram Maya, friends of Kailee. They had already visited Malaysia and come back with a longing to serve returnees from Malaysia and the Middle East, especially those who had become Christians while working overseas. They wanted to help them link up with the Nepali church in Nepal, something that was not automatically easy. Within the first year the number of guests more than doubled, and together we started to build up a network of contacts in Nepal and overseas. For a while there was talk of the government cutting down on overseas migrant work because of the credit crunch, and some countries had already started sending home workers long before their contracts expired. Other migrants returned with medical, social and/or financial problems – cheated by their agents or employers and with no hope of compensation. All this eventually proved a huge challenge for Mitra Niwas and what grew out of it.

Janak BC.

In 2009, with an M.A. to my name, I started to mentor Janak BC, an M.Div. student from Pune who was researching aspects of Nepali migration in the main Indian metropolitan cities. About the same time, although still on a business (not mission) visa, I became the convenor of the INF Diaspora group, looking into various different opportunities in India, South East Asia and the Middle East – something that fitted well into my own growing passion for the diaspora. One of the other members was Sapana, a Nepali married to a Malaysian but then living in Kathmandu. She and her husband Franklin had pioneered Nepali migrant ministry in Kuala Lumpur and were beginning to follow that up among the returnees. They started a monthly prayer fellowship for their contacts and this got linked with the Mitra Niwas group. Then I invited some of my friends who had returned from Qatar – and later Janak (Sharma) from UAE. This brought together the key players for the next stage of God's plan for Diaspora work based in Kathmandu.

As this plan began to unfold, I was excited but also flabbergasted to find I had been invited to Lausanne III in Cape Town at the end of 2010. I went as the only non-Nepali delegate in the Nepali team. The theme of that conference was God Is On The Move – amazingly relevant to my own growing migrant ministry.

Many Nepali migrants in India were seasonal workers; others had their families with them. Not so, those elsewhere. Most were men on their own, but some were women, often working as maids, and in Muslim societies it was especially hard for them. I discovered that many Hindu Nepalis who went to Muslim countries returned home as Christians. What happened was that they were lonely, away from the pressures of home, and so when they were genuinely befriended by Christians, they were open to rethink their own beliefs. These new believers then often returned to Nepal with great enthusiasm but less maturity, keen to attend Bible College and establish new churches, but less sensitive to the needs of their own families and the practicalities of finding a job. Some began to drift back into their old Hindu lifestyles. This spiritual issue, together with a growing awareness of the social, medical and financial problems faced by returnees, was what challenged those of us linked with Mitra Niwas to do more to help them. The outcome was NeMUN – the Nepalese Migrant Unity Network – which soon grew into a registered local Christian NGO, serving through hospitality, advocacy, networking and social assistance as well as prayer.

In the middle of 2010, I was back in Malaysia yet again for a further three-month stint of travels and meetings – with both Nepali migrants and Malaysians involved with migrant ministry. Alongside the teaching I began to promote the work of NeMUN and, together with Sapana and Heike and a group of Nepali Christian migrant leaders and Malaysians, we discussed migrant issues with Dr Rishi and some of his staff. All too soon he was posted elsewhere, that being how the Nepali civil service functions (or dysfunctions – depending on how you look at it) but the problems stayed on in Malaysia. There was much for NeMUN to do.

Many stories demonstrate the immense value of prayer, partnerships and networking in Diaspora ministry, and I think Jung was not exaggerating when he said that, "Diaspora (is) ... God's strategic tool to achieve His Mission."[160] The local Nepali fellowship in Penang secured Ganesh's release from jail and gave him financial help to return to Nepal, where he was welcomed and further assisted by NeMUN members and Mitra Niwas. Smriti, returning from Australia, was put in touch with a counsellor. Gobinda's dad was given details of Nepali contacts in the UK for his son. Dr Narayan's family were linked up with fellow Nepalis on their arrival in Canada. Roshan was given a Nepali Christian contact phone number the very day before he left for South Korea. Jasman was helped to try to find (sadly unsuccessfully) his long-lost brother in Malaysia. Bina was ill-treated by her employer in Kuwait and transferred to Saudi Arabia, but NeMUN contacts were instrumental in obtaining the help of the Nepali ambassador and human rights personnel, and eventually she returned to Nepal.

After Anil, another friend of Kailee's, joined YWAM, he was sent to a village area of Nepal for outreach ministry. When he got there he found hardly any young men. Puzzled, he asked where they were. "They're in Malaysia, Qatar, UAE... working as migrants," came back the reply. God spoke to him through this. If that was where the young men were, then that was where he should go. He went, and spent several years in Penang as 'tentmaker' and then pastor. Now he is back in Nepal and still working with migrants – with NeMUN and Mitra Niwas.

About half of all Nepali households have members working overseas in the diaspora. Maya, whose husband was working with INF/Nepal in

[160] Jung, Connections 2005 Vol. 4 No. 3.

Nepalgunj, was one of them. She travelled to Kuwait, but before long, like so many other ladies in that part of the world, ran into serious trouble. She found herself outside her contracted work and without her passport (doubly illegal), and knew that she could be arrested at any time. Not knowing what else to do, she got touch with her husband – something that is not always possible for ladies in the Gulf. But at such a distance, how could he help? Desperate for some advice, he contacted his ex (INF) boss. Mark also had no idea how to help but wisely asked his wife what he should do! Liz immediately suggested getting in touch with me "as Val knows all about Diaspora matters" – a slight exaggeration although I probably did know more than most other people at that time. Agam, the Nepali pastor in Kuwait, was not contactable by either phone or email, so – what to do? This was important and urgent. Suddenly, I remembered that Judy (my old school friend) had mentioned that someone connected with her church was working in Kuwait. Maybe he could be the link we needed... Fortunately, an email to him brought a rapid response and all of us in NeMUN prayed that his involvement would work out for good. Andrew managed to contact some of the Nepali Christians and they discovered that Maya had by then been arrested and was apparently being held in a certain police station. He duly visited but was told in no uncertain terms that they had no prisoner by the name of Maya. Strange! However, in his heart he felt certain that she really was there, so as he turned to leave the office, he called out in a loud voice, "Maya," and she answered. How this embarrassing situation was overcome I never found out, but I do know that the story had a happy ending. Andrew and others were eventually able to get her out of the lock-up, and later help her get back to Nepal and safety with her family.

When I returned to Nepal in early 2011, for my final term of service with INF, I had yet another new hat to wear – as Diaspora Coordinator, although in practice I was just doing officially what I'd already been doing unofficially for several years previously. I acquired an INF office and was able, in working hours, to indulge my eccentric habit of talking to my computer, but before long I was off once again to Malaysia and that was the year when I taught Bible Yatra a total of 7 times, and also preached 7 sermons in 24 hours in Johor Bahru. I also attended a second HIMGlo conference, this time in Hong Kong. The convenors were keen to forward the Pattaya vision through networking and outreach in Malaysia, Myanmar and Thailand, but as there were virtually no representatives from any of these countries present, nothing much came of this. Looking back, this was probably all to the good, as issues surrounding cross-cultural outreach by Nepalis among Muslim or Buddhist (not even Tibetan Buddhist) communities had not then been addressed.

In February 2012, with Alois, Seeta (from INF) and Shyam (from BaYaN), I attended the IMI networking gathering in Delhi and visited some of their centres in Himachal Pradesh and Uttarkhand. It was not the most sensible choice of dates; it snowed in Shimla and I still marvel how Shyam didn't die of frostbite after he lost his coat. Shortly after that Janak (BC) joined IMI, so doubling the INF staff contribution.

By May I had thawed out and was off to swelter in the UAE. It was a fantastic three weeks! Amazing arrangements and hospitality! I was humbled that the Nepali community there gave me such a gracious and generous welcome: Peter and Roni, and Netra and Dhan Maya, who opened their homes to me; Pratima and colleagues, who arranged fantastic hotel accommodation; and Som and Shyam (yet another Shyam – not my language teacher or the BaYaN one), who fixed the programme. With all these practical details sorted, God was able to bless abundantly – and he did. I taught Bible Yatra in Al Ain, Sharjah and Abu Dhabi and learnt two important things about ministry in Emirates. Transportation to meetings is a serious logistic headache because the migrants live in such scattered communities. Punctuality (no doubt quite a culture shock for new arrivals from Nepal) is vital; when so many different (language) fellowships all share the same church premises, meetings have to start and finish exactly on time.

2013 was my last year in Nepal, and it also included my last visit to Malaysia. No longer could I make Heike's flat in Kuala Lumpur my base as she had completed her studies and left Malaysia. The upside to that was that she was travelling with me. It was great to have a companion, but arranging accommodation for two must have been a headache for our Malaysian hosts. We started in Thailand, where in Bangkok we met Singha, who had been in jail for nearly 14 years – for drug smuggling. A clear miscarriage of justice, all he was guilty of was naïvety and trying to carry a parcel over the border to Malaysia for an agent. Initially condemned to death, his sentence was later commuted, and while in jail he somehow heard about Jesus and became a Christian. Nowadays he is a free man (in every way) and a whole lot wiser. Following that – and a short visit to Chiang Mai – we spent about two months in Malaysia and Singapore, dashing from one group of Nepalis to another, and also attending a third HIMGlo conference on the outskirts of Kuala Lumpur. This time more specific and definite steps were taken in linking Nepalis in south-east Asian countries to help each other in Nepali and cross-cultural ministry. NeMUN delegates (Sapana, Devendra, Janak Sharma, Heike and I) also facilitated a workshop on migrant ministry, but my biggest memory of the conference is of badly spraining my ankle on the way there! The remainder of 2013 is also a bit blurred: I spent it in Kathmandu, working with NeMUN and BaYaN, advising IMI, getting to know people from the NOCF[161] and, in between, starting to pack.

Then on 2nd January 2014, I left Nepal for England, travelling via Emirates and Jordan.[162] Back home in the UK it dawned on me that I was now permanently living in one bit of the Nepali diaspora but one rather different from Malaysia and the Middle East. Around 80,000 Nepalis live scattered all over the British Isles, and so you never know when you might bump into one, not just in the army cantonment areas but on the London tube or in a village pub or... The famous Gurkhas, both serving and retired soldiers, and their families benefitted from Joanna Lumley's advocacy, but sadly, the land they thought was flowing with milk and honey has, for many, turned out to be rancid and bitter. No longer the recipients of army perks, they have discovered how expensive and challenging it is to live in the UK. Many too, especially the older women, are lonely as they cannot communicate in English. The students and professionals have, for the most part, been well able to integrate, so much so that many have been infected by British materialism. Since the end of the Maoist crisis, there have been few asylum seekers, with the exception of a quota of Bhutanese refugees, accepted for resettlement after surviving for eighteen years in camps in south-east Nepal.

---

161 NOCF – Nepali Overseas Christian Fellowship (Nepal branch) formed by a group of ex-migrants from UAE.

162 See Chapter 26.

In September 2014 I hosted Sapana and Janak (Sharma) on their three-week visit, chauffeuring them over 2,000 miles to meet with Nepalis in the north (Bradford, Rochdale, Sheffield and Doncaster), London (Plumstead), Reading, Aldershot and Folkestone. That visit was a real miracle. Janak, as a travel agent, got his visa with no difficulty, but Sapana was only granted hers at literally the 13th hour. Initially refused because she had not provided sufficient information, Sapana was allowed to reapply. I found it almost impossible to advise her how to answer the questions and wondered, are those forms deliberately designed to be so complex that most would-be visitors give up? Sapana and Janak changed their flight dates to give the maximum time for bureaucracy to work its course, but even so, it got to the day before they were due to leave Kathmandu and the visa had still not come. Sapana almost gave up when told to return the next day – the day she should have been boarding an early morning flight to the UK. She had a strange feeling that she should go back to the office that afternoon, but by the time she got there it was officially closed. However, an unusually helpful *peon* took her upstairs to meet the officer who was still on the premises, drinking tea, and he agreed to check one final time, even although nothing had arrived up to ten minutes previously. And – wait for the miracle – the documents had arrived in those ten minutes. Sapana had her visa, but still needed to re-confirm her flight ticket. That office should also have been closed but for once it was still functioning. With little time left to pack, it's hardly surprising that she forgot to include some warm clothes, but early the next day, with visa and ticket (but no sweater), she was safely on the plane and heading for Heathrow. No wonder it was a really fruitful trip!

Sapana Basyal Karong and Janak Raj Sharma.

26

Don't Look Back!

Re-tyrement

(2014 to date)

Sutton Coldfield Prayer Group (2014)
(incl. Janak and Sapana).

I KNEW IT WAS TIME FOR MY FIRST home leave in 1975 when the plastic part of my stethoscope cracked; and I knew it was time to retire when I also began to show signs of aging. So, when I returned to Nepal in early 2011 to establish the INF Diaspora project, I already knew it would only be for three years. INF had agreed that I should 'retire' on my 70th birthday. I knew that this was the right thing to do, that it was what God wanted, but there was no dramatic 'call' as when I went to Nepal. There was no special 'word' from the Lord, no Bible verses, no relevant hymn; it was just that it was sensible, logical and practical – and just occasionally I do what is sensible, logical and practical.

This gave me three years to prepare to leave the land where I had spent most of my working life. That was important not least because I had so much 'stuff' to dispose of – and by 'stuff' I mean mainly books and notes. Even I realised I could not take all of those home with me to the UK, so almost from the first day I was back in Nepal, I started scanning the papers I thought I might want in the future. This was a wise move as it took me almost three years to complete the task – in between daily trips to the office and a few longer trips to Malaysia and the Middle East. Now I have all these documents in digital format (although probably I won't ever look at 99% of them!) This is something I could never have dreamed of at the time I went to Nepal in 1970.

Saying goodbye to friends in Kathmandu could – or perhaps, should – have been quite protracted but, in the end, was squashed into the last month, in between all sorts of other jobs that needed doing. I was still meeting most of these friends regularly so there was no point in saying goodbye until the last minute, but there were a few I needed to visit personally. I found Dr Aryal still going strong at campus (although I understand he has since left), but it was a sad parting from Martha (my former colleague from Ghorahi), then so aged and afflicted by Alzheimer's. She died in 2017. INF, BaYaN, DAI, NeMUN and Ashish Church all insisted on official farewell celebrations – with food and presentations. One of the last things I needed to do was to get a police check. Done too late and the documentation would not be processed in time for me to collect; done too soon and there would be a suspicious time-gap in my record. It worked – and I subsequently acquired UK DBS[163] clearance without any problems.

It was logistically easy to say goodbye to these friends in Kathmandu but I still had many friends I wanted to see in Pokhara before I left. So in October 2013, around *Desai* time, when I knew that people would be on holiday and any Hindus would be gathered with their families for the festival, I went to Pokhara for a couple of weeks. I went on the scooter so that I could whizz around Pokhara and see everyone in record time, but it was a bit sad as I knew it was the last long drive I would make on my little red Mahindra. In the space of about ten days, I managed to visit almost all the friends I have mentioned in this book and of course most

[163] DBS – Disclosure and Barring Service.

of them invited me for *daal-bhat.* Priscilla and Daniel are still faithfully involved in Bagh Bazaar Church. They're now on their own, the grandchildren having fled the nest – to the west, although Pushpa (their daughter) and Luka were at home. I was told that Tika was still working overseas. Now that Rikhman has his second family, it was a bittersweet reunion with Bhim Kumari, but happily, she has good support from two of her daughters: Sarbada, married to Bimal (now pastor of Kunahar Church); and Bindu, married to Bijay (who both worked in Israel for several years). Shyam (Malla)'s family were all gathered for the festival, and so after a long time I met daughter Bindu and her husband as well as the three sons and their families. It saddened me to see that Shyam had become even more devoutly Hindu. I also felt sad saying goodbye to Sonam, as her situation was as bad as ever, partly because of her alcoholic son. It was a poignant meeting with Mithu and Pan Bahadur, knowing I would probably never see her again. Rashmi and Ram Gopal, however, were rejoicing. Their daughter Abuni in America was expecting a baby, and son Bibudh was planning on getting married the following year. They invited me to come back for that but in the end the dates were fixed too late for me to make arrangements to attend. Although many of my former colleagues had moved on from INF/Nepal, I still knew quite a number and they laid on a splendid 'farewell' for me regardless of the fact that I had effectively left many years before.

By staying in Pokhara for two weeks, I managed three Saturdays and so visited all the three churches – Ramghat, Bagh Bazaar and Kunahar – I had attended. They all let me say a little bit by way of thanks and farewell – and, of course, there was some more food! I was gobsmacked to be asked to give the main addresses at one of the joint Pokhara churches' *Desai* conferences – exciting, humbling and a tremendous privilege; something I could never even have dreamed of forty-three years earlier. I bravely tackled some teaching from Hebrews about God's one-and-only, once-for-all sacrifice of his son for us – a sacrifice far more valuable than the annual *Desai* slaughter of goats that the Hindus around us were celebrating. Looking back now, it has been such an honour to have worked and worshipped in Nepal with some of the original pioneer Nepali Christians. Before I left Pokhara I met the three surviving oldies, but since then two have already reached heaven.

The weather should have been fantastic – bright, warm sunny days with the mountains out in all their grandeur – and when I first arrived, it was. But then it became unseasonably and unreasonably wet – *very* wet. I felt sorry for all those trying to celebrate in the rain and mud; and, as every day unveiled itself in mist, I felt sorry for myself too as it looked as though I would be leaving Pokhara without a final glimpse of Fishtail Mountain. I was due to leave on the Sunday morning and had prayed especially that I would for one last time see the mountain that symbolised Nepal to me. Thursday – Friday – Saturday – and it was still wet and foggy, and my faith was being stretched to the limit. But then Sunday dawned sunny and clear and Fishtail was again out in all its majesty. From the roof of Lois' house, I took my last photos and then we sat down to breakfast – but even while we were still eating, the mountains once more disappeared in the mist. I was sad as I had hoped to make their snowy panorama my last sight of the Pokhara Valley. Right up until I left Bagh Bazaar and headed my scooter towards the Kathmandu road, I was still praying that I would see them again, but it was not to be. I forgot that my prayer had actually been answered: I had seen Fishtail that morning before breakfast. Instead, as I drove out of Pokhara, I kept looking back over my shoulder to see if the peaks had peeped out again, and it was then that the Lord spoke to me: "Don't look back." It was not a voice I could hear with my physical ears but still very clear. I was humbled and challenged, and knew that God understood. He had given me my last glimpse of Fishtail and now he had something new and equally exciting lined up for me for the future.

During the last couple of months of 2013, I finally started getting rid of the 'stuff'. About half my books and all the relevant lecture notes I gave to the ATEN[164] library. This was stressful, not only because I hated to be parted from my precious books and notes but also because I had to transport them on the back of my scooter. There were far too many for the bag, and the bag was far too big for the carrier – which is undoubtedly why it threatened to fall off into the ditch. A few other books I managed to sell – for a pittance and nowhere near their real value; and the rest (at least half of the original number) I set aside to bring home to the UK. Thus it was that I ended up with fourteen boxes to freight home and most

[164] ATEN – Association for Theological Education in Nepal.

of them contained books – including extra copies of the ones I had written over the years. I packed virtually no clothes as most of them I had given away – except for an astonishing number of *khastos* I had been given as leaving presents. I'll probably never be able to wear them all, but they did come in handy for packing around the pictures and framed appreciation certificates I had also accumulated. Sadly, despite this carefully insulated packing, the carrier dropped a couple of boxes on their corners which smashed some of the pictures and dented a silver water pot. But at least the 'stuff' all arrived quickly, and it was all present even if not quite correct.

I had been really concerned that the Diaspora work would continue to grow after I left. It was such a small project and I knew Heike was also planning to leave before long. Time went by and there was no replacement for me on the horizon. It seemed our prayers were not being answered. And then we discovered that Paul and Becky would be available. Both had been children of missionary parents, and later spent many years working in Nepal; they had good Nepali (probably better than mine) and a real heart for the Nepali church. Ideal. God's provision. Prayers answered. There was even time for a handover. Subsequently, all the Diaspora work has been completely Nepalised.

The other problem I had concerned my flat. I had hoped that someone in INF would move in, but sadly, no one seemed to want a very nice little flat in a great location with a really friendly landlord and family. I began to think that I would just have to terminate the lease, but this would have been a loss for the landlord and a big hassle for me as I would have had to dispose of all my furniture etc. And then – I heard about an expatriate, working with another group, who was planning to transfer from Pokhara to Kathmandu. My flat ticked all the boxes that she had listed as her requirements. She could even speak the tribal language of my landlord and they 'clicked' immediately. Andrea liked the flat, signed the agreement and even bought almost all of my furniture. This made clearing up so much easier and also meant that I could continue working until the last minute – which of course I did! Then my landlord bought my scooter which meant I could keep riding it until the very last minute – which of course I did! Amazing. Truly amazing. God's provision once again. More answered prayer. All that I still had to do was to sell off a few odd items Andrea did not want and dismantle the 'go bag'. This was the emergency bag INF insisted we all kept ready in case of a catastrophe like an earthquake. For the last couple of weeks, I just had to trust there would be no earthquake – and there wasn't… then!

I left Nepal on 2nd January 2014, forty-three years and one week after I had first arrived. It took me a fortnight to reach the UK as I stopped off in UAE and Jordan. The former had been planned well in advance but then I discovered that the new bathroom that was being fitted in my flat would not be ready by the first week of January. As it was not feasible to arrive home to a flat without a loo, I had somehow to delay my travels – but how? I couldn't change the dates for UAE, but then I hit on the idea of asking if I could visit Jordan, and the suggestion was welcomed. I had a busy – and hot – week in Emirates, which included the very first ladies' seminar for Nepali female migrants in Dubai. It also included a rather 'different' house group fellowship. When they asked me to speak at this, the organisers forgot to tell me one important detail. As we crowded about fifteen to twenty bodies into one small sitting room (which was also my bedroom), two got out their computers and started booting them up. Only then did I discover that I was not just speaking to twenty people in Abu Dhabi but also to about the same number scattered globally, even as far as Canada – by Skype. Jordan was a lot colder, although I was warmly welcomed by the Nepalis, who were working mostly in the north near the Syrian border; and also by my Indian hosts, who made the visit special by taking me to visit the Jordan River and the Dead Sea, something I had not been able to do in 1964/5.

Left to right: 1970s; 1980s; 1990s; 2000s; 2010s.

Returning to the UK was both easy and hard. Easy, because I have many understanding friends, notably Judy who has given me so much practical and prayer support over the years, and because I have a good church (Sutton Coldfield Baptist Church). Hard, because so many things have changed over the years and not all for the better. Political correctness, data protection and the nanny state are some of my pet hates. I had told everyone that there were two things I wanted to get once I hit the UK: a Kindle and some sausages. Those top priorities were soon settled, but then, instead of getting out to visit all my friends, I had to wait two months to buy a car that would fit into my 1960s-size garage. By then I was immersed in the difficulties of sorting out the house and other official affairs, and the visits were postponed. I needed some new furniture, the most urgent requirement being for more bookshelves to get all my many books off the floor. Once the plumbers had moved out, I needed a new bathroom carpet, but the shop got the measurements wrong and the first they delivered was even more minute than my bathroom! Getting a TV (though why on earth did I bother?) was child's play compared with fixing up broadband and the phone with BT. After about a month and three different phone numbers, none of which were my original number as promised, I settled for a new one and moved on to other challenges. Andrew, a friend I had known since he was four, was an absolute godsend, helping me sort out all kinds of odd and even odder jobs I didn't know how to tackle on my own. Placating the tax office after many years of not submitting returns took considerably longer, but in the end was well worth the effort as they actually gave me a generous refund. Extracting my INF pension was by far the most difficult task and took more than a year. Now I'm rich – well, relatively speaking! In between settling all these issues, and by way of relaxation, I discovered where and when the local buses run, where to buy replacement glass for my broken picture frames, when is the best time to pick up bargains at the local supermarkets, and how to use the Internet to get a TV licence and download books for my Kindle. At last my 70th birthday loomed and retirement began to feel like something I could enjoy, but then I remembered I had opted instead for re-tyrement. As Seeta said at my INF farewell in Kathmandu, "I do not think [Val] can sit quietly..."

Fishtail.

Postscript

Many friends who have met me again after a gap of several (or many) years have commented, "You haven't changed a bit." I'm not quite sure what to make of that. My hair is certainly not the same colour it was; and I thought the Bible taught that we are supposed to be being changed "from one degree of glory to another"[165]. Then in my last month in Nepal, many people said such nice things about me and my ministry. My stamina and diligence were mentioned, although perhaps pig-headedness would have been more accurate. Someone said they believed the Lord was saying to me, "Well done, ... faithful servant," (Matt. 25:21) but inside I knew I had not always even done my duty; I was more like the "unworthy servant" of Luke 17:10. I have made mistakes so often. I have learnt far more than I have taught. I have been blessed far more than I have blessed others. I discovered the hard way that one reason why God sent me overseas is because that was the only place where he could teach me the lessons I needed to learn.

Accordingly, this book is not, nor ever could be, like the missionary autobiographies I was brought up on – a deeply spiritual and triumphant story – but I hope you have enjoyed it; that you have laughed with me and perhaps cried a little too. I hope you have spotted those few occasions where, despite my failures, God did use me in some small ways. I hope you have seen how God has worked through the INF medical programmes, and how he has built the Nepali church; and have understood how Bible Yatra has blessed so many young Nepali Christians. I hope you have learnt something about the amazing land of Nepal – its history, geography, politics, culture and religions. I hope you have understood migration – at least in its Nepali context. And, I hope you have got to know some of my Nepali friends better, and that at least some of you will continue to pray for them.

---

[165] 2 Cor. 3:18 (ESV).

O God Most High;
Who crafted all the lofty mountains;
Carved out the lowly hollows.
Who opened up the valleys;
And reigned above the snowy peaks.

Do you no longer love this land?
Why don't you water it with your hand?

The mountains now are lost from view;
Their peaks hidden by haze.
The people still grope for truth,
Not seeing you're by their side.

The washer-man's stream is decayed;
Its waters a river of death.
Priests and people are busy all day,
But not with the water of life.

The nation's wealth is dried, and shrivelled,
Parched with thirst.
Powerful men are full and replete,
Totally regardless.

Myriads of gilded temples
House multitudes of idols;
While many urban poor have
Only tiny squalid shacks.

All men cry "Freedom", but to get
A name that's known throughout the land.
And even some who bear your name
Stand tall, unbending, not like the great bamboos.

Our hearts are heavy for this land,
And breaking for this people.

O God above all gods
Come down and shake this land!

That even hilltop gods may quake,
Watching their ancient homes slip from their grasp,
Like hillsides sliding into the valleys below,
Crumbling and decayed.
Unable to help.

O God in heaven
Come down and touch this land!
That even powerful men may tremble,
Seeing the mighty fallen at your feet,
Stumbling down the hills into the valleys below,
Broken and crippled.
Unable to stand.

O God in heaven; God above all gods
Come down and heal this land!

For, when you come down, we'll see
From the high mountains to the forest plains,
Tribes and Castes together grow.
From the eastern and the western rivers,
Streams of living water flow.

Then will we sing our praise
To God, the God Most High
Whose throne is on the heights.
To the God above all gods
Whose throne is in our hearts.

A Lament for Nepal, which I wrote in 1999, during a time of drought in Kathmandu, and as an assignment for my Theology course. I believe it is still relevant today in the aftermath of the 2015 terrible earthquake.

Appendix

Below are the full lyrics for *The Green Eye of the Little Yellow God,* referred to in Chapter 4, page 44.

The Green Eye of the Little Yellow God

There's a one-eyed yellow idol to the north of Khatmandu,
There's a little marble cross below the town;
There's a broken-hearted woman tends the grave of Mad Carew,
And the Yellow God forever gazes down.

He was known as "Mad Carew" by the subs at Khatmandu,
He was hotter than they felt inclined to tell;
But for all his foolish pranks, he was worshipped in the ranks,
And the Colonel's daughter smiled on him as well.

He had loved her all along, with a passion of the strong,
The fact that she loved him was plain to all.
She was nearly twenty-one and arrangements had begun
To celebrate her birthday with a ball.

He wrote to ask what present she would like from Mad Carew;
They met next day as he dismissed a squad;
And jestingly she told him then that nothing else would do
But the green eye of the little Yellow God.

On the night before the dance, Mad Carew seemed in a trance,
And they chaffed him as they puffed at their cigars:
But for once he failed to smile, and he sat alone awhile,
Then went out into the night beneath the stars.

He returned before the dawn, with his shirt and tunic torn,
And a gash across his temple dripping red;
He was patched up right away, and he slept through all the day,
And the Colonel's daughter watched beside his bed.

He woke at last and asked if they could send his tunic through;
She brought it, and he thanked her with a nod;
He bade her search the pocket saying, "That's from Mad Carew,"
And she found the little green eye of the god.

She upbraided poor Carew in the way that women do,
Though both her eyes were strangely hot and wet;
But she wouldn't take the stone and Mad Carew was left alone
With the jewel that he'd chanced his life to get.

When the ball was at its height, on that still and tropic night,
She thought of him and hurried to his room;
As she crossed the barrack square she could hear the dreamy air
Of a waltz tune softly stealing thro' the gloom.

His door was open wide, with silver moonlight shining through;
The place was wet and slipp'ry where she trod;
An ugly knife lay buried in the heart of Mad Carew,
'Twas the "Vengeance of the Little Yellow God".

There's a one-eyed yellow idol to the north of Khatmandu,
There's a little marble cross below the town;
There's a broken-hearted woman tends the grave of Mad Carew,
And the Yellow God forever gazes down.

J. Milton Hayes (1911)

Glossary

A	*amma*	mother
	arsi	Nepali curved all-purpose knife
B	*baba*	father
	babu	a term of endearment usually reserved for small boys; also occasionally used in place of *baba* – father
	bada din	the great day (Christmas)
	bahini	younger sister; can also mean house-helper
	Bahun(i)	Brahmin
	baidya	Ayurvedic or herbal doctor
	bajai	grandmother
	bandh	strike or stoppage of traffic and/or closure of shops
	bhai	younger brother
	bhatti	small wayside inn, sometimes house of ill repute
	bhauju	sister-in-law
	bholi	tomorrow
	bhurria	porter
	bhut	evil spirit
	bijuli	electricity
	biralo	cat
	buhari	daughter-in-law
C	*chabi*	key, lock
	chapati	thin pancake of unleavened wholemeal bread cooked on a griddle
	chappals	rubber flip-flops
	charpi	toilet
	chaukidar	caretaker
	chha	Hindi for tea (the Nepali is chiya) [*chha* also means 'is' in Nepali]
	chhang	Tibetan-style millet beer supped through a bamboo straw
	chhaupadi	old custom of making a woman 'sit apart' during her times of menstruation
	chhurpi	cheese
	chhuti	holiday

	chichindra	a kind of shrew
	chiya	Nepali tea
	chulo	wood-burning village stove
	crode	ten million
D	*daal-bhat*	lentils and rice (Nepali staple diet)
	daura-suruwal	Nepali men's traditional dress
	Desai	annual Hindu family and sacrificial festival
	dhiki	village husking and grinding machine
	didi	older sister; sometimes also used as a term of respect for an older woman
	digory	usually the doctor's stethoscope; the symbol of our qualifying degree
G	*gaās*	small amount, mouthful
	gali	a telling off
	gargro	big earthen pot for storing water
	geet	song
	ghaās	grass
	ghat	the holy area by the riverside where cremations are carried out
	ghiu	clarified butter
	guhu-ko dolo	lump of excreta
	gundri	mat made from woven straw
	gundruk	dried sour vegetables
	gupha	cave
H	*hola*	perhaps
	Holi	Hindu festival of colour
	hulak	post office
	hut	go away (spoken to a cow or buffalo)
I	*istri*	iron (for ironing clothes)
J	*jankri*	witchdoctor or spirit doctor
	jethi	oldest (or older)
	jhol	gravy
	jhola	shoulder bag
	jhum jhums	paraesthesia or pins and needles sensation
	juicylo kira	furry caterpillar
K	*kaccha*	crude, imperfect
	kanchha ba	father's youngest brother
	kanchhi	youngest (or younger)

	karar	agreement, contract, promise
	karindar	steward
	karma	Hindu belief that you are what you were born and cannot change it
	katam	finished, dead and gone
	ke garne	what to do?
	kera	banana
	khasto	lady's shawl
	khukuri	Nepali fighting knife/sword
	kina	why
	kira	insect/insects
	kiriya	Hindu funeral rites traditionally performed by the eldest son
	kori	derogatory term for a leprosy patient
	kos	the distance that can be walked in 1 hour
	kunni	don't know and don't care
	kurta-suruwal	ladies' top and trousers
L	*lagyo*	beginning to be
	lato	idiot, half-wit (it also means dumb or unable to speak)
	leepnu	besmear with mud
M	*mahila*	woman
	mahabhir	the great hill
	mahinawari	'monthly' – menstruation
	maile	I, me
	maili	second daughter
	mailo	dirty
	mama	mother's older brother
	mana	a pint
	marchha	it kills
	mil	to fit together, be compatible
	momo	small steamed dumpling
	Mongsir	the eighth month in the Nepali calendar – Nov/Dec
	mora	small stool made from bamboo
	mriga	deer
	mrigaula	kidney
N	*nachune*	'don't touch' – menstruation
	nakha-bandhi	blockade of the (Kathmandu) valley

	namaste	Nepali greeting
	niyam	rule, law
O	*oo bhayo*	feeling like death warmed up
P	*paisa*	the smallest Nepali coin, worth 1/100 Rupee; no longer valid currency
	panchhanu	'shun' – menstruation
	panchayat	unit of local government from 1960 to 1990, after which they were renamed Village Development Committees (VDCs) until 2017
	para sarne	'move away' – menstruation
	parsi	day after tomorrow
	patuka	a six-yard length of cloth that villages ladies wrap around their middle and which serves as corset, purse, basket and handkerchief as needed
	pau-roti-ek-rupiya	yeast bread one rupee
	peon	general factotum, odd-job man etc.
	pharsi	pumpkin
	phulne	swelling
	ping	swing
	polne	burning
	Pous	the ninth month in the Nepali calendar – Dec/Jan
	pugya	arrived at
	puja	Hindu worship
R	*rajaswala*	'one who is bleeding' – menstruation
	rakshi	locally made alcoholic drink
	rani aiyo	the queen has come
	rato chiya	lit. red (i.e. black) tea
S	*saathi*	friend
	sasu	mother-in-law (husband's mother)
	sau	big businessman
	stri	woman
	sui	injection
	suitkerrie	delivery case
	sukkha-roti	lit. dry bread – the Nepali name for a chapati
	sukum-basi	squatter on free government land
	swasnimanchhe	woman, wife
T	*tal*	lake
	Teej	Nepali women's festival

	Terai	southern plains of Nepal
	Tharu	a tribe that lives on the Terai
	thulo manchhe	important person (lit. big man)
	Tihar	Nepali Hindu festival of light
	tika	religious mark on the forehead denoting Hindu worship
	topi	Nepali man's hat
	Tundikhel	the old parade ground
	tupi	tuft of hair on a Hindu man's head
	tyessai	just because, without
U	*udghaten*	official opening of a programme
Y	*yagya*	Hindu altar
	yatra	journey
	Yeti	abominable snowman

Other Books by the Author

If I'd been born in Nepal (originally *Daughters of the Millennium*); published by EKTA, Kathmandu

Maps of Nepal – Historical, Ethnographic, Linguistic

Bible Yatra: Basic Bible Survey (Nepali)

Bible Journey: Basic Bible Survey (English)

Sitting in my House; Dreaming of Nepal: Nepal through the eyes of its proverbs – Nepali Proverbs Analysed, Classified and Compared with English Proverbs and also a List of Common Nepali Proverbs; published by EKTA, Kathmandu

Introduction to Study Skills & Research Methods

Introduction to the Bible –

Vol. 1. Bible Survey

Vol. 2. Bible Structure

Vol. 3. Bible Formation

Vol. 4. Bible History, Geography, Customs & Culture

The Nepali Diaspora: Migrants, Ministry & Mission; published by EKTA, Kathmandu

All these books are available from the author, Val Inchley:

Email: val.inchley@uwclub.net

Phone: 07963-787735

Similar Books by the Publisher

Shaped to Fit

Joan Kearney

ISBN 978-1-911086-69-7

When God shapes our lives to fit his purposes, anything is possible!

Raised in a strict Christian sect, with many religious rules and social requirements, Joan struggled to reconcile the lifestyle she was expected to lead with the example that Jesus set for his disciples. Her desire to follow Christ in all things, including 'eating with sinners', soon compelled her to leave behind all that was familiar. A short term 'Mission to Miners' in France stirred a passion within her to become a missionary overseas. Formerly a teacher of severely deaf children, she soon found herself working for Wycliffe Bible Translators in the Amazon forest. Unexpected family joys and deep sorrow were to follow, but through all things God was shaping Joan to be an integral part of his divine masterpiece.

From China Seas to Desert Sands

Jean Goodwin

ISBN 978-1-907509-87-2

A truly inspiring account of a nurse who triumphed over all kinds of adversity, upheld by a vibrant and mature Christian faith. Her family of six graciously adapted to working in five continents over seven decades. It starts with Jean aged nine, captured in China by brutal Japanese soldiers and imprisoned with her family, where she was half-starved, lost much education, and her family life was totally disrupted. She overcame all these deprivations, and went on to a life of selfless devotion to others, supporting her pioneering husband in his leprosy work, his outstanding research, and lecturing in many countries.